# Urban Poverty, Housing and Social Change in China

*Urban Poverty, Housing and Social Change in China* highlights the causes and scale of urban poverty and addresses important questions: how serious are the inequality and poverty problems in Chinese cities? Who are the urban poor? Where and how do the poor live? What are the effects of rural to urban migration on urban poverty? What kind of anti-poverty policies have been developed? How effective are they?

While fast economic growth in China has significantly improved the life of many in China, the benefit of reform was not shared equally in the society. The transition from a socialist planned economy toward a market economy created social change and led to housing and poverty problems. Mass unemployment created by recent industrial restructuring and widespread migration from rural to urban areas formed a new poor social and economic group.

The Chinese experience provides an important comparison to the problems faced by other transitional economies. Unlike many central and eastern European countries, China has followed a progressive reform process which avoided sudden collapse of urban economy and delayed the emergence of urban poverty. Sustained economic growth also enabled the government to develop new social support policies and reduce the extent of suffering of low-income communities. Rising urban poverty, however, has become a major obstacle in the future development of Chinese cities, and demands a pro-poor economic development strategy.

This book is based on a long period of research on Chinese urban development, and benefited from several research projects conducted in Chinese cities. It is an important reference for all those interested in urban and social change and a key text for students of the Chinese economy and society.

**Ya Ping Wang** is Reader at Heriot-Watt University, Edinburgh and has previously taught at Shaanxi Teachers University in Xi'an. His research on contemporary China had been supported by the UK Economic and Social Research Council, UK Department for International Development, British Academy, British Council and his university. He has published widely on planning, housing and urban poverty in China and is the co-author with Professor Alan Murie of *Housing Policy and Practice in China* (1999).

## Housing and society series
Edited by Ray Forrest
*Professor of Urban Studies and Head of School for Policy Studies, University of Bristol*

This series aims to situate housing within its wider social, political and economic context at both national and international level. In doing so it will draw on the full range of social science disciplines and on mainstream debate on the nature of contemporary social change. The books are intended to appeal to an international academic audience as well as to practitioners and policymakers – to be theoretically informed and policy relevant.

**Housing and Social Change**
East–West perspectives
*Edited by Ray Forrest and James Lee*

**Urban Poverty, Housing and Social Change in China**
*Ya Ping Wang*

Forthcoming
**Housing and Social Policy**
*Peter Somerville and Nigel Sprigings*

**Gentrification in a Global Context**
*Edited by Rowland Atkinson and Gary Bridge*

**Managing Social Housing**
*David Mullins, Barbara Reid and Richard Walker*

**Housing Shapes**
Shaping the space of the twenty-first century
*Bridget Franklin*

# Urban Poverty, Housing and Social Change in China

Ya Ping Wang

Routledge
Taylor & Francis Group

LONDON AND NEW YORK

First published 2004
by Routledge
2 Park Square, Milton Park, Abingdon, Oxon OX14 4RN

Simultaneously published in the USA and Canada
by Routledge
270 Madison Ave, New York, NY 10016

*Routledge is an imprint of the Taylor & Francis Group*

Typeset in Times and Frutiger by
HWA Text and Data Management, Tunbridge Wells
Printed and bound in Great Britain by
TJ International Ltd, Padstow, Cornwall

*British Library Cataloguing in Publication Data*
A catalogue record for this book is available from the British Library

*Library of Congress Cataloging in Publication Data*
Wang, Ya Ping, 1957–
    Urban poverty, housing, and social change in China / Ya Ping Wang.
        p.   cm.
    Includes bibliographical references and index.
    1. Urban poor–China. 2. Urban poor–Housing–China. 3. Rural-urban
    migration–Social aspects–China. 4. Poverty–Government policy–
    China. 5. Social change–China. I. Title.
HV4150.A5W35 2004
362.5′0951′091732–dc21                                    2004003840

ISBN 0–415–30738–4

To Dad and in Memory of Mum

# Contents

# Preface

Economic reform in China has significantly improved the life of one-fifth of the world's population over the last twenty-five years. A large proportion of urban residents, in particular, have enjoyed a life which had never been experienced before in the country. However, urban reform has resulted in the widening gap between the rich and the poor, and poverty has emerged recently as a major problem in Chinese cities. Mass unemployment created by industrial restructuring together with many millions of rural migrants formed a new urban underclass. Chinese cities become increasingly divided in both social and economic terms. This book addresses questions such as how serious are the inequality and poverty problems in Chinese cities? Who are the urban poor? Where and how do the poor live? What are the main causes of poverty? What are the effects of migration on urban poverty? What kind of antipoverty policies have been developed? How effective are they?

This book is based on a long period of research on Chinese urban development. A recent project on 'Social Implications of Urban Economic Reform' supported by the UK Department for International Development (DFID), in particular, provided quantitative data for empirical analysis. This project was conducted in two inland industrial cities – Shenyang and Chongqing – between 1999 and 2001, and focused on several low-income community areas. In Shenyang, one area represents the state enterprise residential areas in Tiexi District; two (one in Huanggu District and one in Dadong District) represent the poor traditional housing areas near the city centre; and two villages in the suburban areas were included in the study. In Chongqing, many small poor residential areas were found at difficult locations along the two large rivers – Yangtze and Jialingjiang – which run through the city. Three traditional housing areas in Yuzhong District were selected, all on steep slopes facing the Yangtze River. The other one was a textile industrial factory residential area in Shapingba District. More rural migrants were found in these areas in Chongqing, and migrants were selected along with the official local residents for the study.

Face-to-face interviews were conducted with a sample of households living in these areas. A target sample of about 1000 households was planned (700 official urban residents and 300 rural migrants). This was split equally between the two cities. In each city, the sample was divided between the study areas roughly according to the size and type of these areas. Housing quality in these areas was very poor and most houses were not properly built units, but single rooms. The structure of households in these areas was very complicated. Samples in each area were selected systematically on site. The final sample consisted of 1120 households – 521 in Shenyang (of which 160 were migrant households) and 599 in Chongqing (with 158 migrants). Although this quota sampling method was not ideal, the sample did provide a good coverage in these two cities and was a reliable representation of residents living in these areas. Data collected through household interviews formed the basis for analysis on economic, social and housing conditions of the low-income groups and migrants in Chapters 5, 6 and 7.

# Acknowledgements

The principal funding was provided by the UK Department for International Development through a research grant during 1999 and 2001 (Award Number R7639). DFID supports policies, programmes and projects to promote international development. DFID provided funds for this study as part of that objective but the views and opinions expressed are those of the author alone. The book also benefited from work supported by a British Council China Studies Grant in 2003 and earlier works supported by the British Academy and the Economic and Social Research Council (UK).

During my fieldwork in China I received assistance from many housing and social security officials in both central and local government. These include the Department of Housing and Real Estate Industry of the Ministry of Construction, Housing Reform Offices or Bureaux in Beijing, Shanghai, Shenyang, Chongqing, Guangzhou, Shenzhen, Urumqi and Xi'an. I also received help from several higher educational and research institutions in China, including the Graduate School of Beijing University, School of Architecture of Tsinghua University, School of Economic Management of Liaoning University, and Faculty of Architecture and Planning of Chongqing University. Academic staff and students from Liaoning University and Chongqing University carried out household surveys for the DFID-supported project. Numerous local government and work-unit housing and social benefit officials gave their time for interviews and discussion with me; and over one thousands individuals in Chongqing and Shenyang participated in our household survey. I thank all of them for their kind help.

I appreciate the time and trouble taken by many people to comment on the initial concept for the book and on subsequent parts of the draft text, especially Professor Ray Forrest (Editor for the 'Housing and Society' series) who read and commented on draft chapters. Michelle Green at Routledge has taken particular care to guide me through this publishing process. I would also like to thank my colleagues in the School of the Built Environment at Heriot-Watt University for their continuous encouragement and support in my work on China.

Finally I would like to thank my family, especially my wife Chun, my daughter Fan and my son Kevin, for their love and encouragement.

Ya Ping Wang
Edinburgh

# 1  Introduction

Central Business District (CBD) and traffic on Guomao (National Trade) Bridge on Dong San Hua (Third Ring Road East), Beijing, October 2003.

## Economic reform and urban change

Economic reform has brought significant changes to China over the last 25 years. The reform started from rural areas in 1978 and dismantled the collective agricultural production of communes and introduced the household responsibility system. This liberated the rural workforce and resulted in a rapid increase in rural productivity and improvement of living conditions in the countryside. Rural success was followed by urban reform from 1984 (Croll, 1994). Since then the speed of economic growth and transformation of Chinese society has been remarkable. The old style of socialist economic planning has gradually given way to a so-called 'Chinese-style socialist market economy'. Throughout the reform period, China's GDP growth was maintained at around 10 per cent. Even during the late 1990s, while most Asian countries were in an economic crisis, China still achieved an annual growth of more than seven per cent. Between 1996 and 2002, China's GDP per capita increased by 69 per cent from 4,854 yuan to 8,184 yuan (State Statistics Bureau, 2003).

Rapid economic growth brought a large-scale increase in personal and household incomes. Between 1978 and 1995, per capita disposable incomes more than tripled in cities. During the Ninth Five-year Plan period (1996–2000) average annual disposable income per person in urban areas increased by 47 per cent from 4,283 yuan to 6,280 yuan. By the end of 2002, it had reached 7,703 yuan (an increase of 23 per cent over the two-year period). Income in large cities and coastal provinces grew even faster. In Shanghai, Beijing, and Guangdong, annual disposable income per person had reached 13,250, 12,464 and 11,137 yuan respectively (State Statistics Bureau, 2003). Because of this remarkable economic growth, China has been hailed as the most successful transitional economy.

Economic growth was accompanied by an accelerated urbanisation. Between 1979 and 1999, the number of cities in China increased from 193 to 663 (State Statistics Bureau, 2000). The officially registered urban population had increased from 18 per cent in 1978 to 39 per cent in 2002 (State Statistics Bureau, 2003). This did not include the estimated 100 million rural labourers working in urban areas. Changes in the urban landscape in many cities were also striking. Old industrial facilities of the socialist period and poor-quality traditional houses were replaced by high-rise office blocks and new residential estates. Built-up areas in most cities expanded rapidly. In Beijing built-up areas have more than doubled over the last 25 years. Expansion toward suburban areas was measured by the layers of new ring roads constructed. The city had four rings of fast roads built between 1980 and 2000, and another two are under construction. Some coastal cities and towns have turned into huge construction sites.

Urban economies have also been transformed. There was a steady decline of the state and collective industrial sectors, and an expansion of private and joint-venture businesses. In 1978 almost all urban residents were employed in either the state or the collective sectors. By the end of 2002, over 33 per cent of urban employment was in the private or 'other' sectors, including self-employed (Ministry of Labour and Social Security and the State Statistics Bureau, 2002). Government is no longer the sole job provider, and urban residents have more freedom in choosing their jobs and careers.

This diversification of employment and increased household income has resulted in a significant improvement of the general living conditions in cities and towns.

For 30 years since the communists came to power, housing conditions remained very poor. Average housing floor space stagnated at merely three square metres per person and much of the housing stock was of poor quality and simple construction. The majority of urban residents had no exclusive access to a toilet or kitchen. Reform in the housing provision system and the construction industry revolutionised urban living. Thousands of new residential estates were built each year and average housing floor space in urban areas had reached 20 square metres by 2001. Many families have moved into purpose-built apartments and over 80 per cent of official urban residents now own their homes (Liu, 2003).

## Social implications

In spite of these achievements, the change from a planned economy to a market economy in China has not been a smooth and problem free process (Hussain, 1994). The reforms have encountered many difficulties in recent years and new economic and social problems have begun to emerge. First, early success of rural reform was not followed by further innovation in agricultural development and management. The economic advantages gained by the rural population through the family responsibility system during the early 1980s were soon lost to the fast increase of income in urban areas and cost of industrial products. During the 1990s rural incomes increased very slowly in comparison with urban areas. Between 1997 and 2002, rural disposable incomes rose by 3.8 per cent annually while urban disposable incomes rose by an average of 8.6 per cent (Zhu, 2003). Low demand for agricultural labourers, oversupply of food products and low incomes in the agricultural sector resulted in a massive flow of rural labourers to urban areas in search of work. While this shifted low-paid workers into cities, rural migration generated great pressure on urban infrastructure and facilities such as housing. Most rural migrants lived in slum accommodation in suburban villages of large cities and took up most of the poorly-paid jobs. The presence of large numbers of migrant workers became a distinctive feature of Chinese cities.

Economic reform also had a very uneven effect on the existing urban population. The restructuring of the urban economy resulted in a significant change to the distribution system. While there was a general increase in family incomes after 1979, the gap between the rich and the poor increased dramatically. Living standards among the white-collar professionals and public-sector employees, including those working in government and administration, improved substantially, while some blue-collar workers suffered from rising unemployment.

In the state-owned-enterprise sector, the emphasis on production and management efficiency resulted in reduced job security and income stability. Well-performing enterprises could provide their employees with better pay and services, while poorly performing enterprises could lay off (*xiagang*) some or all of their employees. Although the laid-off workers were not counted officially as unemployed (because their relationship with the employer had not been cut off entirely), they were indeed unemployed people. At the end of 1995, there were 5.6 million people who were registered as 'laid-off' by their employers. One year later, it had increased to 8.1 million. At the end of 1997, the total number of laid-off and other unemployed people in urban areas had reached 15 million (Yi, 1998; Zhang, 1998) It has been estimated that about 30 per cent (24 million) of all employees in the state sector were not working in 1997 (Zhu, 1998).

After 1997 the government adopted tougher policies to reduce the labour force and increase efficiency in the state-owned-enterprise sectors. This led to a dramatic reduction in employment in the state and collective sectors. Between January 1997 and December 2002 the total number of urban residents employed in work units fell by 19 per cent. In the state sector there was a fall of 36 per cent, while in the collective sector, over 63 per cent of employment was lost (State Statistics Bureau, 2001a, 2003). Although there were increases in the number of jobs in other sectors, this expansion did not compensate for the losses in the state and the collective sectors. A similar restructuring policy was recently introduced in the government and public institutional sectors, which could result in a similar reduction of jobs.

Industrial and institutional restructuring and rising unemployment resulted in a dramatic increase in urban poverty. It was officially estimated that there were 30 million urban residents living in poverty in 1996 (Zhong and Wang, 1999). Recent research in some inland cities found that the living standards of many unskilled industrial workers in both the state-owned-enterprise or collective sectors have fallen behind those of officials and professionals (Wang, 2001). In reviewing the social and economic development of the Ninth Five-year Plan period (1996–2000), the State Statistics Bureau reported that the widening gap between the rich and the poor and rising unemployment were the most important problems which could lead to social instability:

> … during the Ninth FYP period, the increase of differences between income groups had slowed down, but improvement among the urban lowest income groups was slow; in some cases, the situation of the poor got worse. The poorer the group, the slower the increase in their income. The proportion of income going to the 60 per cent middle- and low-income groups declined continuously, while the proportion going to the top 40 per cent increased. The gap between the rich and the poor was increasing.
>
> (State Statistics Bureau, 2001b: 6)

Economic and social changes have also been accompanied by spatial and residential re-organisation (Wang, 2001; Wang and Murie, 2000; Wu 2001, 2002 and 2003). Although distinctive functional zones such as administrative areas, industrial areas, and commercial and housing areas were planned, the pre-reform cities were not divided into different residential areas according to income levels. There was also no obvious concentration of poor people in particular districts. After over 20 years of reform a different social and economic structure has emerged. Communities or neighbourhoods of similar income or status have become a key feature. Residential patterns based on socio-economic class have formed, and poor families have been left in either run-down traditional residential areas or housing estates associated with bankrupt enterprises.

There are close associations between poverty and housing. From 1949 to 1979, housing in cities was provided by the government within a socialist system. Since the early 1980s, urban housing reform and privatisation have been gradually carried out throughout the country. During the first half of the 1990s, a large proportion of the public housing stock owned by state enterprises and institutions was sold to sitting tenants. This mass privatisation, on the one hand, improved living conditions of a large proportion of the urban population; on the other, it was part of the cause for emerging urban poverty. New housing was too expensive for many urban residents, particularly those who had no association with the formal state sectors and who were at the lower end of the employment hierarchy. Privatisation has also changed the welfare nature of urban housing provision. There were large-scale increases in rents in both the public and private sectors. (In Beijing, for example, rents for public housing increased from 0.11 yuan per square metre in 1992 to 1.3 yuan per square metre in 1996. From January 2000, housing rent in the public sector was increased to 3.05 yuan per square metre. Meanwhile, rent subsidies were introduced to the key public sector employees.) The increasing housing costs which result from housing privatisation could become a major burden to poor families and could lead to a further deterioration of the living conditions of the urban poor. Along with job security, housing used to be the most important element of the welfare system in Chinese cities. Housing privatisation and the changing housing provision system have therefore had far-reaching social and economic implications.

## Exploring the new urban poor

Issues of income inequality and urban poverty have attracted increasing attention among Chinese officials and academics in the last few years and the new leaders emerged from the Sixteenth National Chinese Communist Party Congress are more concerned about the inequality and poverty problems. Studies have been carried out to establish the links between unemployment and urban poverty (e.g. Zhang, 1998; Zhu, 1998; Zhang, 1999). Regional variations in urban poverty, the relationship between poverty and family income, employment types and economic sectors have also been investigated. These studies have led to new policy development and some change in social welfare provision.

At the international level, the literature on urban reform and transition in China has also grown rapidly over the last few years. Recently published material addresses a wide range of issues, including:

- the economic and industrial changes occurring in cities as part of the country's re-emergence on the world stage (Solinger, 1993; Naughton, 1996; Chung, 1999; Logan, 2002; Wu, 1997);
- the physical and cultural transformation of Chinese societies (Davis *et al.*, 1995);
- changes in the egalitarian distribution and consumption system and the increased level of material comfort (Davis, 2000);
- institutional changes and the role of state in establishing a market economic system (Nee and Stark, 1989; Nee and Matthews, 1996; Nee, 1996 and 2000; Wang, 1998; Winckler, 1999);
- new social and economic class divisions and the persistence of existing power and benefit structures (Chan, 1996; Tang and Parish, 2000);
- regional implications of economic transition (Goodman, 1989; Cannon and Jenkins, 1990; Cannon, 2000; Fan, 1996 and 1999; Yang, 1997).

These works reflect the views of sociologists, geographers and economists, and have made important contribution to the understanding of the development of the market economic system in China. However, there has not been much research on the rising inequalities associated with the transitional process itself (Bian and Logan, 1996; Yao, 1999; Khan and Riskin, 2001; Guan, 2003; Bian, 2002) and on the life of the most disadvantaged groups (Solinger, 1999). There has been very little systematic discussion of urban poverty and living standard of the urban low-income groups (Cook and White, 1998; Cook and Holly, 2001). This book aims to fill this gap by exploring the social consequences of urban reform, and the associated poverty and housing problems. It will:

- review the major changes that have occurred in Chinese cities;
- highlight the emerging problems of urban poverty;
- assess the living conditions of urban families including rural migrants found in major disadvantaged areas in Shenyang and Chongqing – two large inland industrial cities;
- review and evaluate government anti-poverty policies.

The book will address questions such as how serious are the inequality and poverty problems which are emerging in Chinese cities? Who are the urban poor? Where and how do the poor live? What are the main causes of poverty? What are the effects of migration on urban poverty? What kind of anti-poverty policies have been developed? How effective are they? It, of course, will be difficult to provide comprehensive answers to all these questions. The aim of the book, however, is to highlight the seriousness of urban poverty and to make an important contribution to the general debate about poverty and housing problems in transitional economies.

The rest of the book consists of eight chapters. Chapter 2 discusses the general characteristics of transitional economies and changes in cities built under socialist principles. It explores the common problems associated with transitional societies in central and eastern European countries. The aim of this chapter is to provide an international and theoretical background to the specific discussion about China in the later chapters. Chapter 3 includes an overall view of changes that have occurred in Chinese cities with contrasts and discussion of social and economic structures before and during the reform period. Chapter 4 highlights the growing poverty problems in cities with discussion of various disadvantaged groups and major low-income communities. The subsequent three chapters draw on empirical research in Shenyang and Chongqing. Chapter 5 assesses the income and employment situations of the official urban poor. Chapter 6 looks at the housing and living conditions of the official urban poor. Chapter 7 examines the working and living conditions of rural migrants found in these two cities. Chapter 8 reviews and evaluates the recent development in anti-poverty policies, particularly the so-called three lines of defence against poverty – laid-off workers' basic living allowance, unemployment benefits and urban minimum living standard and the new social housing initiative. Urban redevelopment has affected a large number of residents and its impact will also be discussed. The concluding Chapter 9 summarises the key features of urban poverty in transitional societies and examines different theoretical perceptions which could offer some insights over the future of urban poverty in China. Finally, the chapter discusses development policy options for poverty alleviation.

# 2 Society in transition

A 'European style' gated community under construction in an eastern suburb of Beijing, the words on the advertisement hoarding read 'Building the Model Standard of Classical Living in the World', October 2003.

## What is transition?

Economic reform and transition of socialist societies affect more than a quarter of the world's population. The process began with the experiments in some east European countries during the 1960s, which was followed by China from 1978. The fall of the Berlin Wall in 1989 opened the way for comprehensive political and economic transformation across central and eastern Europe and eventually led to the break-up of the Soviet Union in 1992. There is no doubt that this transition represents an important progress in the societies affected and paved the way for a long-term freedom and prosperity among their people. At the same time, the transition has brought with it many social and economic problems, such as a decline in GDP, collapse of the old industrial factories, large-scale increases in unemployment, inequalities in income distribution and the emergence of poverty.

The word 'transition' has been used in different ways and many different definitions for transition can be found, and most of them refer to economic changes. The simplest and most commonly used one is: *transition from socialism to capitalism* or *from plan to market*. According to this, the objective of transition was to introduce capitalism in former socialist economies and to bring these countries, within an appropriate period of time, to levels of prosperity comparable to those of the most advanced industrialised countries. Such an objective is however by no means assured for countries having undertaken the transition process. Recent experiences show that transition involves much more than the switch from plan to market. Economic transition is not possible without simultaneous transitions in political, social and cultural spheres. The large-scale institutional changes involved in transition are among the most complex economic and social processes one can imagine (Roland, 2000). Those countries that had made progress in economic transition had done so because they have been successful in reforming their political and social systems to create the institutions which support economic reform. Transition entails comprehensive processes bringing about new arrangements of market economy as well as of political democracy (Mandic, 1997). To reflect these complex natures of transition, Hare gave a broader definition for transition from centrally planned economies operating under the socialist system into market-type economies operating under the capitalist system in a democratic political framework (Hare, 2001).

Differences in the understanding of what is transition means more differences in the interpretation of what transition involves; where it leads to; how it proceeds and how it relates to the previous histories of the societies in which it takes place. Bradshaw and Stenning indicated that the term 'transition' is problematic because it suggests a change from one known stable state to another stable state. In fact, each version of the Soviet-type system was different. As a consequence, each economy is likely to evolve into its own version of a market system and will occupy a unique position in the international economic system. The word 'transition' may give the impression that transition is 'simply' a short-run policy issue that should take a few years at most. In reality, nobody can tell for sure how transitional the transition is or whether the countries engaged in this process will end up transformed into successful capitalist economies (Bradshaw and Stenning, 2000).

The Chinese government, after many years of reform, worked out its own definition of transition, which includes two main aspects: a social transition from a traditional, rural, agricultural, and semi-closed society to a modern, urbanised, industrialised, and open society; an economic transition from highly centralised planned economic system to 'a Chinese-style socialist market economic' system. According to this definition, Chinese transition differs importantly from the east European one. Apart from moving from planning to market, it included transition from traditional rural society to modern urban society, but excluded change from socialism to capitalism.

## Political changes

Hare (2001) observed that collapse of the socialist system had many important political implications. Several states that existed in 1989 have since split into components or merged with others. The former East Germany became part of the existing German Federal Republic following unification in 1990. Yugoslavia has disintegrated into several countries. Dispute over the nature and pace of economic reforms led to the disintegration of Czechoslovakia into two separate countries – the Czech Republic and Slovakia. From the former Soviet Union, fifteen states emerged: the three Baltic States (Estonia, Latvia and Lithuania), and the twelve states which formed the Commonwealth of Independent States (CIS). Some of these changes happened peacefully, while others with bitter conflict and fighting. With the continuation of political disputes and military conflicts in several locations, the political landscape in the region is far from finally settled. At the beginning of the transition, few observers had predicated that there would be so many break-ups and that they would happen so fast.

Inside each country, there were fundamental political changes. Szelenyi (1996) noted that three major constituents of the state socialist social–economic and political order were dismantled in east European countries:

- The state monopoly ownership of major means of production was abolished. Property laws were introduced to protect private property rights, and privatisation had largely removed the state from the productive sphere, leaving it as the exclusive domain of private entrepreneurs.
- The system of one-party rule came to an end and multi-party parliamentary democracy and elections were introduced.
- The socialism cadre elite has been unseated and replaced by a new political class (Szelenyi, 1996: 308).

Although one-party rule in central and eastern European countries had ended and a western style of democracy was introduced, the systems emerged were not the western style of capitalist formations. A few years after the communists had been evicted from power by the democratic revolutions of 1989, former communists came back to power via the ballot box in several countries. In some the communists had transformed themselves into European-style social democrats (Roland, 2000). Electoral backlash was another surprise of the transition.

In a few of these countries, corruption and organised crime are widespread. On the ruins of the communist government, organised criminal groups started to emerge at an amazing speed. In Russia, the so-called mafia phenomenon has become so serious that it attracted the attention of many international law enforcement organisations. These problems led to a number of interesting and provoking theses describing and explaining the system which is emerging. Stark, for example, described the transition as from *plan to clan* rather than to market (1990), and Burawoy and Krotov characterized the post-communist Russian economic system as *merchant capitalism* (1992).

## Economic changes – the Big Bang and J-curve

In economic terms, transition involved a series of reforms. At the beginning of transition, much of the policy advice received by the transitional countries from the West was derived from the so-called Washington Consensus. Although individual authors tend to differ in terms used to describe the key components of the economic transition prescribed by the Washington Consensus, liberalisation (in particular, price liberalisation), macro-economic stabilisation, privatisation, structural reform (including the financial system), and internationalisation (opening the economy to foreign trade and inward investment) were widely seen as the pillars of economic transition (Bradshaw and Stenning, 2000; Roland, 2000).

According to Roland (2000), the Washington Consensus is rooted in a combination of standard neoclassical price theory, standard macro-economics and experience of stabilisation policy, and the disappointing experiences with partial reform in central and eastern Europe. Since the initial situation is characterised by fundamental inefficiencies and since economic theory predicts that transition will deliver sure efficiency gains, then these reforms should be implemented with faith. We know that capitalism as experienced in the United States or Europe has been proved successful, so it is simply a matter of copying the better models.

In terms of reform strategies, the Washington Consensus political economy emphasises the use of early windows of opportunity or periods of exceptional politics to push reforms through as fast as possible and to create irreversibility. It also rejects any partial reform, because it will create rents for given groups that will be threatened by further reforms. Complementarities in reform are of absolute importance and are an overriding argument, whereby all reforms are introduced in a simultaneous and comprehensive way – the 'big bang' approach (Roland 2000). As the dominant economic ideology, the Washington Consensus has shaped policy recommendations from international financial organisations. Many international agencies and western advisors had insisted upon the notion, 'of the fastest possible abandonment of all aspects of state socialism and its replacement by (neo-)liberal democracy, with the least possible role for the state (and as decentralised an administration as possible) compatible with free markets and the private ownership and exploitation of capital' (Harloe, 1996: 5).

According to De Melo *et al.* (1996), measures put forward by the Washington Consensus should bring about the following changes in a formerly planned economy. The initial collapse of the planned system creates a period of macro-economic instability. For example, the liberalisation of prices may cause a period of high inflation. However, if stabilisation polices are implemented, inflation is brought under control and exchange rates stabilised. The distribution of the planned economy, loss of traditional markets and changes in domestic demand lead to decline in industrial production, referred as 'transitional recession'. In theory, the reallocation of resources, say from an inefficient industrial sector to emergent service sector, eventually creates positive growth; transitional recession gives way to economic recovery (the so called 'J-curve'). At the same time, policies to encourage private sector growth and foreign investment also generate growth. Thus, there is seen to be a process of creative destruction whereby the inefficient and distorted Soviet-style economy is replaced by a more balanced and effective market economy. The main argument in favour of transition was a desire to put the countries in question on a path of sustainable growth. It was assumed that shift of property rights from state to private hands and the shift of allocation mechanism from state to free market would soon enhance savings rates and capital formation, as well as allocative efficiency. Thus it ought also to have contributed to high-quality growth (Bradshaw and Stenning, 2000).

In assessing the progress of transition, Stiglitz (2002) pointed out that seldom has the gap between expectations and reality been greater than in the case of the transition from communism to the market. The combination of privatisation, liberalisation, and decentralisation was supposed to lead quickly, after perhaps a short transition recession, to a vast increase in production. It was expected that the benefits from transition would be greater in the long run than in the short run, as old, inefficient machines were replaced, and a new generation of entrepreneurs was created. Full integration into the global economy, with all the benefits that would bring, would also come quickly, if not immediately. These expectations for economic growth were not realised. In all transitional economies, before any growth has occurred there has been severe contraction, ranging from 20 per cent over three years in Poland, to over 60 per cent in nine years in Ukraine (Kolodko, 1998). Moldova's decline is the most dramatic, with output less than a third of what it was ten years ago. Only a few countries – such as Poland, Hungary, Slovenia, and Slovakia – have a GDP in 2000 equal to that of a decade ago (Stiglitz, 2002).

Although some economists did expect a sluggish supply response to price liberalisation and a mild economic slowdown, the double-digit output fall was quite unexpected. The outcome of privatisation policies was also unexpected by many. Privatisation of former state-owned enterprises benefited mostly the 'insiders' – that is, managers, and sometimes also workers, who were inside the firm before transition started. It was expected that the outsiders (foreign investors and new private entrepreneurs) play a bigger role. Insiders benefiting much from privatisation raise suspicions about the efficiency of some of the privatisation policies (Roland, 2000).

According to World Bank data, in 2000, Russia had a GDP that was less than two-thirds of what it was in 1989. Sustained output fall had transformed Russia quickly from an industrial giant into a natural resource exporter. There is a consensus among researchers that most individuals have experienced a marked deterioration in their basic standard of living, reflected in a host of social indicators. (Stiglitz, 2002) Kornai (1990) describing the 'crisis of post-communist transformation', referred to this as one of the most if not the most severe economic crisis in modern history: sharp fall in GNP and industrial production, increase in unemployment and inflation. These unfavourable results are the consequence of both the legacy of the previous system and the policies exercised during transition, though it is obvious that the latter are of major importance.

## Institutional changes – gradualism

As processes of economic, political and social restructuring unfold, the empirical validity of the Washington Consensus and the 'big bang' theory of the transition were soon called into question. It was realised by many policy-makers in central and eastern European countries that the transition to a market economy will be a lengthy process comprising various spheres of economic, social and political activities. The belief that a market economy can be introduced by 'shock therapy' has been wrong, and in several cases, when attempted, has caused more problems that it has solved (Kolodko, 1998). A market requires not only liberal regulation and private ownership, but also adequate institutions.

At the initial stage of the transition, it was believed once central planning was swept away, that the opening of markets would bring with it the needed institutional structures to make the new market system work properly. This view was soon proved fundamentally wrong (Hare, 2001). As McMillan (1997) put it: 'A market is an institution, which needs rules and customs in order to operate' (p. 222). New institutional arrangements are of key importance for successful transformation. For this reason many believe that transition can be executed only in a gradual manner, since institution building is a gradual process based upon new organisations, new laws, and the changing behaviour of various economic entities.

Many social scientists also did not agree with the view held by proponents of the free-market solution for the former state socialist societies. They emphasised the varied, hence path-dependent nature – 'where you get to depends on where you're coming from' (Stark, 1990; 1992). Harloe (1996) pointed out that we cannot turn our backs on the legacy of the past if we want to understand the present. Nor can we accept, as some do, that 'state socialism' was a cross-nationally identical phenomenon, or that similarly uniform description and analysis can be provided of the transition.

The evolutionary–institutionalist perspective has more support in academic circles than in international policy circles. It was clearly a minority view in the beginning of transition but has gained more and more support over time in the light of the transition experiences. It emphasises strongly the success of the Chinese transition experience, which has followed none of the recommendations of the Washington Consensus vision and poses a challenge to it.

> … Institutions of other countries cannot so easily be copied or imitated, and attempts at imitation may yield unintended outcomes. These outcomes are strongly dependent on the initial set of institutions that form the starting point of transition.
>
> (Roland, 2000: xviii)

Poland became the most successful of the Eastern European countries by employing alternative strategies to those advocated by the Washington Consensus. It started with 'shock therapy' to bring hyperinflation down to more moderate levels, and quickly realised that shock therapy was inappropriate for societal change. It then pursued a gradualist policy of privatisation, while simultaneously building up the basic institutions of a market economy. The Polish government emphasised the importance of democratic support for the reforms, and tried to keep unemployment low, providing benefits for those who were unemployed and adjusting pensions for inflation, and creating the institutional infrastructure required to make a market economy function (Stiglitz, 2002).

In Russia the change has happened at such a pace that the political, administrative and law enforcement systems were struggling to enact appropriate laws and develop appropriate regulatory and enforcement agencies. When new agencies such as the Federal Tax Police Service were established, it was expected to identify, investigate and control tax evasion. These functions were of special significance with reference to the severe economic crisis resulting from the serious shortfalls in revenue. The operation of this service was however very different from that in established western societies. *The European*, in its issue of 9–15 February 1998, referred to a raid on corporate premises in these terms:

> Two heavily armed men in leather jackets and helmets ran up the stairs of the building and pushed open the door of a Moscow trading company. 'Nobody move!' they shouted. They pointed guns at the terrified employees and demanded to know where the safe was. They emptied it and removed everything from the office that looked valuable. This wasn't a visit from the mafia but a call from Moscow's tax police.
>
> (Gregory and Brooke, 2000: 433–4)

Many social scientists also do not agree with the view that privatisation involves a simple transfer of rights of ownership from the state to private individuals and enterprises. Ownership, as Marcuse (1996) noted, is not a simple concept rather it refers to a bundle of rights which were divided between the state and individuals under state socialism, as they are under capitalism. The privatisation process, therefore, involves frequently conflictual repartitioning of these rights. The process of transition involves a complex struggle between contending groups for economic advantage, political power and social position. The privatisation of former state assets is a key part of all this. The lack of a stable legal framework or a system of planning regulation, means that there are many opportunities for interest groups to manipulate the situation, to gain advantages for themselves, and to convert the advantages that they enjoyed under state socialism into private property ownership in the new regime.

Studying the transition of east European housing systems, Struyk (1996) found that, paralleling other developments in the post-socialist society, those who had privileges in the former system tended to gain most from housing privatisation, and this adds to resentment among the rest of the population. Privatisation is not a socially just or equitable process. Some gain and others lose out, and many of the former are in this position by virtue of their ability to convert advantages gained in the old system to ones enjoyed in the new system. Housing privatisation involves a profound shift in housing consumers' attitudes, from those associated with property rights under socialism – linked to considerations of security of tenure and the ability to pass tenancies on to family members – to those associated with capitalism, in which housing is seen as a commodity with value in the market and a source of income and wealth.

It is also argued that the older western capitalist democracies have generally had mixed economies rather than pure market systems. State and non-profit sectors are very large and the private sector regulated and subsidised. The post-socialist market models often bear little comparison with the realities of the non-socialist systems elsewhere.

Differences in the progress made by the central and eastern European transitional countries and the success of reforms of the socialist system which failed in Europe, but still work in Asia, have very much reinforced the institutionalist perspective, emphasising the importance of the various institutions underpinning a successful economy. It is also accepted that within each political system there is room for some variation. As for structural adjustment, institutional reform, and behaviour change, they will take a long time under any conditions. More recently, further considerations were called for the important roles played by transitional governments. Drawing on the success in Poland, Kolodko claimed that

> Market economies do not expand without a wise government-led development policy and well designed institutions, both types of economies, i.e. European and former Soviet economies in transition as well as the reformed economies of China and Vietnam, have a chance to succeed in their market endeavors. … If the state fails to design a proper institutional set up, then

market failures prevail and informal industrialisation takes over. Instead of a sound market, a 'bandit capitalism' does emerge.

(Kolodko, 1998: 15–16)

In the very long term, the transition should be seen as a major instrument of development policy.

## Urban transition

Key principles of socialist urban development include: socialist and 'scientific' ideologies; industrialisation, particularly in the heavy industry sector; under-investment in housing, community facilities and other general infrastructure; central control through economic planning and public projects. This resulted in poor urban living environment, low level of utilisation of land in central area, uniformity of architecture and urban landscape manifested by the factory-built estates of flats in the outer ring. Szelenyi pointed out that socialism produced distinctive urban patterns, not necessarily according to the designs of socialist planners, but due broadly to 'the consequences of the abolition of private property, of the monopoly of state ownership of the means of production, and of the redistributive, centrally planned character of the economic system' (1996: 287). Features of socialist cities included under-urbanisation (relative to capitalist systems at the same industrial level), low levels of spatial differentiation, unusually low density in central areas, and few signs of socially marginal groups. Old neighbourhoods were allowed to deteriorate, while new construction was focused in high-density blocs in peripheral zones (Logan, 2001).

Bachtler et al. (2000) examined the regional implications of transition and concluded that reform has produced relative winners and losers, and transition has increased levels of inequality between regions and individuals. National differences have become increasingly apparent as individual countries have made their reform choices against unique historical, political and institutional back-grounds. Transformation has created new spatial patterns of economic and social inequality. Capital cities, for example, are usually flourishing, with relatively low unemployment rates, high levels of new firm formation and concentrations of foreign investment. Old industrial areas have particularly suffered from the closure or rationalisation of outdated and inefficient enterprises, often with a critical social cost. While emerging regional disparities have certain common elements – deep-seated historical and cultural factors, ethnicity – the specific influence of central planning and national characteristics all influence the ability of individual regions to adapt to the changing economic environment (Bachtler et al., 2000).

Since 1990, the most important administrative reforms impacting on urban development in central Europe have been that of decentralisation of power and a re-emergence of local authorities as the main decision-making entities with respect to urban functions and development (Enyedi and Szirmai, 1992; Keivani *et al.*, 2001). Decentralisation of power, however, has also brought issues of conflict, competition and rivalry between different layers of local government. De Melo and Ofer studied the nature and variety of transition in ten regional capitals of Russia. They found that all cities had experienced radical changes in their institutions and economies – changes associated on the one hand with the abolition of central planning and the introduction of freer markets, and on the other hand with political decentralisation and the introduction of local elections. These changes had led to a wide diversity in economic and social outcomes, reflecting differences in the central government's (inequitable) economic relations with regions as well as differing local and regional policies. They also found that there were significant variations in transition among these cities. Ulyanovsk was clearly lagging on market reforms, and Saratov represented a model of liberalisation without institutional support. Both extremes had failed, but as far as the concern with social consequences the failings of the Saratov model appear to be worse than those of the Ulyanovsk model (de Melo and Ofer, 1999).

Privatisation in urban areas in east Europe has generally followed two basic stages: small privatisation and large privatisation programmes (Ghanbari-Parsa and Moatazed-Keivani, 1999). The former was largely carried out through auction whereby small retail units, restaurants, service and manufacturing firms were sold to domestic investors. The latter, on the other hand, focused on medium-sized and large state-owned enterprises through tenders and direct sale and was open to both domestic and foreign investors. In some countries, the processes had been open to abuse as vehicles for accumulation of vast wealth by individuals and financial groups, thereby creating major problems in terms of inefficiencies in corporate governance and the operation of firms, rental windfalls to a few and the exclusion of large parts of civil society, the increasing social division.

Reviewing the literature on urban development of eastern European cities in the 1990s, Ruoppila (1999) identified two main features: gentrification and commercialisation of the urban core, and suburbanisation. The most remarkable change in eastern European cities had been the rapid renewal of urban cores. In general, the residential status of the historical cores of the cities was rather modest at the end of the socialist era. The urban renewal had been implemented through the relocation of the old tenants. In medieval city centres the gentrification had accompanied an overall decline of the residential population as part of the old residential spaces had been redeveloped into business or office use. There was the booming of the tertiary sector looking for space in central locations, but increasing international tourism, leading to gentrification of services, and 'touristification' of medieval city centres. In capital cities, part of the residential gentrification related to foreigners' demand in the housing market (Ruoppila, 1999). Contrary to potential foreign influence in the gentrification, the accelerated process of suburbanisation had been very local. Also the process of suburbanisation had been argued to be socially highly selective comprising mainly the wealthy residents, who seek an attractive living environment from the detached housing areas behind the city borders.

Parallel to the above tendencies, a concern had been expressed about the decay of socialist panel housing areas. The need of urban planning to prevent the slums was expressed especially by western writers. Studying the accelerated decline of status of the newer and more distant socialist housing estates of Budapest, Szelenyi (1996: 315) argued that 'those who can afford to move are beginning to escape, leaving the poor and ethnic minorities to concentrate in them'. There is a growing recognition in post-socialist cities of the trend towards an increasing concentration of disadvantaged households in certain neighbourhoods. The best examples of deprivation and social erosion in post-socialist cities were provided by high-rise housing estates. New social exclusion is the outcome of the capitalist transformation of labour market and the housing market. Poorly educated people, with low and irregular incomes were increasingly marginalised within society. Studying one of the poor housing estates – Havanna in Budapest – after privatisation, Egedy and Kovacs found that:

> From the beginning of the 1990s Havanna started to function as the dead-end of the housing chain, it was very easy to get into a flat, but it was very difficult to get rid of it. For those who had no chance to improve their position on the labour market it became really the final station in their career independently from their age, or race.
>
> (Egedy and Kovacs, 1999: 15)

Szelenyi predicted, in 1996, that east European cities will experience far-reaching changes in all the three dimensions of urban development where it was possible to detect 'socialist characteristics': the urban–rural relationship which evolved under state socialism is at breaking point and major dislocations of the population may be expected as the crisis of post-communist transformation evolves; the 'urbanism' of post-communist cities has already undergone spectacular changes; change can also be detected in urban forms and in patterns of social segregation (Szelenyi, 1996). Though there is little sign of a post-communist *landflucht* (flight from land), under-urbanisation continues to be reproduced, even though its social-economic and political basis has been undermined. The reasons for this are, first, a weak push from the rural communities and second, an even weaker pull from the urban centres, which sooner or later may result in major geographic shifts of the population. In terms of urbanism, there is an expansion of the tertiary sector, increasing ethnic diversity, increase in urban marginality, homeless people, sharp increase in crime, confusion and legitimacy problems of law enforcement agencies. Urban forms change more slowly than urban diversity. It is obvious, though, that social inequalities are increasing sharply, and this is beginning to affect patterns of urban social segregation as well (Szelenyi, 1996: 311–14).

Restitution of private property and privatisation was an important aspect of the east European cities. In the Czech Republic and Poland (excluding Warsaw) original owners or their heirs could apply to the courts for restitution of property confiscated after the 1945–9 communist take-over or could ask for compensation (Keivani *et al.*, 2001). In Prague, for example, the vast majority of buildings in the city centre (70 per cent) had been returned to the original owners by 1994 (Sykora and Simonickova, 1994). This process plus high demand for office, retail and general commercial activity in central areas of the city led to large price differentiation between the central and peripheral locations.

Hasty urban reform policies were based on a simple assumption: privatisation will facilitate the process of redevelopment of the city; and housing privatisation will accelerate the formation of the market. Because social ownership was the vital point of the previous institutional and ideological order, it had a very strong symbolic meaning and the sale of social rental accommodation signalled that the fortress of social ownership was definitely crumbling and was giving way to new arrangements (Mandic and Stanovick, 1996).

## Inequality and poverty

Transition in central and eastern European countries has important consequences to the social and economic orders established during the socialist period, and has led to increasing polarisation of population in those countries. Summarising the main social characteristics, particularly with regard to poverty, in the Russian Federation in the mid-1990s, the World Bank found that many households have been seriously affected by inflation-induced erosion of real transfers (especially minimum pensions and unemployment benefits), the decline in wage-earning opportunities, and a distinct widening of income distribution. The incidence of poverty has increased significantly since the onset of transition. Moreover, regional variation in poverty and unemployment is widening. Spulber observed that at the end of the first privatisation drive in 1994, on the basis of the 1991 level equalling 100, wages stood at 34 per cent and pensions at 22 per cent of their previous levels. In the mid-1990s, between 33 to 40 per cent of the population in Russia fell below the official benchmark for poverty. If using the unofficial standard proposed by the Russian Centre for Public Opinion, poverty could include around 85 per cent of the population. Real pensions were terribly eroded by inflation and various kinds of official regulations and limitations, and a minimum of 10 million pensioners (out of some 37 million) received less than the minimum subsistence income set for pensioners.

> The shrinkage and deterioration of the safety net have not been due to an ad hoc policy objective; rather, the conclusive processes of socio-political and economic transformation have pushed unrelentingly toward the decline and the debasement of welfare.
>
> (Spulber, 1997: 124–7)

By late 1998, more than 40 per cent of people in the country had less than $4 a day, and more than 50 per cent of children lived in families in poverty according to a survey conducted by the World Bank (Stiglitz, 2002). Following the collapse of communist control, the socialist goal of economic justice has been dismissed. The distributional aspects of transition were a secondary consideration (Andrusz *et al.*, 1996). It was assumed that privatisation and other macro-economic adjustments would benefit some people more than others, and those who worked hard and produced well would reap the rewards for their efforts. However, it was expected that Russia would be spared the inequality arising from inherited wealth. Without this legacy of inherited inequality, there was the promise of a more egalitarian market economy. Reality is very different from this expectation. Russia had a level of inequality comparable with the worst in the world (Stiglitz, 2002).

Other post-communist countries have seen comparable, if not worse, increases in poverty.

> In 1987, two years before the fall of the Berlin Wall, some 2.2 million people lived on less than US$1-a-day in Eastern Europe and the former Soviet Union. In 1993 – a mere six years later, with economic reform in full swing throughout the region, that number had risen almost sevenfold to 14.5 million. Over this period, and with respect of that poverty line, the region had recorded by far the largest increase in poverty of any region of the world.
>
> (Ferreira, 1997: 7)

This increase in serious poverty was due fundamentally to two effects of economic transition on its income distribution: a fall in average household incomes, sustained during the period of output collapse; and an increase in income and expenditure inequality. The output declines have now been completely or partially reversed in most countries. Though they were severe and their impact on living standards was dramatic, they were essentially transitory phenomena. The same cannot so confidently be said of the substantial increases in inequality. Whilst this transition will not hurt the poor – unless it somehow leads to an increase in public sector employment – it is likely to benefit the rich much more than the poor. Substantial changes taking place in the labour market are certain to affect the distribution of final incomes in transitional economies. Greater efficiency is not sufficient to imply higher social welfare; it is likely to lead to greater inequality and, in some cases, higher poverty (Ferreira, 1997).

State socialism is characterised as an economic system integrated by redistributive mechanisms, where capitalism is a market-integrated economic system (Szelenyi 1987). Many researchers had predicted a change of social order in former socialist countries. Nee indicated in 1989 that if the transition from redistribution to the market mechanism involves changes in the mode of allocating and distributing resources, the transition will probably change the stratification order.

(Nee, 1989: 663)

According to Szelenyi (1983), inequalities under one system can be reduced by introducing the alternative as a counterbalancing mechanism. Thus, the penetration by market factors will undermine the socialist inequality created by redistribution. However, with the market becoming an influential, or even dominant, mechanism, it will eventually lead to new inequality. For this reason, Kolodko believed that

During transition income policy and government concern for equitable growth has great meaning. Whereas increasing inequality is unavoidable during the initial years of transition, the state must play an active role, through fiscal and social policies, controlling income dispersion. There is a limit of disparity beyond which further expansion of overall economic activity becomes constrained and growth starts to slow or recovery is delayed. If disparity growth is tolerated for a number of years during contraction, when the standard of living is improving for a few and declining for many, then the political support for necessary reforms will evaporate. Hence, large inequalities turn against crucial institutional and structural reforms.

(Kolodko, 1998: 24)

## Differences between eastern Europe and China

Roland, Stiglitz and many others believe that the most positive surprise of transition is the success of Chinese economic reforms. China had presented a different model of socialism in the past and has followed a different route in transition. Economic reform and marketisation was carried out in a pragmatic way in contrast to the so-called 'big-bang' approach adopted by some eastern European countries. The control of the Communist Party has been preserved as well. Despite the lack of democratisation, there was no major backlash against economic reforms that brought prosperity and increased incomes to hundreds of millions, despite the associated increase in income inequality.

Whether this divergent trend was due to differences in initial conditions or deliberate choices of policies were hotly debated. One school of thought emphasises policy issues including design and sequencing of policy implementation. McMillan and Naughton (1992) and Perkins (1991) demonstrated the merits of 'gradualism' and argued that China provides a strong case for evolutionary reform. Stiglitz (2002) identified several differences in reform policies and practice between China and Russia.

- China's reform began with a partial privatisation in the agricultural sector, with the movement from the commune system of production to the 'individual responsibility' system.
- China used a two-tier price system which avoided the pitfall of large-scale inflation.
- China unleashed a process of creative destruction – of eliminating the old economy by creating a new one. Millions of new enterprises were created by the townships and villages. Meantime, foreign firms were invited into China to participate in joint ventures.
- China simultaneously, created the 'institutional infrastructure' – an effective securities and exchange commission, bank regulations, and safety nets.
- China did not follow the simple textbook models of policy development.

Singh also believed that China was correct in starting reforms from agriculture and small enterprise (1991). Economic reform was first kicked off with the very poorest quarters of the population and moved gradually upward, which effectively avoided unnecessary social and economic suffering and instability. Rural reform of the late 1970s and the early 1980s brought many villages out of poverty and solved the long-standing food shortage problems. It also released surplus labour for urban development. Urban reform began in the 1980s with the opening up of free markets (mainly grain, vegetables, fruit and other food products), which brought immediate benefits to the poor urban residents outside the state sector by setting up shops using their own property or street stores. The first group of the urban rich (the so-called 10,000 yuan households) were created among the bottom social and economic groups. Industrial reform started with the decentralisation of some decision-making powers to each enterprise aimed at improving efficiency. This allowed enterprise managers to use their own resources to give workers extra pay or bonuses. This action increased incomes among relatively low-paid workers and did increase the productivity of the existing industrial establishment. These early waves of reform reduced the inequalities in the society and created a more relaxed political, economic and social background for more in-depth and aggressive restructuring of the society. If a 'big bang' approach was followed right at the end of the Cultural Revolution period and everyone was pushed into the market at the same time, a large proportion of the population, especially the poor would have experienced a very difficult time. In territorial and political terms, China may have broken into several different units.

Others contested that China put economic reforms ahead of political reforms, while the order was reversed in eastern Europe. Spulber observed that from 1978 onward the Chinese reforms have been kept firmly under central control while achieving the crucial purposes of decollectivising agriculture, shrinking the state sector in industry and services, expanding complex non-state sectors, increasing the country's participation in world trade, and yielding very high rates of economic growth.

Harvie (1998) also highlighted a number of interesting and important lessons from the process of economic transition in China, in terms of the reform strategy to be pursued – its pace, sectoral emphasis, sequencing and key ingredients. First, the initial point determines whether a more gradual or 'big bang' approach is appropriate. China started its reform process in a relatively advantageous position. While the economy was not performing as efficiently as it could have, and many distortions existed from the planning system, it was already experiencing economic growth; it had low inflation, low budget deficits, high savings and low external debt. The reform process could therefore proceed in a gradual and incremental fashion. There was no need for the economy to start the transition process with a stabilisation program. In addition China maintained centralised political control in the hands of the Communist Party, unlike other transition economies in Europe which saw the demise of their communist governments. For China political reform was not on the agenda. Hence the starting point for economic reform was one in which there was both relative economic and political stability. Second, the focus of reform was initially placed upon a sector of the economy where success was most likely. Third, there should be an opening-up of markets to competition from various types of enterprise owner-ship, such as town and village enterprises (TVEs) and non-state sectors. Fourth, rapid integration with the global economy. The experiences of its dynamic regional neighbours played a major role in convincing the Chinese government to pursue such a strategy. China with its cultural, family and historical connections to Hong Kong and Taiwan, was in a particularly advantageous position in this regard. The open-door policy had enabled China to gain access to western technology and ideas through foreign investment. Fifth, China had made the clear decision to move towards a socialist market economy; the attainment and viability of such a socialist market economy in which there will remain extensive public ownership. Finally, China's experience with gradual approach to transition highlights the prospective problems with such an approach, including macro-economic cycles, weakening budgetary revenues, corruption, and rising income disparities across regions.

In contrast to these above explanations, Sachs and Woo (1994) argued 'it was not gradualism, nor experimentation, but rather China's economic structure … that has proved so felicitous to reform'. According to them, China's problem was the classic one for a less-developed country. The problem for such a labour-surplus economy was moving the surplus from low-productivity agriculture to high-productivity industry. China's strategy had accordingly involved a two-track approach. The first goal was to facilitate the flow of peasant-workers into a new labour-intensive, export-oriented sector that is largely outside state control; the second, to keep most of the state enterprise workers in their privileged positions. According to them, gradualism was not feasible in east Europe. The only suitable approach for east Europe would be the 'big bang' reforms.

Berliner (1994) advanced entirely different reasons for the Russian–China contrast. According to Berliner, Gorbachev had actually adopted the Chinese model

– or tried to when he launched *perestroika* – but because of the different economic conditions, the result was the deterioration of the economy. Russia was not China simply because the latter had maintained a powerful structure of authoritarian management, was not a federal state, and had no separation of powers. China's success was based on its 'cruel suppression' of attempts by the opposition to 'destabilise the situation' and on the state apparatus maintaining its grip over a united country. China had delayed the chaotic situation to a later stage.

Rana saw that both initial conditions and policies were important in explaining the difference in economic performance between the Asian transitional economies and countries in east Europe (Rana, 1995). It was wrong to presume that a free market would develop overnight if central planning was eliminated and the market freed. Scrapping the central planning system was obviously a necessary step toward the evolution of a market economy, but unless existing institutions can readily be converted to facilitate production and distribution under market conditions, the transitional process will be difficult and lengthy.

Two further points should be mentioned here. First, China started reform earlier than most east European countries. The east European experience shows that earlier reform was also a key advantage. Those countries began their reform before 1989 prepared them well to face the sudden changes caused by the collapse of the communist system. Second, though China remains a communist state, the political system functions now are very different from old-fashioned communism. Apart from the one-party system, not many political and economic policies conform to the traditional communism ideologies. Much openness, accountability and internal democracy had been introduced into the administrative system.

With sustained economic growth during the reform period, China had not experienced the so-called transitional recession. There were significant improvements in the quality of life among the Chinese population. The country also saw the largest reduction in poverty in history in a short time span, from 358 million in 1990 to 208 million in 1997. This however does not mean China has avoided all the problems experienced by the east European countries. The World Bank (2001) reported that China has also had significant increases in inequality – between town and country, and between the coastal areas and inland China. These inequality and poverty problems will be discussed in following chapters.

# 3 Urban change in China

Oriental Plaza – the famous Wang Fu Jing shopping area after redevelopment, Chang'an Avenue, Beijing, October 2003.

Chinese cities have experienced two dramatic transformations since 1949. When the communists came to power, the country was predominately a rural society with a very poor urban network. There were only 69 settlements with official city status, which included about 11 per cent of population. Cities also had distinctive land-use patterns and internal structures derived from the historical sequence of Chinese imperial and western-associated colonial treaty port eras. Land use in cities dominated by palaces, gardens, government buildings, traditional houses, western settlements (concessions) and some industrial establishments concentrated in the coastal regions. Between 1949 and 1976, cities experienced the first major transition. Under the leadership of Chairman Mao, semi-feudal and semi-colonial cities were transformed into socialist industrial bases. Centralised economic planning and strict population movement control maintained a relatively low level of urbanisation (Kirkby, 1985).

Since 1978 Chinese cities have witnessed another major transformation. Under the banners of an open-door policy and economic reform, cities have moved gradually away from the socialist planned industrial bases to liberal market places and focal points for mass consumption. New changes included the move to a more heterogeneous population, rural to urban migration, spatial reorganisation, large-scale new housing development, globalisation, suburbanisation, and changes in the spatial/administrative systems of cities (Ma, 2002; Cook, 2000). This chapter looks at this latest Chinese urban transition in more detail.

In western societies, distinctive features of the upper class, the middle class and the working class and the mobility between classes were important elements of social research. There was no such clear division of population and comparable study of social structure on China. Most research in the past focused on political and class struggles and the rise and fall of particular political figures and associated groups. Broad-brush classifications such as urban residents, rural residents, the leaders, the communist party members and the masses were used to describe Chinese population. The internal structure of urban society and the relative advantage and disadvantage of different socio-economic groups were not given sufficient attention. This chapter will focus on the official division of labour, the social and economic status and the distribution of benefits and rights among different social groups.

## Pre-reform social structure

### Rural and urban division

Pannell (1990) outlined the theoretical principles that underlined the early Chinese communist ideologies. First, there existed an ideological/theoretical commitment to equality and egalitarianism inherent in a Marxist/socialist system. Second, there was the strong belief and commitment to central planning and policy-making that provided the operational thrust for implementing policies that create a more egalitarian society. In practice, Chinese socialist urban policies did not conform to normative Marxist values. Urban areas had been heavily subsidised throughout the socialist period because most urban residents were employed in the state-managed sector of the economy.

In the first few years of the communist government, no formal control was imposed on rural to urban migration. Millions of rural labours moved to industrial cities for employment. Population in some cities had doubled in a very short period (Day and Xia, 1994). In Xi'an city, for example, population increased from about 400,000 in 1949 to 1,000,000 in 1957 (Wang and Hague, 1992). This large-scale increase of population in urban areas and the lack of new investment as a consequence of the breaking relationship with USSR caused serious unemployment problems which resulted in a major policy change. From 1958 onward rural to urban migration was controlled strictly through the *hukou* (residence registration) and food rationing system. Moving from rural to urban area (even for a very short period of visiting a hospital) had to be approved by the authority.

The *hukou* system was initially introduced in 1951 to monitor movement and residence of urban population, and later expanded to cover both the rural and urban populations in 1955 (Cheng and Selden, 1994). The system classified all the people in the country into two main categories: the agricultural (rural) households and non-agricultural (urban) households (Chan and Tsui, 1992). The non-agricultural population mainly lived in cities and large towns and were guaranteed certain supplies of daily necessities, ranging from food grains and edible oils, to clothes and other rationed items. They were also entitled to state-provided education, social and medical services, jobs and housing. On the other hand, agricultural households lived in villages and did not have any of these benefits and opportunities. Neither were they permitted to move out of their villages. Children were only allowed to inherit *hukou* status from their mother (Chan, 1996). This rural and urban division was obviously structured on fundamental inequality (for details on the *hukou* system, see, Johnson, 1988; Goldstein and Goldstein, 1994; Murphey, 1980; Ma and Hanten, 1981; Kirkby, 1985; Pannell, 1990; Chan, 1992 and 1996; Wu, 1997).

## Cadres and workers in the state sector

Absolute equality was not pursued in urban areas either. Although policies aimed at reducing inequalities between different groups were promoted from time to time, inequalities were allowed to exist and sometimes intentionally or unintentionally increased. During the first few years of the new system, as a continuation from the wartime practice, most government officials and leaders were covered by a supply system. They lived in public housing and ate in canteens. In the industrial sector, old employment relations and capitalist-style businesses were allowed to continue, and industrial workers received wages from their employers. With the expansion of state-owned industries, a unified national labour and salary system was gradually introduced from 1955 onward.

This system divided all urban employment into two categories: cadres and workers. The cadre category included all government and party officials in urban areas. It also included professionals such as engineers, technical, managerial and administrative personnel in state enterprises, government-owned institutions and organisations. The workers category included skilled and unskilled employees engaged in industries or other public organisations. The cadre or worker status was recorded in official personnel documents which became the most important indicator of social status in urban areas. Cadre was a superior status to worker and a change from worker to cadre (very rare) would constitute a significant promotion.

Cadre and worker difference was the second most important social division after the rural–urban distinction. When the first salary system was introduced in 1955, it included 30 grades on the cadres' scale, varying slightly between regions. Grade 1 was the highest and grade 30 the lowest. Government leaders at all levels including the party chairman and the premier were paid according to this scale. Placement on the scale depends on experience, years of service and official rank. Initially the difference between the highest and the lowest grade was about 31 times. Later, the salary at the top was reduced on several occasions while the lowest grade salaries were increased (Ma, 1990).

For the worker category, an eight-grade scale was used. Grade 1 included inexperienced workers and grade 8 included the most experienced workers. Below grade 1, there were trainee workers who had just joined the labour force. Although the low-grade workers' salary was similar to that for the low-grade cadres, the higher graded workers' salary was much lower than the highly paid cadres.

The grade of cadre was particularly important to government and party officials. There was correlation between a cadre's salary and his/her office rank. A promotion in the office would move up the salary grade. Cadres with a grade 1–10 were usually referred at as leading cadres who enjoyed more privileges and benefits in housing, personal security, use of personal cars, secretary, and servants. To them the normal salaries became less important because of many extra benefits. The mid-rank cadres (11–18) occupied major administrative and party posts throughout all levels of government and had some privileges in housing provision and other services. Low-rank cadres and general officials occupied the grades above 18. College and university graduates automatically became cadres when they began to work. Workers were recruited by the government among urban school leavers and sometimes among rural youth, and were allocated initially to each state enterprise as trainee workers. The main recruitment criteria were merit and political consciousness. Official corruption in recruitment or 'getting in through the back door' became a main feature of this system during the 1970s. The salary and grade systems were adjusted several times in the following years, but the division between cadres and workers remained.

## Collective enterprises and 'outsiders'

Apart from cadres and workers, there were other groups outside the state sectors. In the early years of communist control not all urban enterprises and businesses were nationalised. Small establishments set up before 1949 were collectivised.

This has been referred to as the collective sector ever since. The state imposed less control on this sector in terms of planning and management. Collective sector enterprises made important contributions to the local economy, but they had less influence over the general condition of the national economy. The urban collective sector also provided employment opportunities to many non-skilled people. Local authorities, particularly the district government, played an important part in organising the collective sector. Apart from the leaders and managers, most employees in the collective sector had a low social status compared with the state-sector workers. Their jobs were low grade or no grade at all, poorly paid and less secure. They received fewer social and economic benefits. Because of the small scale, collective enterprises did not have their own housing estates and did not provide housing to its employees. Most collective sector workers lived in their traditional private homes.

There were also people who were not employed by either the state or the collective sectors. It was common for woman to stay at home as housewives before the communist era. Some women retained this status and relied on incomes from their husband or children. People not employed by the formal state sector usually lived in old houses in central areas. These people outside the state sector were given a special social status by the government: *shi ming* (urban citizens). In some cities, they were referred by others as *xiao shi ming* ('Little Citizens'), a term conveying discrimination.

It is obvious that pre-reform Chinese urban society was a highly divided one. In terms of class structure, the upper class would include party and government leaders at all levels, directors of various public academic and professional institutions and managers of large state enterprises. These people were the key decision makers. The middle class would consist of middle-rank government officials, lower level managers and professionals and academics. The direction of career progress of this group was toward the upper class. These upper- and middle-class people form the basic structure of the state organisation. The working class consisted of industrial workers, general service staff, etc. During the pre-reform period, the political status of the workers (as 'the core group of the Chinese Communist Party') was promoted from time to time without the associated economic benefits. There was also an urban under-class, the outsiders of the state sectors. They were the original poor urban residents (the little citizens) living in the old central areas, who failed to find a position in the state sector. The numbers of this group declined continuously during the pre-reform period through the expansion of the state and collective sectors.

## Distribution of benefits

Marshell (1973) has distinguished three types of rights associated with the growth of citizenship in western societies:

1   Civil rights: freedom of individuals to live where they choose; freedom of speech and religion; the right to own property and the right to equal justice before the law.
2   Political rights: the right to participate in elections and to stand for public office.
3   Social rights: the prerogative of every individual to enjoy a certain minimum standard of economic welfare and security. They include such rights as sickness benefits, social security in the case of unemployment and the setting of minimum levels of wages.

This framework is applied here to assess the distribution of benefits among Chinese urban population before reform. Table 3.1 summarises the rights enjoyed by different social groups. The enjoyment of the rights was judged subjectively and a value of full rights, some rights or no rights was assigned to each group. The assignment is only an indication of the relative situation because most of the benefits or rights are difficult to quantify. They were also taken as an average situation across the group.

Leading cadres enjoyed more benefits and rights than middle-level and general cadres; cadres enjoyed more benefits and rights than workers; workers enjoyed more benefits and rights than the other urban residents outside the state system and rural residents. The table also shows that there were differences between different sets of rights. Formal state-sector employees including the workers and cadres enjoyed more social rights; while the cadres enjoyed more political rights than the workers, one could be elected and the other could only vote. Both the urban 'little citizens' and rural residents enjoyed fewer social rights, limited political rights but more civil rights in speech, and owning of properties. In the pre-reform system, the civil rights of the state sector were limited by the public ownership of housing, which limited the options of where to live and deterred home ownership. In justice and law, theoretically speaking, everyone was the same, but in practice, the powerful cadres usually had more influence in this area than other powerless individuals.

## Work units and social integration

Although there was clear and distinctive social division among urban residents in pre-reform Chinese cities, this did not result in serious spatial segregation. Prior to economic reform, most urban residents in China were associated with a work unit (*danwei*). Work units were defined as independent accounting units in official statistics (Bian, 1994), and were classified into three categories based on their primary functions: a) government or party organisations (*dangzheng jiguan*), b) enterprises (*qiye danwei*), and c) institutions (*shiye danwei*). Government or party organisations represented the state and assumed the central administrative role in Chinese society, while economic enterprises and institutions were owned in varying

**Table 3.1** Social benefits and rights distribution in China, 1949–78

| Occupational class | | Civil rights | | | | Political rights | | Social benefit and rights | | | | |
| --- | --- | --- | --- | --- | --- | --- | --- | --- | --- | --- | --- | --- |
| | | Where to live | Speech and religion | Ownership of a property | Equal justice in law | Participate in voting | Being elected | Free child education | Sickness benefit | Job security | State pension | Minimum wages |
| Cadres | Leading | ++ | – | – | ++ | ++ | ++ | ++ | ++ | ++ | ++ | ++ |
| | Middle-level | – | – | – | ++ | ++ | ++ | ++ | ++ | ++ | ++ | ++ |
| | Ordinary | – | + | – | + | ++ | + | ++ | ++ | + | + | ++ |
| Urban Workers | Skilled | – | ++ | – | + | ++ | – | + | + | + | + | ++ |
| | Unskilled | – | ++ | + | + | + | – | + | + | – | – | – |
| Other residents | | – | ++ | + | + | – | – | + | – | – | – | – |
| Rural residents | | – | ++ | ++ | + | – | – | – | – | – | – | – |

Key: ++ Full rights; + Some or partial rights; – Minimum or no rights.

Note: Citizens' rights categories based on Marshall's work (1973) described by Giddens (1996: 312).

degrees by the state and were administrated directly or indirectly by the government (Wu, 2002).

Work units played a key role in the organisation and management of urban society (Walder, 1986, 1992; Bian, 1994). They were not simply a production organisation as the name indicates. Apart from providing employment, work units were also political organisations. The Communist Party had branches in all work units. Party leaders were involved in all major decision-making, and were responsible for political affairs in all work units. This ensured the party line being followed by all levels of government and industrial and professional establishments. The political nature of work units was also reflected in the election of local representatives for the party and the government. Large work units functioned as election constituencies. In elections, candidacies were usually selected through work units. This political nature of the work unit was not only reflected by the relationship between the employer and employee, it was also apparent in other relations. The relationship between students and their host institutions, for example, was not as simple as that in the west. Political correctness was an important criterion to gain entry into higher education. Once inside the campus, political studies were an important part of the curriculum. During the Cultural Revolution period, students actually played a more important part in controlling universities and organised attacks on professors and lecturers.

Chinese work units were also social organisations and the basic cells of the socialist urban structure. Most large work units provided housing, medical care, pensions and child care/education facilities. They functioned like independent urban communities, sometimes isolated and surrounded by walls. Inside each work unit compound, various facilities (shops, banks, post offices) could be found. In land-use terms, each work unit could have several different functional zones: production or office areas, housing areas and public facility areas (e.g. nursery school, primary school, high school, sports facilities, communal canteen, etc.). Housing estates in cities did not automatically form the western-style urban communities. It was a special social organisation based on employment relation-ship. Residents in a particular housing estate were normally employed by the same work unit. Social relationships were woven into political and economic relationships established through the work unit. The relationships between neighbours were affected by the working relationships of the adults in their offices. A person with access to a work unit did not only have a job, but a whole package of a particular style of urban life.

The resources that a work unit could offer its employees were also contingent upon its structural position in the socialist hierarchy. Resources at a work unit's disposal varied with its type. The redistributive system tended to favour state-owned work units because they were considered the base of the communist regime. Like the individual salary grade system, each work unit had a rank in the hierarchy; the higher the rank of a work unit, the more power it had in bargaining with its government supervisor (Bian, 1994). Because of the different functions assigned to each work unit, there was a strong association between social class status and categories of work unit. Some work units had a higher proportion of cadres and leading cadres such as the central government, while other work units had a higher proportion of low-grade factory workers such as the textile factories. The general relationship between social class status and work unit is summarised in Table 3.2.

The complex nature of the work unit also had a significant impact on Chinese urban administration and governance. The wide economic, social and political powers assigned to the work unit actually left limited powers to the municipal government. Cities were fragmented into small independent units which made the municipal government itself irrelevant to most urban residents. The city government was only important at the macro level of economic management, and very weak at provision of services to residents. In this sense the work unit became an important tier of local administration. Most government social policies in urban areas were implemented through the work units. Family planning or the policy of 'one family, one child', for example, was more successful in urban areas than in rural areas. Without the economic, social and political leverage of the work unit, the effective implementation of it would be impossible (Lu, 1989). The work unit was the crucial vehicle of social administration and social control. It was there that most government policies were implemented.

As such a complex organisation, the work unit offered many different types of job opportunity and required many different kinds of people. It also required a high level of social integration and mixing. Although there were clear social divisions among the employees of a work unit, people tended to recognise the differences and accept the fact that different classes enjoyed different benefits. Spatial differences within a work unit were insignificant. Social mix within a work unit however did not mean everyone was equal. Taking housing as an example, the differences in entitlements between cadres and workers, between highly ranked professional and low skilled technicians were real and significant (Wang and Murie, 1999). The basic criteria for housing were normally office status in the cadre category and years of service in the public sector. Factors affecting family living conditions, such as the size of the household and the number of dependent children, were not taken into consideration.

## Land use and spatial patterns

Socialist cities were planned and developed according to socialist principles. Basic planning principles included separation of functional zones, living near to work, the use of public transport and equal living standards and distribution of job opportunities. Gaubatz (1995) observed that spatial organisation of the Chinese city during the Maoist period was strongly influenced by a 'generalised' ideal of urban organisation. In spatial terms, each district of the city ideally was to be

**Table 3.2** Social class and employment in Chinese cities

| Employment sector and work unit type | | Social classes | | | |
|---|---|---|---|---|---|
| | | *Upper class* | *Middle class* | *Working class* | *Under-class* |
| | Party/government organisation: central and local | Leading party and government officials | Senior and junior officials | General permanent service staff | |
| State sector | Public institutions | Leading professionals and engineers | Professionals at middle or lower rank | General permanent service staff | Temporary service staff |
| | State enterprises | Managers of large firms | Lower-level managers | Shop floor workers | Trainee workers or short contracted workers |
| Collective enterprises | | | Managers or directors | | Shop floor workers or handicraftsmen |

relatively self-sufficient, offering its residents all or most general functions such as housing, employment, and the provision of subsistence goods and services. The city would consist of many such districts, all relatively indistinguishable from one another. In China the generalised form was embodied in the work unit compound in its ideal form, in which the work unit would provide a wide range of services for its employees. In a society without many family cars, work units brought many social and economic welfare services near to their employees.

Several work units were normally planned together to form a special industrial district or functional zones. In Xi'an city, for example, several functional zones had been built outside the historic walled city (Wang, 1992, 1995; Wang and Hague, 1992). These included an electronic instrument manufacturing district in the west, a machinery manufacturing district in the east, a textile industrial district in the east, and a high education, research and cultural district in the south. There were also a few special industrial districts located in the outlying suburban areas.

As a general pattern, most pre-reform Chinese cities consisted of two very distinctive land-use zones: a core of poor-quality traditional housing and commercial and office areas, and a zone of work units built during the socialist period. The central area experienced different degrees of renewal with some modernised shopping streets and a few public buildings and government offices. The condition of traditional housing remained poor because of no investment and bad maintenance. One of the most significant structural changes in the Chinese city during the 1949 and 1978 period had been the development of these industrial districts and relatively self-sufficient work units. The planning and development of a textile factory district in the eastern suburb of Xi'an was one of the successful planning stories in the 1950s. The district was planned to host several factories (from weaving and cloth-making to printing) along with a power station. This plan allowed for products of one factory to be used as raw materials by another with very little transportation. Comprehensive planning of different land uses was achieved, including railway links, workshops, housing and other facilities such as hospitals, schools, open space, and administration. The advantages of this kind of development were obvious: journey-to-work distances were minimised, while the publicly owned factories and housing areas could be easily managed together by the industrial authority.

## Social and spatial change since 1978

The pace of urbanisation in China increased substantially during the 1980s and the 1990s. In 1952, about 12 per cent of the population lived in cities. This increased to 17 per cent by the end of the Second Five-year Plan period in 1962 (State Statistics Bureau, 1998). As a result of strict controls on population movement and the 'sending down' of urban youth to the countryside, no major increase was recorded in subsequent years (Kirkby, 1985). In 1978 about 18 per cent of the population was classified as urban residents (non-agricultural). Economic reform had since changed the rural urban balance and brought a higher level of urbanisation. The 2000 census put the total urban population at 456 million – about 36 per cent of the total population of the country. The number of cities also increased. In 1978, only 193 settlements had city status. At the end of 2000, there were 663 cities across the country; 40 of them had a population over one million and another 53 between half a million and one million (Table 3.3). The most rapid urban expansion was in coastal areas. In Guangzhou, for example, total population increased by 44 per cent over the period from 1980 to 2002, while the officially registered non-agricultural population living in built-up areas had doubled from 2.5 million to 5 million (Guangzhou Municipal Statistics Bureau, 2003). In Shanghai (the largest city), the total population living in the administration area increased by 16 per cent from 11.5 million to 13.3 million over the same period, while the non-agricultural population increased from 7 million to 10 million, an increase of 43 per cent (Figure 3.1). Pannell (2002) identified several factors which contributed to this rapid urbanisation: continuing, although diminishing, population growth; migration of rural people; rapid structural shift in employment activities and the decline of farm employment; foreign trade and foreign investment; restructuring of state-owned enterprises and growth of private enterprises and activities; and allocation of domestic funds in fixed assets for urban infrastructure.

## Rural to urban migration

Government policy was an important determinant of migration patterns since the founding of the People's Republic of China in 1949 (Johnson, 1988; Goldstein and Goldstein, 1994). In the first few years of the communist government, no

**Table 3.3** Number of cities in China

| Year | Very large (1 million+) | Large (500,000– 1 million) | Medium (200,000– 500,000) | Small (< 200,000) | Total no. of cities |
|------|------|------|------|------|------|
| 1952 | 9 | 10 | 23 | 115 | 157 |
| 1982 | 20 | 28 | 71 | 125 | 245 |
| 1985 | 22 | 30 | 94 | 178 | 324 |
| 1993 | 32 | 36 | 160 | 342 | 570 |
| 2000 | 40 | 53 | 218 | 352 | 663 |

Sources: Various sources in Chinese including: State Statistics Bureau's Urban Social and Economic Survey Team, 1995, 1999 and 2001.

Note
Populations used for city classification include only non-agricultural urban residents.

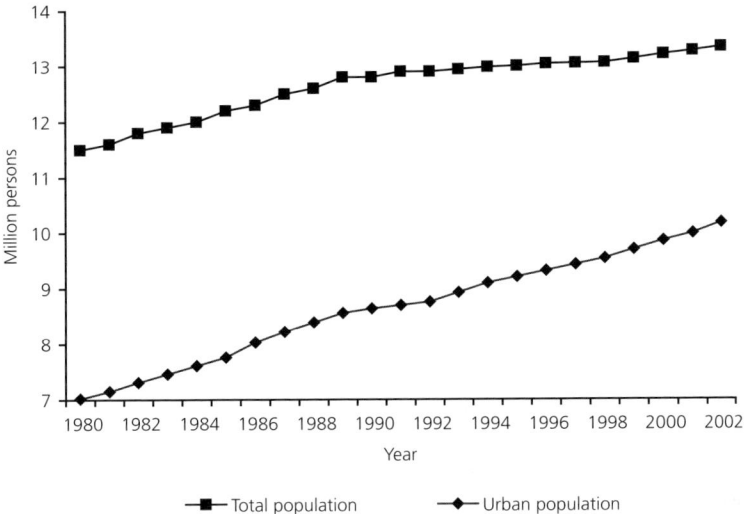

**3.1** Population in Shanghai: 1980–2002

Source: Shanghai Municipal Statistics Bureau, 2003.

formal control was imposed on rural to urban migration and millions of rural labourers moved to new industrial cities for employment. This large-scale increase in urban population caused many problems, which led to strict population control in subsequent years. From 1958 to the end of the Cultural Revolution, any move from rural to urban area had to be approved by the local authority. The open-door policy and rural economic reforms of the early 1980s resulted in a huge number of excess labourers in rural areas, and increase in the mobility of rural population (Xu, 2001). In 1984, the government permitted rural people to work and live in townships and designated towns as long as they brought their own food supply with them (Chen and Chen, 1993). In the following year, rural migrants were allowed to register as temporary population in other urban areas (Shen, 2002). Rural to urban migration had since become a very important part of urban development (Knight and Song, 1999).

When free market trade of agricultural products was restored in cities, food rationing quickly became unimportant. This removed a major obstacle in rural to urban migration. After 1985, many large cities began to allow rural migrants to run shops and set up stalls within their confines. Household domestic services also opened the job markets for young female migrants. During the 1990s, large-scale property and infrastructure development in cities attracted many young people from the countryside to work at construction sites. In some large coastal cities, rural to urban migrants were found in millions (Liu and Liang, 1997; Xiang, 1993). It was reported that at the beginning of 2003, there were 3.8 million migrants in

Beijing, 3.9 million in Shanghai and over 4 million in Guangzhou (*Peoples' Daily* Overseas Edition, 29 January 2003: 8). In Shenzhen Special Economic Zone, 'temporary' residents had outnumbered the official permanent residents by three to one.

The 2000 population census shows that there were 121 million people living away from their registered residence place, of which 90 million were found in urban areas and 88.4 million originated from rural areas (State Statistics Bureau, 2002a). In Anhui province alone, 6 million rural labourers worked outside their village in 2002, of which 5 million went to other provinces. Main destinations included Yangtze River Delta, Pear River Delta, Beijing and Tianjin. Anhui is an agricultural province with 63 million people. This means that 10 per cent of rural people had migrated (*Peoples' Daily* Overseas Edition, 23 January 2003: 2).

After 1992, some local governments (i.e. Shenzhen, Shanghai and Guangzhou) introduced new policies to allow some non-local people to apply for a special, blue-seal (normal official seals on resident status were red) resident card. Migrants had to buy a commercial house in the city and paid a large lump-sum charge (for using the urban infrastructure and facilities) in order to meet the condition for a blue-seal card status. The charge could be up to 10,000 yuan per person (Fan, 2001; Shen, 1995, 2002; Wang, 2000). This policy had the aim of extracting monetary and human recourses from a very small number of elite migrants (Wong and Huen, 1998).

The recent surge of rural to urban migration in China showed some important differences from the migration patterns observed in other developing countries. Although the government had relaxed the restriction on population movement, the residence registration system, which effectively identifies people with their birthplace, was not changed fundamentally. Rural residents may move to cities searching for employment or business opportunities, but they were not treated as equal to the original urban residents (Chan, 1996; Christiansen, 1990, 1992; Goldstein and Goldstein, 1996; Solinger, 1999; Yang, 1993, 1996; Knight and Song, 1999; Xu, 2001). Rather than getting equal social and economic support to that offered to urban residents, the vast majority of rural migrants continue to be rendered inferior and subordinate to urban residents because of the *hukou* system, which denied them urban citizenship even if they managed to live in the city for many years (Fan, 2001).

## Changes of employment structure and work units

During the 1980s and 1990s, work units continued to play an important role in urban development. There was a diversification and an increase in the number of work units in all cities. With the introduction of market economy, many different types of employment organisations emerged, including private and family businesses, joint-venture enterprises and foreign companies. Figure 3.2 shows the

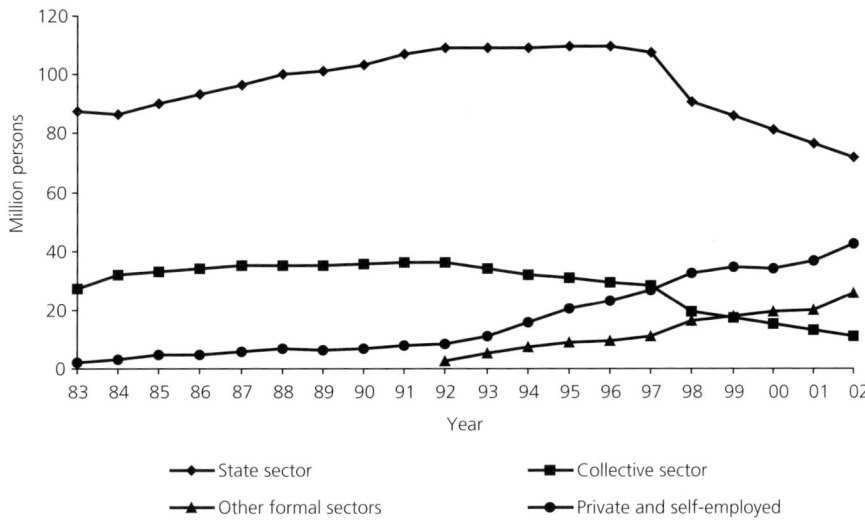

**3.2** Change in urban employment between sectors in China

Data sources: State Statistics Bureau, *China Statistical Yearbook*, 1994; 1998; 2000, 2001 and 2003.

changes of composition of urban employment. The state was the dominant employer in cities in the 1980s and early 1990s and the number of people employed in the state sector increased steadily between 1984 and 1992. The collective sector was the other big employer over the same period, with private businesses and self-employment playing a supportive role. Major changes happened after 1992 when the collective sector began to decline while other non-state sectors began to increase. The restructuring of state enterprises from 1997 onward had a major impact on the urban employment composition. The number of employed in both collective and the state sector declined sharply.

This shift of employment from the traditional sectors to the new market sector was a major cause of other social and economic changes in cities. There was a reduction in job security in both state and collective sectors over the reform period. In the pre-reform urban employment system, most people were employed on a permanent contract. Once a person was assigned to a factory or institution, he or she was expected to work there for the whole of their life, and the employer had responsibilities in looking after the person when he or she retired. There was no formal employment contract between the employee and the employer. This system of job security was often referred as 'iron rice bowl'. During the reform period, more and more young people were employed on short or renewable contracts. In 1983, less than 1 per cent of people were employed under the contract system. By

1993, about 22 per cent of workers in the state sector were on fixed contracts. By the end of 1997 over 50 per cent of employment in state and collective sectors were on contract (State Statistics Bureau, 1998: 150).

In comparison to the old permanent employment system, contracted workers were in a disadvantageous position. Apart from industrial workers employed by state or collective factories, low-level support staff in government and professional organisations could be recruited through the contract system. Work which involved hard labour could be contracted to rural migrants. Very few jobs in cleaning, cooking and security were offered on a permanent basis. In state-owned enterprises, labour-intensive jobs were often given to contracted workers. In construction, steel, mining, shipbuilding and many other industries, most labourers at the frontline of production were migrant workers. Permanent workers were either foremen or team leaders. The 'iron rice bowl' was a feature only for people with permanent contracts; most of them began their work in state factories before economic reform. The total number of these people fell gradually.

There was some degree of depoliticisation of workplaces and deregulation of economic life (Davis *et al.*, 1995). With the introduction of market elements into the urban economic system, the welfare of work units began to vary from sector to sector. The first benefits from reform for work units in the state sector had been some decentralisation of decision-making power from the government. Work units were allowed to retain a portion of profit and to distribute it at their discretion to employees as bonus. While base salaries remained largely regulated by the government, the ability to generate bonus funds and to reward employees varied considerably from one work unit to another. Variation in bonus had become a main source of inter-organisational inequality (Wu, 2002). Work units involved in all levels of administration experienced relatively fewer changes in comparison with the public-owned institutions and state-owned enterprises. The incremental decentralisation policy enabled public institutions and state enterprises eventually to evolve into entities with relative autonomy (McMillan and Naughton, 1992). The ability of each state-owned enterprise to perform in the market became an important factor in determining the income levels of its employees. Throughout the 1990s, employees in enterprises engaged in the new technology sectors such as electronics, automobiles and oil and gas enjoyed improved pay, while incomes of workers in other state-owned traditional factories, such as textiles, declined.

New firms formed in the market sector tended to be more efficient and profitable than the older ones. As a result, employees in the well performing market sector were more likely to receive high wages than employees in the poorly performing state sector. Moreover, as marketisation proceeded, new firms gained economic advantages and pushed many state firms into marginal positions in market competition. The privileges that state enterprises used to enjoy in a homogenously redistributive economy were fading away (Naughton, 1999). Towards the end of the 1990s, it was recognised that most of the old industrial sectors had become unnecessary to modernisation of the economy. New policies were introduced to allow some of these state enterprises to go bankrupt. A significant number of state enterprise workers were laid off.

There were important spatial implications of these changes. The rationally planned industrial functional zones became highly irrational over a very short period in the market system. The concentration of a particular employment type made large parts of urban areas undesirable, socially and economically. In Xi'an city for example, the model textile district mentioned earlier experienced many economic and social problems. Many workers had lost their jobs or were laid off because of industrial restructuring and declining of textile industries. In the large electronic manufacturing district located in the western suburb, similar problems emerged, although to a lesser extent. The spatial distribution of the new wealth created by economic reform was not equally distributed among the work units and the reform had very different impacts on different areas developed during the planned economy period.

## Changes in welfare provision

One of the most dramatic changes in urban life since the introduction of market reforms in the 1980s had been the erosion of the 'iron rice bowl', the social contract between the government and the people. The promises of socialism had gradually given way to the promises of the market. Throughout the reform period, more and more emphasis was put on the efficiency of work units. This led to initiatives that aimed at separating some of the social services that the work unit provided to its employees, such as the management of retirement pensions, health care and housing. These welfare services were either gradually 'socialised' to the municipal level or privatised. The aims of these reforms were to reduce the burdens of state enterprises and make them compete with private firms on equal terms. Socialised management of welfare provision also aimed at solving problems created by bankrupt enterprises.

These changes had different implications for different types of work units. In the government administration sector, the changes were less destructive, and socialisation of benefits, such as health care and pensions, had no major negative effect for most employees. In the enterprise sector, the effects were important. With reduced government support and the intense market competition from the private sector, many state enterprises and most collective enterprises experienced difficulties in providing the necessary services to its employees. Even after socialisation, some enterprises and their employees could not afford to pay their share of contributions, which resulted in pension or health care payments for some retired persons not being paid at times. The negative impacts were not limited to individual employees, but often the whole family, because different generations from the same family usually worked in the same factory.

## Diversification of social and economic groups

As discussed earlier in this chapter, the urban social and economic group structure in the pre-reform period was very simple. The majority of urban employees fell into two categories: cadres or workers. Although this cadre and worker distinction and the associated salary grades remained an important feature of the urban employment system, the socio-economic structure in cities is much more complicated than the worker–cadre division. The state-regulated salary system had also become more complicated than the grade systems used in the 1950s. By the late 1980s, there were 24 grades on the cadre salary scale, with grade 1 the highest and grade 24 the lowest at a difference of about 12 times. This wage scale system was reformed during the 1990s with the introduction of new systems for different sectors. For example, there are different charts for government official personnel, engineering personnel, higher educational and research personnel, secondary and primary teachers, and workers. There are also more complex charts of a combination of general grade and administrative post/professional status-related scale.

New socio-economic groups were created by the expansion of market sectors outside the redistributive planned economy. Jiang Zemin, the then General Secretary of the CCP, in his Report at the Sixteenth National Congress of Chinese Community Party identified six new socio-economic groups, which the Party should represent. These include:

- pioneers, founders and professionals of the non-state-owned scientific and technological research establishments
- managers and technical staff employed by foreign firms
- owners of family businesses
- owners of private enterprises and companies
- professionals employed by various brokers or middlemen organisations
- self-employed (Jiang, 2002).

Many western commentators viewed this as a significant change in Chinese politics, and capitalists were invited to join the Communist Party. The importance given to these groups by the party did indicate their economic and political strength. Many Chinese sociologists referred to these new groups and the existing senior administrators and professionals in the public institutions as the new Chinese middle class. Indeed, though their proportion was still small, they were the dominant groups in economic, social and political affairs. The power and privileges enjoyed by the traditional socialist working class were in continuous decline.

Apart from the return of capitalists to Chinese urban societies, there was also diversification of other social groups. During the pre-reform period, political allegiance and job status were the key criteria used to identify population groups. Despite the planning of distinctive functional zones such as administrative areas,

| Pre-reform groups | New urban social groups |
|---|---|
| Government and party officials | Government and party officials |
| | Civil servants |
| | Owners of large private businesses |
| Directors/managers of state-owned enterprises | Managers of joint ventures or foreign companies |
| | Directors/managers of state enterprises |
| Professionals and academics in state-owned institutions | Professionals of private consultancies |
| | Academics and professionals in public institutions |
| Managers of collective enterprises | Managers of collective enterprises |
| Workers in state enterprises | Workers of state enterprises |
| | Workers of collective enterprises |
| Workers in collective enterprises | General staff employed by joint-ventures or foreign companies |
| | General staff employed by private business |
| Other general urban residents | Self-employed and family business owners |
| | Rural migrants |

**3.3** Social and economic groups in cities

industrial areas and commercial and housing areas, cities were not divided into different residential areas based on household income. There was also no obvious concentration of the poor in particular areas. Although political reliability is still a very important condition for senior party leaders and government officials, political classification of residents has become less significant as a result of economic reform. Instead, a different social and economic structure has emerged in urban areas. Communities or neighbourhoods of similar income or status have appeared.

Figure 3.3 lists the major social and economic groups before and since reform. It also shows that some of the new groups were related to the old ones while others emerged from the market economic system. At the top of the social hierarchy is a new rich class. It includes senior government and party leaders, directors and managers of the new private businesses and foreign companies, and some small business owners who made a fortune during the early years of urban reform. The lifestyle of this group is very different from the traditional working class. New cottage housing was built in almost all large cities to accommodate this group.

## Spatial re-organisation

In contrast to the generalised urban form developed during the pre-reform period, cities are becoming increasingly specialised. New urban landscape consists of many new functional zones and districts, such as central business districts (CBDs), high-tech development areas, special economic development areas, residential districts, manufacturing districts, foreign enclaves and tourist districts. The continued increase in spatial and functional specialisation in Chinese cities is strongly tied to increased autonomy and diversity in the social and economic spheres. Whereas the pre-reform city was predicated on a static population and a very specific ideal of urban life and space, the new city is developing in a context of greater socio-economic and individual mobility, and changing into an increasingly complex economic organisation and urban form (Gaubatz, 1995, 1996).

Urban reform policies which have a direct impact on spatial re-organisation are related to residence and housing. Pre-reform period cities were not divided into different residential areas based on residents' income levels. As a result of reform, a different spatial structure has emerged, in which communities or neighbourhoods of similar income or status have appeared, alongside the legacy of the old socialist cities. Figure 3.4 provides an indicative model of the new urban land-use and residential distribution. In large cities, several different land-use zones developed under different modes of production can be identified. Central areas had a history of pre-communist period, which consisted of small shops, government buildings and traditional housing. Because of the central location and higher land values, most central areas had be redeveloped into high-rise commercial

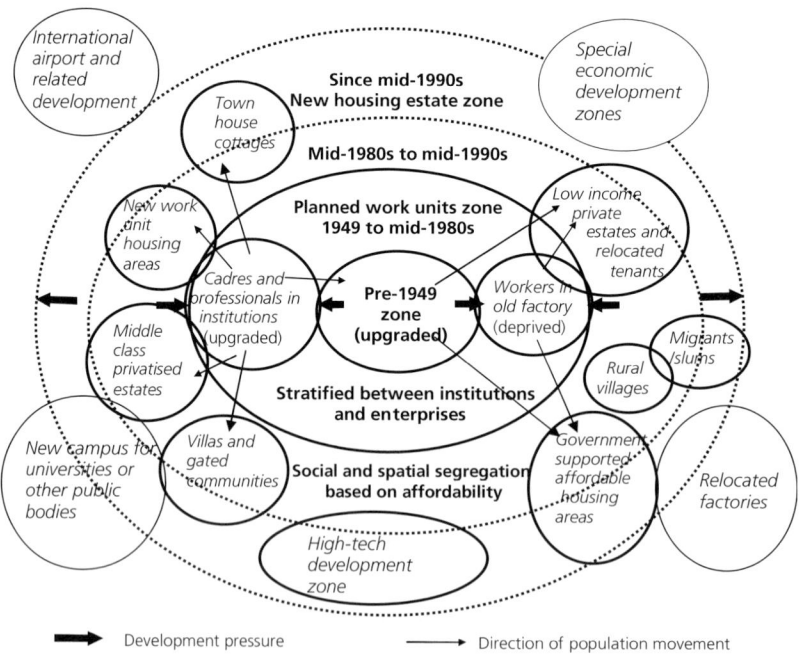

**3.4** Spatial and residential differentiation in cities

and office buildings and luxury residential apartments. Outside these historical cores lie the socialist planned work unit zones. Different functional areas were originally planned, such as industrial areas, warehouses, housing and public institutions. Major upgrading in this area was carried out at work unit level. Because of differences in financial powers between work units, there is spatial stratification within this zone. Some large well-performing institutions carried out comprehensive redevelopment on the land under their control and improved their housing and living environment, while other work units, particularly old industrial factories, experienced difficulties in holding onto their position. Some were forced to 'sell' their land to developers and move out of the urban areas.

A chemical factory located in a south suburb of Beijing was forced to close down in 1997. The land occupied by the factory was sold to a property developer. The managers of the factory hoped to use the money to buy another piece of land further from the central area to set up a new factory for their workers. The deal became problematic after the old factory buildings were demolished and a new piece of land bought. The developer ran out of funds. By the end of 2003, there was no progress in negotiation while most of the factory's original employees were laid-off. Urban expansion led to many of this type of factory being relocated to suburban areas. Part of the reason for this move is the increased land value in cities. Industrial production is less profitable than real estate development. Old factory areas had to give way to real estate development.

Apart from industrial relocation, much of new development happened on green-field sites. This is where the post-socialist zone lies. In large cities, this zone could be further divided into two rings. The inner ring comprised mostly high-rise moderate-standard commercial or work unit housing areas; while the outer ring consisted of high-standard private housing built in the last few years. Housing estates, specifically those for the rich, can be found in this ring. This ring is also home to most high-tech or special economic development zones. Some government-supported affordable housing schemes (usually very large ones, such as *huilongguan* for 300,000 residents in Beijing) are located in this ring as well. Urban sprawl also brought many rural villages into urban built-up areas. These villages maintained their original courtyard housing land-use patterns. Some of them had become the prime location for rural migrants.

Suburbanisation is continuing over the last few years. In some cities one of the most important driving forces behind the urban sprawl was the expansion of higher education. With an increase in student numbers and associated incomes, many large universities carried out a sizeable development programme, some on their original campus, others on new sites in suburban areas. As a strategy to increase the high-tech components of the local economy and enhance its national standing, Shenzhen city built a large complex of high educational facilities to be used by major national universities. Both Beijing and Tsinghua Universities were invited to set up a postgraduate school in this complex. As a key high education centre in the inland, Xi'an city is host to many important universities. A few of them developed new campuses over the last few years. One of these new campuses is about ten kilometres from the existing campus. The new area is more than twice as large as the old campus. Good agricultural land has been put out of use and the original farmers relocated, though the full development of the new campus is going to take many years. Several other universities did the same at nearby sites.

After nearly 25 years of development, much of the transformation of the central areas had been completed. Only small patches of traditional housing areas in difficult locations were left. The outer zones of commercial properties were the result of the new market economy. The future development of cities depends much on changes made to the middle zone of socialist work units. Specific land-use pattern in cities varies from place to place according to local historical features, regional economic and physical geography and political will of local leaders. However, these zones representing different periods of development can be identified easily. In some cities, these zones could be discontinuous areas rather than complete rings.

Because of the economic planning during the 1950s and 1960s, some cities had a concentration of state-owned industrial establishments, while other cities, particularly those at the coastal regions, were starved of industrial investment during the socialist period. In terms of time scale, different cities will have different courses for change in the future. Large coastal cities with relatively smaller work unit zones may find the transition to a market economy easier and shorter, and large industrial towns located in the inland areas will find the transition more difficult and will take a longer time. Possible transitional patterns in different cities are presented in Figure 3.5.

## Distribution of reform benefits

The social impact of urban economic reform changed through time. The general pattern had been a shift of benefits from one group to another. As Harvie (1998) pointed out, the first group to benefit from reform was of people engaged in informal sectors and the population at the bottom of urban society. In the late 1970s and early 1980s, urban residents who lived in central areas began to benefit from policies that encouraged small private businesses. Many households took the opportunity and set up shops and restaurants. Although these people were still outsiders to the socialist system, they had become an important economic force in cities. Some of them later developed their businesses into sizeable enterprises. The locational advantages of this group were later curtailed by the invasion of commercial property developers and the urban renewal process. Realising the high land values in central areas, local governments began to take advantage of their legal land ownership. Large-scale commercial and office blocks were developed in the central areas and original residents were relocated to other less expensive areas; some of them were

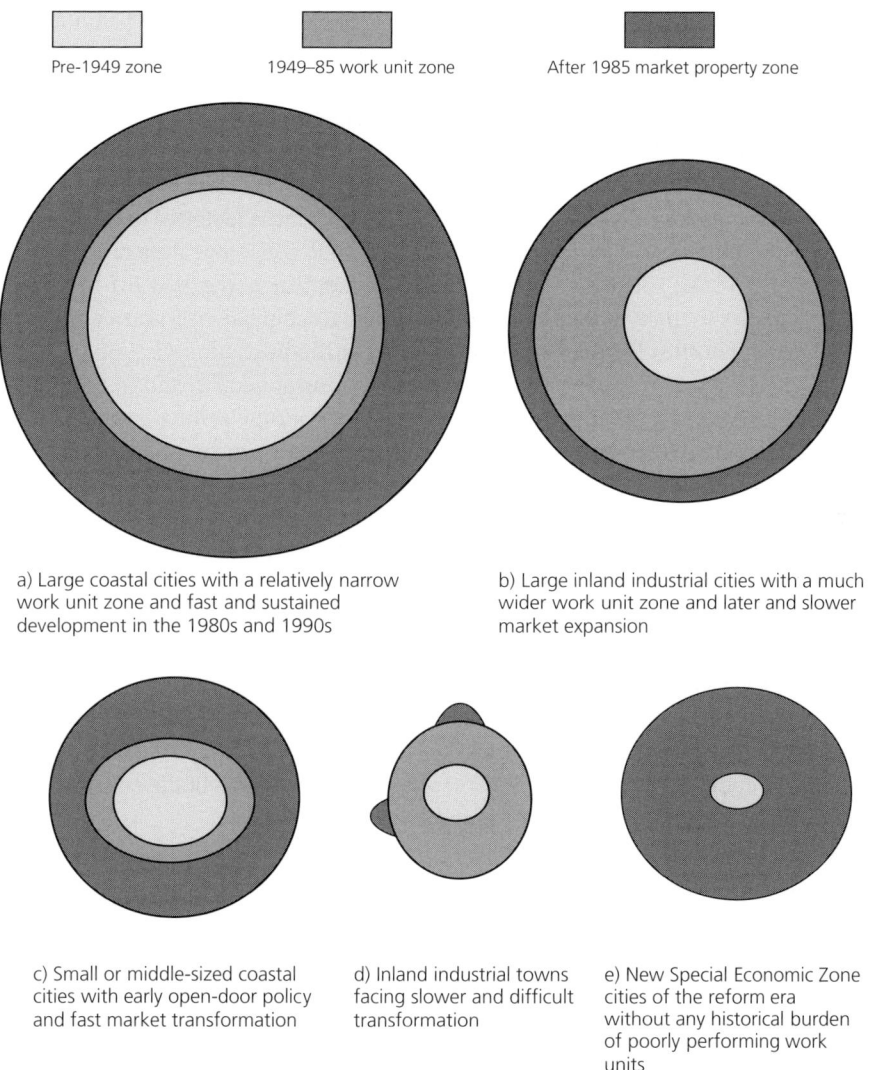

Pre-1949 zone | 1949–85 work unit zone | After 1985 market property zone

a) Large coastal cities with a relatively narrow work unit zone and fast and sustained development in the 1980s and 1990s

b) Large inland industrial cities with a much wider work unit zone and later and slower market expansion

c) Small or middle-sized coastal cities with early open-door policy and fast market transformation

d) Inland industrial towns facing slower and difficult transformation

e) New Special Economic Zone cities of the reform era without any historical burden of poorly performing work units

**3.5** Spatial change in different cities

displaced to peripheral housing estates. Although there was significant improvement in housing conditions for these people through relocation, they lost the prime location for business opportunities.

The next group which benefited from reform was state factory workers. For years they were required to work at a very low salary. In a drive for efficiency, bonuses were re-introduced as an incentive to encourage hard work. With the overseas market still closed, products of state factories were the main consumer goods available in the market in the early 1980s. Many factories expanded their production. Workers and other factory employees were direct beneficiaries. This situation changed with further opening up to international markets and the development of new firms that used modern technology. The products of the old state factories soon lost favour in the market. More and more state enterprises ran into difficulties. The new policies introduced by the government in the mid-1990s to stop financing loss-making enterprises and to allow these factories to go bankrupt had shifted the economic pressure to the industrial zones developed during the early years of the socialist system. Unemployment or being laid off became a serious reality to many industrial workers. Real hardship had become a reality for some urban families for the first time since the difficulties around 1960.

Professional and academics in public institutions responded to reform cautiously. During the early 1980s, they were almost observers of the reform process. For a time, university professors earned less than street stall runners and taxi drivers. Towards the late 1980s, they began to participate more actively. Professional skills and knowledge were used to gain additional incomes either for their institutions or for themselves. In the 1990s, many professionals and academics engaged in second jobs outside their normal employment in the public sector. Professional architects and urban planners, for example, made a fortune in helping developers to design projects.

The group enjoying the greatest benefits through the reform process was government officials, particularly those at local levels. The initiatives of privatisation and expansion of the market into the state sectors had created more business-like government services. Various charges had been turned into bonuses. Corruption and bribery were other sources of income for officials.

In studying the pre-reform urban social groups, Hou (1997) emphasised the important differences between those inside and those outside the state system. With the continuation of Communist Party control and the socialist political system, these differences had been largely preserved during the reform period. The groups who had benefited most from urban reform tended to be the core insiders of the state system (such as the government officials) and those with strong links with the government (such as academics and professionals). These without good links with the state (such as the industrial workers in the state-owned and collectively-owned enterprises) had only gained benefit for a relatively short period (Wang and Murie, 1999, 2000).

## Continuities and changes

Chinese cities were built according to particular principles during the early years of communist control. In contrast to the traditional communist principles of equality, urban society was divided according to employment categories which were reflections of the personal qualities measured by the level of education. The differences between cadres and workers were official and important. Grades within each of these categories were other important factors in determining the social and economic status of urban citizens. In such a divided system, social stability and integration were achieved through another particular feature of the system – the work unit. Work units as the basic cells of urban society provided various social and economic services to their employees directly. This reduced municipal governments' responsibility to a minimum.

Urban economic reform in China had produced far-reaching results and taken the sector-by-sector approach within the communism framework. It had profound effects on the urban society. However, it is important to note that many distinctive features established during the planned economy period remained. The most important one is the continuation of the work unit and the social class division between cadres and workers. So far efforts were made to separate general social services from business or administrative functions, but the organisation of the work units as an economic body, political body and social administrative body continued. This is particularly true in the government administration and professional/institutional sectors which still employed the most influential and powerful population in the country.

Traditional socialist planning segregated different land uses and had important social consequences. However, the division had not shown clearly because of economic and political integration between different groups and work units. In the transition to a market system, rationally planned areas based on technical criteria can become highly irrational in terms of integration and distribution of urban social groups. The conditioned stability under the planning system could become very fragile once the conditions had been removed. In cities in western countries, it normally took some years for a community to degrade into socially problematic areas through the selective movement of the population. In the Chinese case, an area could become a socially problematic area over a short period. Because of the linkage between living and work, the prosperity of the residents was dependent on the viability of the enterprises that employed them. This was also one of the main reasons why the reform of state-owned large enterprises had become the key concern of the overall economic reform programme. The difficulties of the reform could only be fully understood by knowledge of the existing integration of working and living.

Urban changes in China shared some of the common features of transition in the former east European socialist countries. The general trend was moving from a planned economic system toward a market economic system. During this transition privatisation of public assets, commercialisation of state production and operation, and opening up cities for international investments were key policies pursued by both east European countries and China. Beyond this general trend, important differences exist between the two. As Chapter 2 shows, east European countries saw the collapse of the Communist Party and the entire re-organisation of government and administration, while the Chinese Communist Party remained in power throughout the reform period. Western observers emphasised the differences between the 'big bang' and gradualist approaches. The gradualist idea may not necessarily grasp the whole idea of the Chinese situation. In China, there were social and economic reforms in many areas; there was also continuation in many other areas. The rapid growth of the Chinese economy was often contributed to the reform policies. The contribution from elements derived from the previous system was not given sufficient attention. It was the balance of change and continuation that sustained the development of the Chinese economy. There are different views on the roles played by the Communist Party in maintaining social and organisational stability, which provide a peaceful environment for economic development. The practice of some old policies did contribute to the prosperity of cities. The continuation of the urban and rural population registration system and the unfavourable conditions attached to rural residents played an important role in sustaining urban development. Because of the exclusion policy, rural migrants offered a large quantity of cheap labour in cities and posed no major threat to the fragile urban infrastructure and social support system. The continuation of state ownership of most large enterprises and institutions and the associated work unit benefit system avoided large-scale poverty and suffering at the beginning stages of reform, though income inequality and poverty increasingly became a major problem in cities.

# 4 The emerging problem of the urban poor

A poor residential area in central Chongqing, October 2000.

Poverty has a long history in China, but had been mainly associated with rural areas until very recently. In 1978 there were 250 million rural people living in poverty. Early success in economic reform had brought about a significant reduction in rural poverty and, by 1993, those living in poverty in the countryside had declined to about 80 million. Fast economic growth during the 1990s brought further reductions in rural poverty. By 2002 the official figure for rural people living in poverty had reduced to 28 million. (It was widely acknowledged that China had been very successful in reducing rural poverty. The number of people in poverty, however, is disputable. The official figures quoted here are based on the official poverty line of 625 yuan per person per year. This is much lower than the commonly used US$1 a day. Rural income data was also not very reliable and may include necessary investment for the following year. Using an adjusted poverty line of 1,200 yuan per person per year, Wu (2003), estimated that about 150 million rural people might still live in poverty in mid-2003.) As discussed in previous chapters, living standards among ordinary urban residents was more or less equal before economic reform. After 25 years of reform, there was diversification of the urban population and income distribution. While many urban residents became richer, some at the bottom of the urban society had become very poor.

Though urban poverty is a new phenomenon in China, it has become an important policy concern over the last few years. At the National People Congress meeting held in March 2003, many delegates raised the issue of urban poverty. Apart from rural poor, it was reported that there were about 100 million poor rural migrants, 20 million poor suburban farmers who lost their land as a result of urban expansion, and 20 million original urban residents who became poor as a result of industrial reorganisation. This chapter will review the increasing gap between the rich and the poor, identify different poor groups in cities and outline the common features of poor urban communities.

## Urban income inequality

Official statistics on income distribution in China usually divide urban populations into different percentage bands. The top 20 was referred to as the high-income group and the bottom 20 as the low-income group. In the middle were the medium-high, medium and medium-low income groups. The low-income group was sometimes further divided into very low-income group and low-income group, each with 10 per cent of the total population. The bottom 5 per cent were referred as families with difficulties. Table 4.1 compares the average income in each group. Between 1995 and 2002, the average income per person in urban areas increased by 90 per cent. Only 20 per cent of the population had an increase above this national average. While earnings of the lowest income group (first decile) only increased by 16 per cent, income of the richest (top 10 per cent) increased by 145 per cent. In 1995, the income of the top 10 per cent was only 3.8 times that of the bottom 10 per cent of the population. This has increased to 8 times in 2002. When the income of the rich increased steadily over the period, the income of the poor was actually in decline in the last two years. In 2000, with some slow improvement, annual incomes for the first decile reached 2,653 yuan per person and it then began to fall. If we focus on the 5 per cent poorest population, the picture is even more worrying. The change over the

**Table 4.1** Annual income per person in households, 1995 and 2002

| Income group | Average income (yuan per person) | | |
| --- | --- | --- | --- |
| | 1995 | 2002 | Increase (%) |
| Total | 4,288 | 8,177 | 91 |
| Lowest: 10 per cent | 2,178 | 2,527 | 16 |
| Of which the very low 0–5 per cent | 1,985 | 2,063 | 4 |
| Low: 10–20 per cent | 2,778 | 3,833 | 38 |
| Middle to low: 20–40 per cent | 3,364 | 5,209 | 55 |
| Middle: 40–60 per cent | 4,074 | 7,061 | 73 |
| Middle to high: 60–80 per cent | 4,958 | 9,438 | 90 |
| High: 80–90 per cent | 6,036 | 12,555 | 108 |
| Very high: 90–100 per cent | 8,231 | 20,208 | 146 |

Source: State Statistics Bureau, 1996, 2003.

seven years is ignorable. If taking into inflation consideration, income levels of the poor were in constant decline.

These general national trends can be observed at city level as well. In Shanghai, for example, the average annual actual income per capita increased four times from 2,198 yuan to 10,989 yuan over a 10-year period from 1990 to 1999. At the bottom of the low-income group, the first decile, income only increased three times from 1,404 yuan to 5,645 yuan, while the tenth decile – the richest group – the increase was six times (from 3,468 yuan to 24,006 yuan) (Figure 4.1). After 2000, when the rich became much richer, the income of the poor actually declined.

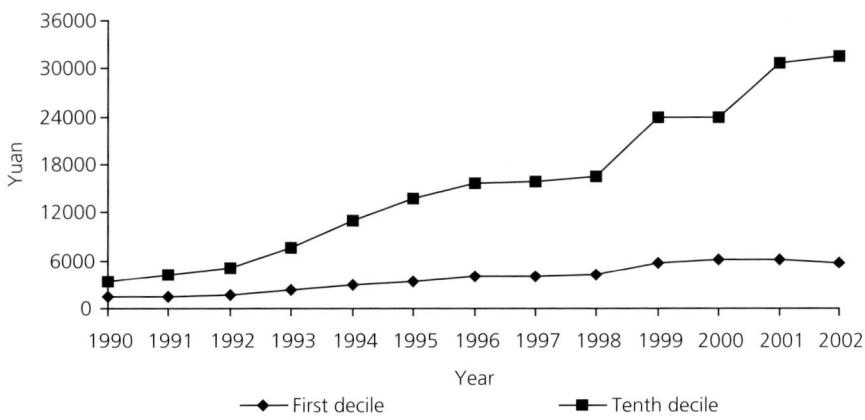

**4.1** Annual personal income in Shanghai, 1990–2002

Data Source: Shanghai Municipal Statistics Bureau, 2003: 107.

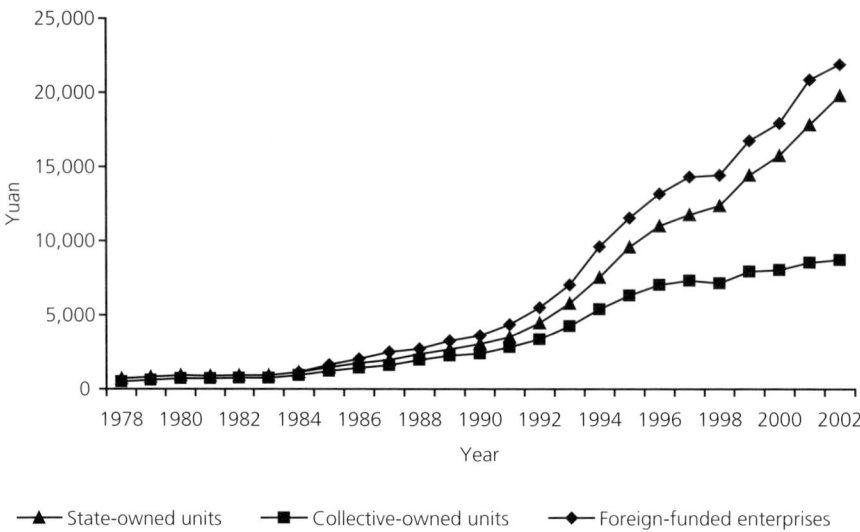

**4.2** Average annual salaries of different economic sectors

Source: Shanghai Statistics Bureau, 2003: 96.

Income differences for employees in different sectors also increased (Figure 4.2). The collective sector, after several years of decline, still employed more than 10 per cent of staff and workers in the city. Income of the collective sector workers showed little change since the middle of 1990s while earnings in the other two sectors climbed rapidly.

In Shenyang city, the Municipal Labour and Social Security Bureau carried out a survey of 255 major employers about employment and salaries in 2003. It found that the highest paid enterprise manager earned 129,490 yuan a year; a highly paid technical engineer earned 31,211 yuan a year; and a lowest paid shop assistant earned 5,197 yuan a year. The highest salary was 25 times that of the lowest (Wang, S., 2003).

Income and living standards in cities located in different regions also varied significantly (Table 4.2). Average income in major coastal cities and the national capital were much higher than inland cities. Between 1998 and 2001, incomes in all cities increased. However, the amount of increase varied from city to city. In 1998, Shenzhen had the highest salary, and three years later, with an increase of almost 90 per cent, Shanghai had overtaken Shenzhen as the city with the highest pay in the country. Shanghai's average salary was 2.7 times of that in the inland industrial town of Liupanshui. Among the cities with data, Jieyang and Yichun were ranked at the bottom with an average annual salary just above 5,000 yuan (State Statistics Bureau, Urban Economic and Social Survey Team, 2003).

**Table 4.2** Average annual salary in selected cities

| Region | City | 1998 (1,000 yuan) | 2001 (1,000 yuan) | Increase (%) |
|---|---|---|---|---|
| National capital | Beijing | 12.7 | 19.5 | 54 |
| Major coastal cities | Shenzhen | 18.4 | 25.9 | 41 |
| | Shanghai | 13.8 | 26.2 | 90 |
| | Tianjin | 10.2 | 14.5 | 42 |
| | Guangzhou | 15.5 | 23.5 | 52 |
| Selected major inland cities | Chongqing | 7.0 | 10.4 | 49 |
| | Shenyang | 8.0 | 11.6 | 45 |
| | Xi'an | 7.2 | 11.2 | 56 |
| | Urumuqi | 8.2 | 12.9 | 57 |
| Selected inland industrial towns | Liaoyang | 7.2 | 10.2 | 42 |
| | Liupanshui | 6.1 | 9.7 | 59 |

Source: State Statistics Bureau, Urban Economic and Social Survey Team, 1999, 2003.

**Table 4.3** Gini coefficient changes during the reform period

| Year | Whole country | Urban areas | Rural areas |
|---|---|---|---|
| 1978 | | 0.16 | 0.212 |
| 1980 | | 0.16 | 0.241 |
| 1985 | | 0.16 | 0.227 |
| 1990 | | 0.23 | 0.310 |
| 1995 | 0.389 | 0.28 | 0.342 |
| 1996 | 0.375 | 0.28 | 0.323 |
| 1997 | 0.379 | 0.29 | 0.329 |
| 1998 | 0.386 | 0.30 | 0.337 |
| 1999 | 0.397 | 0.295 | 0.336 |
| 2000 | 0.417 | 0.32 | 0.354 |

Source: State Statistics Bureau, China Statistics Information Network, 2001.

The State Statistics Bureau reviewed income distribution in the country in 2001. The report accepted that the Gini coefficient figure was a good indicator for income distribution (Table 4.3) and acknowledged that the common international warning level was 0.4. It however emphasised differences between rural and urban areas, and suggested looking at these areas separately. It insisted that, taking the country as a whole, a Gini coefficient level 0.45 or even 0.5 would be acceptable. The figure for China as a whole in 2000 was 0.417 (*China Daily*, 12 March 2003). In the last two years, the gap between the rich and the poor had increased again particularly in urban areas. No recent official Gini coefficient figures were published. It was widely believed that the overall figure could be over the accepted warning level of 0.45 for the country as a whole, and the figure for urban areas could be over 0.4 as well, particularly if the poorly paid migrant workers were taken into consideration.

## Identifying the poor

The term 'urban poor' did not feature in official documents until very recently. An alternative term, the medium to low-income group, was used, which included the majority of public-sector employees and their families (about 80 per cent of the urban population). In the early years of reform, most adult residents were in employment and only a small proportion of people were relatively poor. The term of 'medium- to low-income group' was useful in developing policies aimed at the majority of the urban population. When income distribution spread more widely and poverty became a major issue, the term of 'medium- to low-income' became less relevant. In the last few years, terms specifically referring to the poor, such as 'low-income group', 'weak social and economic groups' (*ruoshi qunti*) and 'urban poor residents' (*chengshi pingkun jumin*) were accepted and appeared in government documents. Specific groups were also identified as poor, such as the traditional 'three no' individuals (no ability to work, no source of income, and no relatives or dependents), unemployed and laid-off workers. The following sections describe the characteristics of the main poor groups which emerged in cities.

### Traditional poor

Although urban poverty was not a main issue in China during the early period of communist government, there were some poor people in urban areas. There were about 4 million unemployed people in large cities when the communists came to power in 1949. Most of them lived in slums. The new government adopted a relatively flexible employment policy in the early 1950s to facilitate rapid economic recovery. It encouraged economic development and employment in all sectors including private business, despite this being in contradiction to communist ideology. These policies proved to be successful and the urban unemployment problem was quickly solved. Large-scale economic expansion also attracted many rural labourers into urban-based factories and services.

After the failure of the Great Leap Forward movement (1958–9) and with-drawal of support by the USSR, both urban and rural economies experienced a major recession period. This led to a dramatic reduction in urban employment in the early 1960s. A large number of urban employees returned to their rural origins. At the same time, the government moved gradually to control and plan urban labour supply by assigning jobs for university and college graduates. This later extended to all urban school leavers. By the middle of the 1960s, about 10 per cent of urban labourers were out of work; most of them were young graduates. During the Cultural Revolution period (1966–76), unemployed youth were sent to rural areas for 're-education'. By the early 1970s, about 10 million urban young people were working in rural areas. This temporarily released the employment pressure in urban areas (Gao, 1998).

This programme ended with the death of Chairman Mao and the end of the Cultural Revolution in 1976. Most urban young people who were sent to rural areas gradually returned to cities. Urban unemployment problems intensified. Urban labour management authorities were unable to find jobs for all these returnees. With the increasing numbers of new school-leavers, the planning approach to urban employment was, in practice, unworkable. This forced the government to abandon the single-minded job planning system. Various measures were used to create jobs for the young. This included the expansion of collective sectors. Local labour service companies were set up by street committees or large state-owned enterprises to create jobs for young people in service sectors such as retail or restaurants. Special arrangements were also made for public-sector employees to retire earlier on condition that their employer would take on their children. These new measures did not solve the surplus labour problem, and 'waiting for job' (*daiye*) became a major phenomenon in Chinese cities and towns. In 1980, 1.2 million working-age residents in cities were waiting for jobs. Apart from a few privileged families, most households had one or more young persons who had no job. Although urban youth unemployment was a serious social problem in cities, it did not result in poverty for most families. Unemployed young people mainly stayed with their parents. While general housing conditions were poor, food and clothing were not a problem for most them.

The urban poor in the 1950s mainly consisted of two types: 'three no' people and people who had no connection to any work unit, which included solders and army officers of the previous governments, returned overseas Chinese and some infectious-disease carriers (Fei, 1999). Between 1960 and 1978 three more categories were added to the urban poor list: 1) redundant workers from the economic recession of early 1960s, mainly the old and disabled who had no rural homes to return to; 2) economically inactive young people returned from the rural areas because of injuries or disease; 3) political victims of the Cultural Revolution. The government provided some relief for these people through work unit or street committees. Official statistics shows that in 1985, 3.8 million urban residents benefited from government relief fund (Table 4.4). Another 534,000 persons who did not work because of illness and disability also received support from work units (State Statistics Bureau, 1994). These figures give a rough indication of urban poor families during the socialist planned economic period.

## Unemployment and laid-off workers

Up to the early 1990s, the Chinese Communist government saw unemployment as a feature of the capitalist system. In socialist societies, no one should be allowed to be unemployed. Therefore, there were no official references to unemployment in policies or other official documents. Urban youth without jobs were only 'waiting for job' (*daiye*). When the government adopted the ideas of 'socialist market economy' in 1993, the term *daiye* was gradually replaced by unemployment. In 1994, unemployment rates appeared in a government report for the first time.

Table 4.5 shows the urban unemployment situation between 1978 and 2002. The official unemployment rate was high at the end of the Cultural Revolution. In 1978, urban unemployment rate was 5.3 per cent (according to data published after 1993). This declined quickly to less than 2 per cent by 1985. Since then, there were some increases, but it remained below 3 per cent. Throughout the 1980s, most unemployed persons were school leavers. The official unemployment rate remained low during the 1980s. Various job creation programmes and the expansion of urban economy in general were the main reasons. Several other factors were also important in maintaining the low unemployment rate. With less emphasis on efficiency and more emphasis on full employment, most public-sector enterprises and organisations employed more people than they should. Work that could easily be done by one person was handled by two or more, and over-staffing was a main

**Table 4.4** Traditional urban poor (million persons)

| Year | Persons receiving relief and subsidies | Early retired and disabled persons receiving relief |
|------|------|------|
| 1985 | 3.77 | 0.53 |
| 1990 | 6.33 | 0.56 |
| 1992 | 9.08 | 0.54 |
| 1993 | 2.00 | 0.55 |
| 1994 | 2.26 | 0.54 |
| 1995 | 3.75 | 0.54 |
| 1996 | 2.61 | 0.54 |
| 1997 | 2.68 | 0.53 |
| 1998 | 3.32 | 0.55 |
| 1999 | 1.57 | 0.52 |

Source: State Statistics Bureau, 2000.

Note: The sudden decline in 1993 reflects a change of definition and unemployment was counted separately.

**Table 4.5** Urban unemployment

| Year | Total number of unemployed persons (million) | Of which unemployed school leavers and youth (million) | Unemployed youth as % of unemployed | Unemployment rate |
|------|------|------|------|------|
| 1978 | 5.30 | 2.49 | 47.0 | 5.3 |
| 1980 | 5.42 | 3.82 | 70.6 | 4.9 |
| 1985 | 2.38 | 1.97 | 82.6 | 1.8 |
| 1990 | 3.83 | 3.13 | 81.6 | 2.5 |
| 1991 | 3.52 | 2.88 | 81.9 | 2.3 |
| 1992 | 3.64 | 3.00 | 82.4 | 2.3 |
| 1993 | 4.20 | 3.32 | 79.0 | 2.6 |
| 1994 | 4.76 | 3.01 | 63.2 | 2.8 |
| 1995 | 5.20 | 3.10 | 59.7 | 2.9 |
| 1996 | 5.53 | | | 3.0 |
| 1997 | 5.70 | | | 3.1 |
| 1998 | 5.71 | | | 3.1 |
| 1999 | 5.75 | | | 3.1 |
| 2000 | 5.95 | | | 3.1 |
| 2001 | 6.81 | | | 3.6 |
| 2002 | 7.70 | | | 4.0 |

Sources: State Statistics Bureau, 1998, 2000; Ministry of Labour and Social Security and State Statistics Bureau, 2003.

feature of the socialist work unit system. Early retirement and replacement by children were other factors. Many workers and low-ranked cadres gave up their jobs for their sons or daughters when they had not yet reached retirement age.

During the 1990s, two changes in unemployment can be observed. First, while the unemployment rate remained low at around 3 per cent, the number of unemployed people doubled from 3.5 million to 6 million. Second, the proportion of school leavers declined gradually while other unemployment became more prominent. These changes had important implications to urban poverty. Under the old system, once a person found a job in the public or collective sector, he or she had found an 'iron rice bowl'. Unless the person committed a serious crime or went to prison, he or she could stay in their job for life. Losing a job or becoming unemployed were rare. The reduction of school leavers among the unemployed means there was an increase of adults who lost their jobs. These relatively older people normally had families (children and parents) to look after. Loss of job and income meant a lower living standard.

The number of unemployed persons has increased since 1994. By the end of 2002, 4 per cent of working-age people were officially registered as unemployed in cities and towns. The total number was 7.7 million. These figures actually do not give the true scale of unemployment, since they do not include the laid-off workers in the state sector. Since the middle of the 1990s, industrial restructuring was carried out in both state and collective sectors with the aim of increasing efficiency by a reduction of the workforce. Poorly performing factories were allowed to be merged with others or to be closed down. These policies led to large-scale reductions of employment in both the state and the collective sector.

People who lost their jobs either completely or partially from state-owned enterprises, were referred to as laid-off workers. They were not counted as unemployed. Laid-off workers retained an employment relationship with their former employers and received a laid-off subsidy. Being laid-off could be a result of selective redundancy by a viable state organisation or enterprise or a result of closure of inefficient state or collective enterprises. In the latter case, responsibility for laid-off workers was handed over to the local authorities.

Between 1997 and 2000, on average about 6 million industrial workers were laid-off each year. A few of them returned to their posts or were assigned different jobs, while most of the others were in similar situation to the unemployed. Initially, the government and employers set up various Re-employment Service Centres to help the laid-off workers to find new jobs or to learn new skills. Because of the scale of the lay-offs, this initiative failed to arrange work for everyone. By 2001, there were about 30 million laid-off workers in the whole country (State Statistics Bureau, 2001a).

Job losses in state and collective sectors were the main causes of poverty among urban residents in Chinese cities. Subsidies received by laid-off workers were far from enough to sustain the normal standard of life. The average income per person in households headed by laid-off workers or other unemployed was only 272 yuan in 2000, which was about 52 per cent of the overall average income in urban areas (State Statistics Bureau, 2001a). Without jobs for several years, most laid-off workers used up all their savings.

## Pensioners

Poverty among retired people is another problem in Chinese cities. The ratio of pensioners to those employed in formal work units was 1:30 in 1978. This ratio declined very quickly to 1:7.5 in 1985 and 1:3 in 2002. There were over 42 million pensioners in cities and towns at the end of 2002, 13 times the figure for 1978 (3 million) (Ministry of Labour and Social Security and State Statistics Bureau 2003). Though China had avoided large-scale inflation during the last 20 years and managed pensioners' benefits more successfully than some other transitional countries, there were inequalities between pensioners and the majority of retired industrial workers were either just above the poverty line or in serious poverty (see Chapter 5).

Pension provision was the responsibility of work units in the past. Many poorly performing state or collective enterprises had financial problems during the restructuring period. Some of these enterprises found it difficult to pay the wages of their existing employees, and pension payments would be a lower priority. Some of these enterprises, particularly the collectively owned ones, became bankrupt though poor management and performance. Pensioners who had retired from these enterprises had great difficulties in claiming their pensions. Theoretically speaking, these older people could get help from their children. In industrial areas, different generations of family members could be associated to the same enterprise as a result of the replacement policies of the 1980s. Older people with pension problems might live with laid-off child(ren). Recent pension reform aimed at centralising pension management to the municipal level and avoiding the problems caused by bankrupt enterprises. The new arrangement could have a major impact on future generations of pensioners, but it is too late to deal with those already experiencing hardship.

## Poor students

Poverty among university and college students has attracted some attention recently. Students have always formed a special group in Chinese cities. Universities and colleges offered a special route for social mobility under the *hukou* system. With strict control of urban labour supply by the government, enrolling into a university or joining the army were the only ways for rural or small-town young people to move into cities. A university degree can help rural young people to cross the urban–rural division and sometimes skip several steps along the social hierarchy in cities.

During the 1980s, living costs were low and there were no fees charged. Most university students also received a grant from the government for accommodation and food. Once graduated, they were guaranteed a job and cadre status. Most of these privileges had been removed in the 1990s. Apart from studying several specialised subjects, students have to pay tuition fees and the costs of living. A report showed that in Hubei Province, 22 per cent (93,000) of students had problems with tuition fees and living costs in 2001. These students also had difficulties paying for books and getting access to computers, which in turn affected their general academic performance. The Hubei Province Urban Surveying and Research Team (2002) identified two main reasons for student poverty. University fees increased out of proportion to general income increases. Between 1998 and 2001, university fees increased by an average of 13.7 per cent, while urban and rural personal income in the province increased by only 6.7 and 2.7 per cent respectively. The expansion of intake by universities was another reason for the increased numbers of poor students. In 1998, 65,000 students entered universities. This had more than doubled by 2001 with an intake of 159,000. The total students on the campus increased from 210,000 to 421,000.

It was estimated that in the country as whole, there was about 3 million poor students who could not afford to pay the fees and living costs in 2002, and the proportion of poor students ranged from 20 to 50 per cent between different universities (Xinhua News Web: 21 March 2002). Most of those students came either from poor rural areas or from urban low-income families. Many poor students could not afford university accommodation and rented poor-quality rooms in the private housing market. In some cities with a concentration of universities, poverty among students had become a main factor in social instability. Because several urban disturbances were started by students, poverty among this group had caused much concern to both central and local governments.

## Landless suburban farmers

With large-scale expansion of built-up areas (including airports, motorways and infrastructure for various economic development zones) and the sprawl of commercial housing into the surrounding rural areas, landless farmers living on the edge of cities became a sizeable group. Under the socialist system, urban land was owned by the municipal government and suburban land was owned by village farmers collectively. Individual farmers had the rights to use the land for housing and production, but did not have ownership. Land required for urban development was managed by the local government directly. There were policies for municipal government to take over agricultural land from villages. In the 1980s, when land was taken over, the municipal authority or the new land users had to pay compensation to the farmers and also assign jobs to working-age farmers. Urban-based jobs provided an alternative way of life to agricultural production. This practice was more acceptable to farmers because it provided them an opportunity to change to a new life as urban residents.

Land for development had become an important issue in China during the early 1990s. When various development zones or districts were set up, about 10 million *mu* of agricultural land was lost to urban development each year (*mu* is a Chinese unit for land, 1 *mu* = 666.7 m$^2$ or one-fifteenth of a hectare). With regard to food production, strict rules were applied later to protect agricultural land. Since the mid-1990s, about 2 to 3 million mu of agricultural land was converted to urban use. According to the average holding of land by farmers, this means around 2 million farmers lost their land each year. The cumulative figure for landless farmers was estimated at around 20 million (Ge *et al.*, 2003).

Under the new market economy, the role of government in job arrangements was very limited. Cash or housing replacement became the main ways of compensation to farmers. In a Xi'an suburb, a whole village's agricultural land was taken over by a property developer to built cottage houses in 2001. The paddy fields and orchards were the village farmers only source of livelihood. The new houses were designed to a very high standard, each with 300 to 500 m² of floor space and a private swimming pool and garage. To enhance the local amenity, a man-made lake was planned for the estate as well. These new houses were marketed at the price of 5,000 yuan per m² of floor space. Compensation of 6,000 yuan per person (less than a year's average salary in Xi'an city or slightly more than the price for one m² floor space of the new houses) was paid to the villagers for the loss of land they had used for generations. Despite strong objections from the farmers, development went ahead under heavy police presence (Li and Chen, 2003).

To urban authorities, cash compensation is easy to manage. In fact, urban government lost nothing from development. It was the responsibility of the new users to pay the compensation. Urban government received land lease or use fees from developers. To reduce development costs, developers tended to pay the minimum compensation to farmers. To attract outside investment into their cities, municipal governments tend to approve projects and compensation schemes which might discriminate against the farmers. Chinese farmers were relatively poor and most of them had never dealt with large sums of money. Land ownership was not at an individual household level. Farmers were either tempted by a few thousand yuan compensation or were forced to accept the conditions and give up their right to the land. Most of them did not have any long-term plans. Once they lost this basic living resource, they quickly spent the compensation money and many joined the army of migrant workers or ended up in poverty.

## Rural migrants

Although the government had relaxed restrictions on population movement, the residence registration system was not changed fundamentally until very recently. Rural residents could move to cities for employment or business, but were not treated equally to the original urban residents (Fan, 2001). Government policies referred to rural migrants as a 'temporary' or 'floating' population. As temporary urban residents, they were not included in official statistics nor in the calculation of other major urban indicators such as average income, housing floor space, unemployment, etc. Migrants were normally barred from taking up good and secure jobs. In Beijing, for example, rural migrants were not allowed to take up jobs in the following areas in 2001: finance, insurance, accountancy, cashiering and banking, post office work, management, telephone switchboard, price control, vehicle drivers including taxis, ticket sale and collection, nurseries, lift or elevator operators, computing and data entry, air stewarding, typing, meter readers, quality controlling and measurement, machine testing, drawing, store caretakers, shop assistants in department stores, all posts in starred hotels and restaurants. Without access to these jobs, the only thing left for migrants was hard, dangerous and dirty physical labour-intensive work.

Migration was seen as an important way to increase rural income. It was estimated that the total income of rural migrants was about 527.8 billion yuan in the whole country in 2002 (this gives an annual average income of 5,615 yuan/ migrant worker); about 62 per cent of this income (327.4 billion yuan) was sent home (an average of 3,482 yuan/person) (*People's Daily* Overseas Edition, 2 April 2003: 1). Officials in Anhui Province estimated that the total income from their migrants could be 24 billion yuan (based on annual salary 4,000 yuan per migrant). Migrant labour had been one of the main sources of income in some villages. Money earned through migration counted for 30 to 40 per cent of household income (*People's Daily* Overseas Edition, 23 January 2003: 2).

Such positive views do not always represent the real situation of all migrants. Due to many employment control policies imposed on them, most rural migrants work in poor employment conditions. They have no access to social and economic benefits in cities, but have to pay high charges for their stay in the city. *People's Daily* (Overseas Edition) reported that an 18-year-old girl from a small town in Jiangsu Province went to Hefei in Anhui Province to work in a factory in July 2002. She paid a 2,000 yuan deposit for the job at the beginning, and signed a contract with the employer. The employer promised that the monthly wage for the first two months would be 360 yuan and thereafter 500 yuan. By the end of November 2002, she only received 300 yuan in total. The case was brought to the Labour and Social Security Department of Anhui Province. The authority ordered the employer to repay the deposit and all wages in arrears by the end of December 2002. By the middle of January 2003, she had received no payment from the employer at all (*People's Daily*, Overseas Edition, 15 January 2003: 4).

Such poor treatment of migrant workers was not an isolated case. Many similar stories could be found in the news every week. Incomplete statistics show that the construction industry in Beijing alone owed 2,200 million yuan of migrant workers' wages in 2002 (equivalent to 261,000 workers' pay for a year). The municipal government introduced several special measures to solve the problem. Construction companies that owed migrant workers' wages, could be excluded from bidding for new projects or disqualified. One such enforcement in the year led to the payment of 1,400 million yuan in wages (*People's Daily*, Overseas Edition, 16 January 2003: 4).

Because the problem was so widespread, the State Council organised a special check on payment of wages to migrant workers from 15 December 2002 to 15 January 2003, using special phone lines and official visits. It covered 23 provinces and cities with large numbers of migrant workers. It quickly uncovered 13,000 cases of wage under-payment and found that non-payment or wages owed to migrant workers was a serious and widespread problem (*People's Daily* Overseas Edition, 23 January 2003: 4). The State Council subsequently issued a special notice, which required all local labour and social security authorities to monitor and implement the 'Labour Law' in relation to migrant workers. The document particularly required local authorities to check the timely payment of wages to the migrant workers (*People's Daily* Overseas Edition, 16 January 2003: 4). In December 2003 there were again reports and articles in the media urging urban employers to pay migrants their hard-earned wages in order for them to return to the villages for the Chinese New Year festival.

Unemployment among migrants had been increasing. Some rural labourers went to cities searching for jobs but found only disappointment. With so many migrant workers to choose from, urban employers increased their requirements for experience and education levels. A recent report shows that in Shandong province, 80 per cent of ordinary job vacancies in joint-venture and private enterprises require a high-school education. Of the migrant workers found in the province in 2002, only 27 per cent finished high school (Xinhua News Agency Shandong Branch, 2003). This mismatch has important implications for the migrant job market. There was report that because of the high level of competition and over-supply, wages for migrant workers had also declined in the last few years and working conditions were getting worse, while overall income among official urban residents increased. Living conditions for migrant workers were normally measured according to standards designed for the rural areas. Migrants were excluded from the urban poor group and the social support system, while there is no dispute that rural migrants are the poorest paid workers in cities. If measured by the urban living standard, the majority, if not all of them, will fall into the poor group (Wu, 2003).

Government policies still referred to the rural migrants as 'temporary' or 'floating'. The authorities believed that ambitious rural people came to cities to earn some money and would return to their rural home. As temporary residents, they can be excluded from social or economic support; they can be barred from good and secure job opportunities so as to reduce the competition with urban residents; they can be given the hardest and dirtiest jobs that no urban residents want; and they can also be expelled from the land they occupy without compensation and even evicted from the cities when their labour is perceived by the authority to be no longer required. The 'temporary' nature of the migrants was sometimes supported by research findings based on data collected from the street or temporary shelter where most of the new arrivals and the seasonal workers stay. The answers about their future plans given by most migrants were often based on the assumption of the continuation of the strict control on the change of official residence.

The unfair treatment of rural migrants in cities had drawn the attention of some academic researchers. Poverty among migrants has also attracted some media attention recently. Some policy developments were also made in relation to the *hukou* system. Experiments in small towns were carried out since 1997 to grant rural migrants permanent resident's rights, valid only locally, to those who have had stable jobs, income and housing for two years. However, this policy has not, so far, been extended to most large cities. With the increasing pressure of unemployment and laid-off workers from the state and collective sectors in major cities, accepting a large number of migrants formally into the urban resident category and providing them with equal social and economic benefits enjoyed by official urban residents are unlikely in the near future.

## Areas of poverty

As discussed in Chapter 3, spatial differentiation and segregation were important features of Chinese cities. The urban poor, both official and unofficial, were increasingly concentrated in certain areas. These areas include old traditional housing districts, poor-quality public housing estates associated with problematic state or collective enterprises, construction sites and the so-called 'urban villages'. The following sections describe each in turn.

### Traditional old housing areas

The property boom over the last 25 years and the urban redevelopment programme has brought about a big change in all cities and much of the old town areas have been redeveloped. Poor-quality housing in city centres has been replaced by skyscrapers and mulit-storey shopping and office blocks. Most of the original residents were relocated to other areas. However, in almost every city, pockets of old housing areas remain. These areas have become the prime location for the urban poor. In Shenyang city, for example, large areas of old housing remained in 2000, though the government earlier made ambitious plans to eliminate all slum housing by the end of the century. The district around the historic railway station of Huanggu Tun was a very large area of low-quality traditional housing. The area had a long history before the communist period and private ownership was dominant. Because it lies beside the Tiexi industrial district, the majority of the residents were industrial workers.

Guangming Lu was the poorest area in this district. The street was a narrow strip of poor houses between the railway and several larger factories. The area was originally built in the 1930s and 1940s during the Japanese occupation. These 'houses' were actually small single-storey rooms (*pingfang*), each accommodating one family. The original density of these houses was not very high and there were sizeable open spaces between rows of housing. Because of the population increase, each family made additions at both the back and the front of the original room to enlarge internal floor space. The open spaces between buildings were gradually covered up and only narrow passages of 1 to 2 metres were left. There were about 2,000 households living in the Guangming Lu area. Most of them had three generations with four to six people. A large proportion of the working-age residents in the area were laid-off by their employers. Local residents testified that income levels were very low. Many residents received no laid-off subsidy (*xiagangfee*) or pension from their employers. Because of this it was one of the poorest residential areas in the city, the municipal government having a plan to redevelop it. Demolition had already started in 2000. A large area had been pulled down. Timber and other materials had been collected together for sale by the demolition company. Some local residents collected wood and bamboo from the ruins to be used for heating in winter.

There was another large old housing area in Dodong (east side) District in Shenyang. The living conditions in this area were similar to those found at Huanggu District. Most of the core housing existed before 1949. Not much improvement had been made apart from an increase in density by additions and insertions. There were about 7,000 households in this area alone with more than 25,000 people. The majority of these residents were also industrial workers engaged in different enterprises rather than associated to one particular factory.

When visited again in November 2003, much of the area in both Huanggu and Dadong had been redeveloped. Cash compensation had been given to these families but there was no relocation arrangement. Residents had to find their own accommodation. New commercial housing was under construction. Local housing officials acknowledged that it would be difficult for the original residents to move back into this area. New apartments were too big and too expensive for most of them. At the beginning of the redevelopment, local officials had hoped that increased compensation would enable these residents to find a new home in the housing market (e.g. small and older one-bedroom flats). With 90,000 homes demolished within a short period of few months, the price of small flats increased substantially during 2003. Many of these households had to find accommodation in the rented market; some went to villages on the edge of the city. Redevelopment eliminated poor houses from the city centre, but not the problems of poverty associated with them. Poor people had been forced to relocate to other less expensive locations.

In another major inland industrial city, Chongqing, poor housing areas at difficult locations were found in 2000. Jiaochangkou and Shibanpo were two old housing areas less than 10 minutes walk from the central square Jiefangbei. They were both located on steep slopes with high-density, poor-quality traditional houses. Because of the central location, these areas were very active in economic terms with small shops and a street market. Minor streets in these areas were stairs, some of them very narrow, and impossible to move large furniture through. Timber was the main construction material. Most houses had more than one floor. Some had been designated as 'dangerous housing' by the local authority, but were still occupied. Wooden stairs and floorboards had not been properly maintained for many years. The infrastructure of the areas was very poor, with water pipes running along the street and sewage in open or covered drains. The majority of families did not have indoor kitchens or toilets; and many families cooked their food on stoves outside the house.

## The problem of the urban poor

The residents of these areas were a mix of original urban families and rural migrants. Most original urban residents were generally poor and without stable jobs. The unemployment rate was higher and the nature of the residents was shown by the names of new businesses such as Xiagang Chashe (Tea House Run by Laid-off Workers) and Xiagang Banyong (Removing Company Organised by the Laid-off Workers), etc. Most of the migrants living here either worked as *bangbang jun* or as small traders selling farm produce such as vegetables and fruit in the street. *Bangbang jun* – a special term in Chongqing – refers to porters in river ports, railway and bus stations and outside shops in the city. All of them carry a wooden or bamboo bar (*bangbang* in Chinese) and a rope. They are extremely useful in a hilly city where other transport is difficult. It was reported in 2003 that there were more than 10,000 *bangbangs* working in the city.

### Poor state enterprises housing estates

Although many early housing estates owned by state enterprises were either redeveloped or renovated during recent years, housing areas associated with poorly performing factories became another type of area for the urban poor. Gongrencun (Workers' Village) was one of the first public housing estates built in Shenyang in the early 1950s to accommodate industrial workers in Tiexi Industrial District. It initially included 72 three-storey tenements of two or three room flats. The area was designed to a high standard with a low density of housing and good facilities, such as children's playgrounds, nurseries, schools, etc. During the planned economy period, these houses provided homes for the privileged officials, managers and senior workers. Ten to fifteen years ago, the area was still one of the best residential areas in the city. In the new urban market economy, some of the factories performed badly and some had to be closed down. As a result, this housing area began to become run down. Because of poor maintenance and repairs, a few buildings had become the so-called *san-bu-guan* houses (which neither the work unit, the district nor the municipal government took responsibility for). A couple of them did not have running water or any heating. Most residents in these buildings were either old or poor, and some of them refused to pay their rent.

Textiles was one of the heavily hit industrial sectors in the 1990s. Tuwan area in Chongqing was the site of two large state-owned textile factories. They were still running in 2000 but performed badly which resulted in many employees being laid-off. The factories' main residential areas consisted of both old and new houses. The older houses were small and offered a single room for families. The occupiers were mainly manual workers and many had retired. They complained about the poor living conditions, maintenance and high charges for repairs. There were some redevelopment activities in these areas. Older houses were demolished and new ones built on the land cleared. Not all residents welcomed such changes. Mofancun (Model Village) was one of the old housing areas built in 1953 and used by retired workers. The condition of the buildings was not at all bad in comparison to nearby private housing. Because of the relatively large open spaces between houses, residents built extensions at the front of their houses to create more rooms. The managers of the factories decided to redevelop this area. A commercial development company was contracted to demolish the houses but some residents refused to move. Two types of arrangement were made available for the existing residents:

- to move back to a new flat when completed and pay part of the redevelopment cost (*jizijianfang*);
- to move to another older house owned by the factory. These houses were generally poor quality and could only be a temporary arrangement.

Some old residents were not happy, because they found it difficult to pay the cost of moving back. Factory managers put various types of pressure on these residents, including threatening to make family members (sons or daughters) unemployed.

## Urban villages

The most prominent areas occupied by the poor in Chinese cities are the so-called urban villages – *chengzhongcun*. Urban villages were originally rural settlements located in suburban areas. Because of urban expansion, the village's agricultural land was gradually taken over for infrastructure and property development and these villages became physically parts of the urban built-up area. However, due to different population registration systems applied to urban and rural areas, these villages maintained their rural organisation and most farmers remained outside the formal urban management system. Because of their rural background and fewer planning restrictions and regulation, housing in these settlements became the prime locations for the poor, particularly rural migrants. Villagers built poor-quality rooms, one on top of another – some reaching five or six storeys – and rented them to migrants. Rural migrants also found the living conditions more acceptable and less intimidating because landlords were farmers. The rent was normally cheaper than in other areas.

'Urban villages' are not a few isolated cases, but common phenomena in all large cities. In fast urbanising regions, such as the Pearl River Delta and the Yangtze River Delta, a large proportion of rural settlements ended up as urban villages. Residents no longer depend on agricultural activities but engage in commercial or property-related business. In other cities, though the scale was smaller, hundreds of such villages can still be found. In Xi'an, for example, over the 190 square kilometres of built-up area, there are 187 such villages, 55 of which are inside the second ring road. Some of them are actually located quite near the city centre. These urban villages are home to over 200,000 official local residents (Ma and

He, 2003). If migrant workers who rent housing in these villages were included, the total population would be much larger.

The best known urban village was Zhejiangcun (Zhejiang Village) in Beijing. Located in the south of the city, Zhejiangcun was an area used mainly by migrants from Wenzhou in Zhejiang province. The whole area covered about 24 administrative villages. It was estimated that about 100,000 migrants lived in this area in 1995, of which 80 per cent were from Wenzhou (Liu and Liang, 1997). Zhejiangcun represents a shanty town typical of those found in many developing countries. At the centre of this area was a wholesale and retail market. Various sorts of vehicle crowd the main streets. Apart from the main street, other roads were unpaved and became muddy in the rain. Housing quality was poor, most not being purpose-built. Monthly rents per room were from 300 to 400 yuan in 1998. This was about the same as the monthly wages for many migrant workers in the city. At this level, only those who engaged in business could afford to occupy an individual room. Others had to share rooms so as to reduce costs. Sometimes married couples were found sharing with single men or other families. The only private space was the bed. Bedside curtains or mosquito nets were used to maintain some privacy. There is no heating in these rooms and the winter is very cold. Some young migrant couples had to raise their children under these conditions.

## Construction site dormitories

Various styles of dormitories around major construction sites were other locations where the urban poor, particularly migrants, could be found. In Beijing, about 20 per cent of migrants lived on construction sites. One group which worked at Beijing University in August 2000 provides some idea about life at work sites. This group consisted of about 25 men (aged between 20–40) from Shandong province. They worked for a leader from the same area who normally looked for work in the city. Their work at the university was to refurbish an old building. They brought their own quilts and slept on wooden boards in the building they were refurbishing. This way of living reduced their living costs substantially because they did not pay rent. Food was arranged by the team leader and brought to the site in a big container on a trolley. Meals were a mixture of rice, vegetables and some meat. They ate at the roadside using their own bowls or cups, chopsticks and food vouchers. They worked about 13 hours each day: getting up at 5 am and finishing breakfast before 5:30 and starting work from 5:30; lunch from 11:30 am to 1:30 pm; work in the afternoon from 1:30 to 6:30; dinner from 6:30 to 7:00; evening work from 7:00 to 10:00. There were no weekend breaks or holidays. Since the leader was from the same rural area, there was no contract between these workers and their leader. Though the work was hard, they had flexibility if they had to go home for any reason. After paying for food, they could earn about 700 yuan each month (the average salary in the city in 1999 was 1,148 yuan per month). Most of

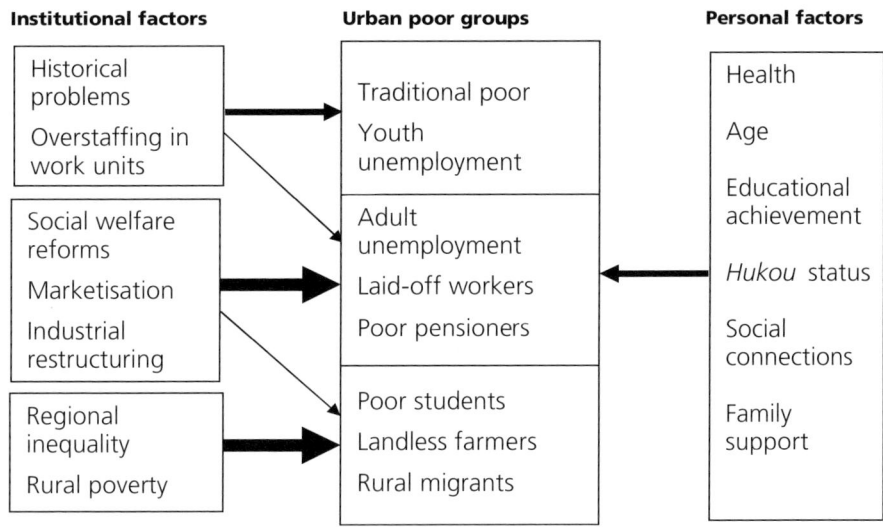

| Institutional factors | Urban poor groups | Personal factors |
|---|---|---|
| Historical problems<br><br>Overstaffing in work units | Traditional poor<br>Youth unemployment | Health<br><br>Age<br><br>Educational achievement |
| Social welfare reforms<br><br>Marketisation<br><br>Industrial restructuring | Adult unemployment<br>Laid-off workers<br>Poor pensioners | *Hukou* status<br><br>Social connections |
| Regional inequality<br><br>Rural poverty | Poor students<br>Landless farmers<br>Rural migrants | Family support |

**4.3** Causes of urban poverty

these men were married with children. Very sad expressions appeared on their faces when they were asked about their families. This was a well-organised group. Their wages were better than many others. They also had the advantage at this job of being able to sleep inside the building rather in than the temporary shelters used by many other construction workers.

## Causes of urban poverty

The discussion above indicates several of the main causes of urban poverty. These include historical and inherited problems such as the 'three no' individuals and disabled people; the pursuit of full employment in urban areas; and overstaffing in the public sector. However, these historical problems did not result in serious urban poverty under the planned economic system. The number of poor people inherited from the preceding period was also relatively small (Figure 4.3). The increase in urban poverty was not the result of falling production, but a direct result of the market economy and the withdrawal of social benefits by work units and the state. While mass unemployment was caused by industrial restructuring, slow expansion in the private sector failed to absorb the unemployed and increase the labour force. In the new private sector, apart from a few large and well-established companies, most people were employed by less stable small enterprises. Inflation and income increases for the employed also led to a decline in living standards for retired workers who relied on low pensions.

Poor health and lack of family support were other reasons for poverty. Age, educational background, social connections and other personal capital become more important factors for competition under the market system. However, compared with institutional factors, personal qualities are less important. Unemployment, for example, affects some industrial sectors more seriously than others. Workers in textile and manufacturing industries suffered heavily throughout the whole country. These workers were laid-off because of problems in the industrial sector they worked in, rather than because of their personal qualities. The so-called '4050 group' as a whole (females in their forties and males in their fifties) experienced employment problems under the market system. It is true that they were the 'sending down youth' during the Cultural Revolution period, but it is unreasonable to think that personal qualities of this group was poor.

Historical features of the Chinese society were other important reasons for urban poverty. The low rate of urbanisation and the large population base resulted in continuous migration of rural poor labourers to urban areas. This put great pressure on both the infrastructure and social support facilities. With the overall urbanisation level being very low, migrants had been a main source for urban poverty. All these facts indicated that urban poverty is a long-term problem in China rather than a short-term problem associated with transition.

In comparison with Russia and east European transitional countries, gradualist reform slowed down and delayed the emergence of the urban poverty problem. The approach also allowed the government to develop and test some anti-poverty measures and policies. Several new social security systems had been established. Some were based on previous practices, others were innovative and drawn on experience from other countries (see Chapter 8). There is no doubt that these new social support systems and policies had played a very positive role in reducing the scale and extent of poverty in cities.

# 5 Social and economic profile of the urban poor

Housing (built in the 1950s) in New Workers Village in Tiexi District, Shenyang, November 2003.

Emerging urban poverty problems were discussed in the last chapter. This chapter and the two following will look at the urban poor in detail using data collected in poor areas in Shenyang and Chongqing in 2000 and 2001. Shenyang is the political, economic and cultural centre of Liaoning province in the north-east of China. Its central urban districts cover an area of 3,495 km² with a built-up area about 230 km² in 1999. The total population in the central urban districts was 4.8 million, of which 3.9 million were official non-agricultural urban residents (Shenyang Statistics Bureau, 2000). Chongqing, situated on the Yangtze River in the Sichuan basin, is the major political, economic and cultural centre in south-west China. The new Chongqing Municipality (one of the only four cities directly controlled by the central government) was designated in 1997. It includes the city of Chongqing itself, four other small cities and 23 rural counties. The total area controlled by the municipal government is quite large (82,403 km$^2$) and the central built-up area was about 175 km$^2$ in 1996 (Chongqing Master Planning Office and Chongqing Urban Planning and Design Institute, 1998). The population in the central urban districts was 8.36 million in 1998, of which 3.5 million were official urban residents (State Statistics Bureau, 2000).

Both cities were important regional and national industrial bases during the planned economy period. Industry concentrated in the traditional sectors of manu-facturing, engineering, chemicals, steel and textiles. Recent industrial restruc-turing policies had a dramatic impact on these old industrial establishments many of them became loss-making and a large proportion of workers were laid-off. Official statistics show that between 1996 and 1999 the number of persons employed by the state and the collective sectors had declined by 17 and 42 per cent respectively in Shenyang and 13 and 29 per cent in Chongqing (Shenyang Statistics Bureau, 2000; and Chongqing Statistics Bureau, 2000).

The municipal government made ambitious redevelopment plans for their cities. Large-scale redevelopment had been carried out in both cities. The urban landscape, particularly in the central areas, was predominantly modern with flourishing shopping and other facilities. However, in comparison with cities along the coast, urban development was slower in Shenyang and Chongqing. Many older poor residential areas remained in 2000. The following discussion, unless otherwise specified, is based on the study of seven areas in these two cities (the poor residential areas located in Tiexi, Huanggu and Dadong in Shenyang; Jiaochangkou, Shibanpo, Wangjiapo and Tuwan in Chongqing) and a survey of 802 families (official residents, not including rural migrants).

## Household characteristics

Family size is an important factor in poverty studies. The size of urban households in China has been falling since the early 1980s. In 1999, the average household size was three people in both Shenyang and Chongqing. In the poor areas studied, the average family size was 3.58 persons (Table 5.1). The proportion of house-holds with one or two people was small, while 40 per cent of households had more than three people. Two-generation households (married couples living with young child(ren)) were the largest group, and the proportion of adults living with married child(ren) and/or grand child(ren) was high as well, at 27 per cent.

The proportion of retired people in the urban non-agricultural population was about 16 per cent in Shenyang and 14 per cent in Chongqing in 1999 (Shenyang Municipal Statistics Bureau, 2000; Chongqing Municipal Statistics Bureau, 2000). There was a relatively high proportion of elderly people in these areas. Over 24 per cent (Table 5.2) had retired and over 40 per cent of heads of households were over 60 (the official retirement age is 60 for men and 55 for women). Of the single person

**Table 5.1** Size and type of household

| | Number of households | % |
|---|---|---|
| Number of persons in household | | |
| 1 person only | 46 | 6 |
| 2 people | 144 | 18 |
| 3 people | 288 | 36 |
| 4 people | 145 | 18 |
| 5 people | 97 | 12 |
| 6 people | 26 | 3 |
| 7 people | 27 | 3 |
| 8 people or more | 29 | 4 |
| Household type | | |
| One person household | 46 | 6 |
| Married couple | 111 | 14 |
| Married couple with young child(ren) | 319 | 40 |
| Adults living with married children and/or grandchildren | 219 | 27 |
| Couple or single (with or without children) living with parents (including in-laws) | 74 | 9 |
| Other | 33 | 4 |

**Table 5.2** Adult employment situation and children (as percentage of the total population in the sample)

| Study area | Employed | Laid-off | Retired | Pre- and school-age children |
|---|---|---|---|---|
| Shenyang | 26 | 26 | 27 | 20 |
| Tiexi | 26 | 25 | 30 | 18 |
| Huanggu | 23 | 28 | 24 | 23 |
| Dadong | 29 | 27 | 25 | 19 |
| Chongqing | 23 | 23 | 22 | 19 |
| Tuwan | 23 | 19 | 33 | 21 |
| Jiaochangkou | 23 | 24 | 19 | 19 |
| Shibanpo | 20 | 25 | 23 | 19 |
| Wangjiapo | 26 | 23 | 15 | 18 |
| Total in all areas | 24 | 25 | 24 | 19 |

households shown in Table 5.1, 63 per cent were aged over 60; and of the married couple only households, 58 per cent of the heads of households were aged over 60. Among all households surveyed, 57 per cent had one or more retired persons.

The proportion of children in these areas was much lower than national average. The 1994 *China Population Statistics Yearbook* shows that on average 26.3 per cent of urban residents were under 18 (Population and Labour Department of State Statistics Bureau, 1994: 14). The proportion of persons under 18 in these study areas was only 19.3. Of the households interviewed, 43 per cent had no dependent children; 58 per cent had one or more school-age children; and only 8 per cent of households had pre-school-age children.

Another important feature of these communities, as shown in Table 5.2, was the very high unemployment rate. At the end of 1999, 42.4 per cent of the non-agricultural population in Shenyang and 53.6 per cent in Chongqing had jobs (Shenyang Municipal Statistics Bureau, 2000; Chongqing Municipal Statistics Bureau, 2000). In these areas, only a third of the adult population had a job; this was substantially lower than the overall figure in these cities. Age distribution was an important factor which affected the employment situation. The proportion of those in work declined with age. Among the 21 to 30 age group 63 per cent had a job; in the 31 to 50 age group about 44 per cent had a job; and in the 51 to 60 age group only 25 per cent had a job.

Educational levels of the heads of households and their partners in the study areas were relatively low in comparison to the general urban average. Over 41 per cent of the heads of households had either no school education at all or only attended primary school. Another 37 per cent had middle school education. The proportion of those with high school or advanced training was very low. There was not a single person who had postgraduate study experience. The general educational level of the partners was similar to the heads of households.

The health of key family members was another problem in the areas. Of the households surveyed, 13 per cent of heads of household, the partner or both of them reported health problems.

## Employment

Unemployment was a major problem in these areas, and nearly 44 per cent of households had no one in employment. About 60 per cent of these jobless families resulted from recent industrial restructuring when family members had been laid-off by their employer (Table 5.3). Unemployment was widespread and more than half of the households were affected. Some households had three people or more who had lost jobs.

The economic sectors which employed most of the residents in the study areas were mainly industrial factories owned by either the state or collectives. In Shenyang, 22 per cent of heads of households in the sample were employed in the collective sector, and 63 per cent in state factories. In Chongqing, 31 per cent were in collectives and 43 per cent in state factories (Table 5.4). The share of collective-sector workers, in Chongqing in particular, was much higher than that in the city as a whole. The number of people employed by government agencies

**Table 5.3** Persons in employment and laid-off in household

|  | Number of households | % |
|---|---|---|
| **Employed people in the household** | | |
| No one | 351 | 44 |
| One person | 264 | 33 |
| Two people | 154 | 19 |
| Three people | 21 | 3 |
| Four or more people | 12 | 1 |
| Total | 802 | 100 |
| **Laid-off people in the household** | | |
| No one | 370 | 46 |
| One person | 234 | 30 |
| Two people | 152 | 19 |
| Three people | 27 | 3 |
| Four or more people | 19 | 2 |
| Total | 802 | 100 |

**Table 5.4** Employment sectors of heads of households

|  | Number of respondents | % |
|---|---|---|
| State factory | 394 | 53 |
| Collective enterprise | 198 | 26 |
| Other state sector | 52 | 7 |
| Self-employed | 39 | 5 |
| Private enterprise | 18 | 2 |
| Joint venture | 13 | 2 |
| Government institution | 13 | 2 |
| Small business | 11 | 1 |
| Public professional | 5 | 1 |
| Foreign company | 2 | <1 |
| Other | 4 | 1 |
| Total | 749 | 100 |

Note: For those who were retired, the employer before retirement was recorded.

and professional institutions was extremely low, less than 3 per cent. The total number of heads of households who worked in the private sectors was about 11 per cent, slightly lower than that in these cities as a whole. Employment in joint ventures and other new private business was very low. The majority of people who identified themselves as private-sector employees were actually self-employed or working for other family-based businesses.

Employment in the collectives and state enterprise sectors was affected by the recent industrial restructuring. About 32 per cent of heads of households employed in the collective sector and 23 per cent employed in state enterprises had been laid-off when interviewed. The collective sector in particular was affected the most seriously. Of the heads of households employed in the collective sector, only 27 per cent were still working full-time when interviewed.

In relation to official employment status in cities, the overwhelming majority of adult residents in the study areas were workers. Nearly 78 per cent of heads of households in the sample were workers. The proportion of workers in Chongqing (82 per cent) was higher than that in Shenyang (73 per cent). The proportion of cadres and enterprise managers was very low, about 20 per cent in Shenyang and 10 per cent in Chongqing. Among the partners of heads of households, a similar pattern was found. Of those households in which both partners identified their employment status, 64 per cent of them were both workers; 18 per cent either the head or the partner was a worker; in only 3 per cent of households, both head of household and partner were cadres. Of those heads of households who identified themselves either as cadres or enterprise managers, 68 per cent actually had retired or been laid-off.

In terms of employment or office rank, residents interviewed also showed a very poor profile. Among the heads of households who were workers, 88 per cent had no grade and were the lowest-ranked shop floor workers. Among the partners who were workers, the percentage of no grade was even higher, at 93 per cent. Among those with a grade, most of them only had either a primary or middle grade. In the entire sample, only one person claimed to have a senior technician grade. Among the heads of households who were cadres or enterprise managers, 46 per cent were general office clerks without any ranking in their offices.

Because of similarities in age, employment status, grade and ranks, many spouses shared the same situation as their partners in terms of employment (Table 5.5). Of the 623 cases, in 207 both the heads of households and their partners were retired; 80 couples had both been laid-off; 5 couples had never worked; and 73 couples were both working when interviewed.

Despite their low status in factories or offices, most adult residents in the study areas had a very long working experience. The average number of years of service (up to the year 2000 or before retirement) was 27 for the heads of households and 24 for their partners. The proportion of residents with less than 10 years of work experience was less than 10 per cent. Low status and long service meant that these

**Table 5.5** Employment positions of head of household and partner

| | Partner of head of household | | | | |
| | Never had a job | Laid-off or unemployed | Retired | Has a job | Total |
|---|---|---|---|---|---|
| Head of household | | | | | |
| Never had a job | 5 | 11 | 10 | 3 | 29 |
| Laid-off or unemployed | 18 | 80 | 23 | 44 | 165 |
| Retired | 30 | 6 | 207 | 13 | 256 |
| Has a job | 17 | 63 | 20 | 73 | 173 |
| Total | 70 | 160 | 260 | 133 | 623 |

people had not experienced any promotion in their work. The chance of being laid-off was higher among people with shorter work experience than those with longer working experience. The laid-off rate in the sample was 47 per cent among people with less than 10 years of working experience, 41 per cent for those with 11–20 years, 23 per cent for those with 21–30 years, and 7 per cent for those with 31–40 years. The type of employment contract was also an important factor in job security. Of those who still had a job, the majority had a long-term or permanent contract.

Being laid-off in these areas were not a temporary or short-term arrangement for most of the people affected, and about 85 per cent of heads of households and 92 per cent of partners who were unemployed when interviewed had been laid-off more than a year earlier. Future prospects of those who had been laid-off were not very good. Because of their poor educational and skill profiles not many could find new jobs. As Table 5.6 shows, very few laid-off workers had actually found long-term employment. About a third of them only found temporary jobs and the majority of them were either looking for jobs, staying at home or didn't know

**Table 5.6** Employment after being laid-off

| | Head of household | | Partner | |
| | Number of respondents | % | Number of respondents | % |
|---|---|---|---|---|
| Found permanent job | 5 | 3 | 2 | 2 |
| Found temporary job | 51 | 32 | 40 | 29 |
| Looking for job | 44 | 28 | 24 | 17 |
| Stay at home | 40 | 26 | 67 | 48 |
| Don't know what to do | 17 | 11 | 6 | 4 |
| Total | 157 | 100 | 139 | 100 |

what to do. Of those who had not lost their jobs, insecurity was also a problem. More than half of those in employment felt their jobs were insecure.

Low status and insecure jobs were accompanied by other poor employment conditions. Official reports showed that important progress in the social security (such as health, pension and unemployment) systems were made in cities in the last few years, which had benefited most mainstream urban employees. These benefits had not reached everyone in these low-income communities. Although the unemployment rate was extremely high in these areas, less than 5 per cent of the adult population had joined the unemployment benefit system. Only 29 per cent of the heads of households had a pension scheme and less than 9 per cent had medical insurance. Nearly 60 per cent of heads of households had not joined any insurance scheme at all. The figures for the partners were even lower.

## Income

Heads of households and their partners were the main source of income for most households. When asked who had the highest income in the household, 56 per cent answered the head of household, 20 per cent the partner. Although only 24 per cent of heads of households had a job, 85 per cent of them reported having received some sort of income in the previous month. Of the partners, the proportion of those who had a job was even smaller, but still 75 per cent of them had some income in the previous month. Apart from the head of household and partner, 36 per cent of households had income from other family members – mainly adult children. The number of other family members with an income ranged from one to five. In these low-income areas, the proportion of people with a stable salary was very small. Personal income came from various sources.

Being laid-off by an employer had a direct impact on a person's income. About a third of heads of households who had been laid-off by employers had no income in the previous month. The rest had some money from either salary from employer, laid-off subsidies, income from business, or wages from a new job. The average monthly income (356 yuan) for the laid-off workers was about 56 per cent of those with a job (637 yuan). The average income for those laid-off was also lower than the average pension of those who had retired (375 yuan).

In comparison with overall average income in Shenyang and Chongqing, the monthly income of the heads of households in these areas was about 10 and 24 per cent lower respectively in October 2000 (Table 5.7). Official salaries usually do not include other income. The income data collected through interviews included salary (if the person still had a job) and all other income and in some cases it was an estimate only. Direct comparison could be misleading, but the general patterns are interesting. Only for those who had a job was the average income higher than the overall average salary in their city a year earlier. Incomes among all other groups were much lower than the city average.

The problems of these areas could be seen more clearly by the comparison of household income per capita between the sample and other household surveys carried out in these cities. Chinese municipal governments normally carry out a small sample survey of households each year and the data are published in the official statistics. A comparison of these official data with the sample data on household income per capita is presented in Table 5.8. The income per capita in the study areas was substantially lower than that in the official survey despite the study being carried out about one year later and there being salary increases in these cities. The data also show that, using the overall standard for the city, more than half of the households in these areas in Shenyang belong to the low-income group (the bottom 20 per cent). In Chongqing, about 80 per cent of the households in the sample belong to the low-income group.

Social security and income support policies were introduced in these cities in the late 1990s. In October 2000, poverty levels were set at 195 and 169 yuan per person per month in Shenyang and Chongqing respectively. Households with a monthly per capita income below this level could apply to the municipal social security department for benefit (if using the World Bank $1 a day benchmark as poverty line, 47 per cent in Shenyang and 57 per cent in Chongqing in the sample were living in poverty). Nearly 32 per cent of the residents interviewed had a personal income below the local poverty level and should have been eligible to claim low-income benefits. In reality, not many households had actually done so.

**Table 5.7** Income: comparison between cities and the samples

|  | Shenyang | Chongqing |
|---|---|---|
| *Average monthly salaries in the city as whole in 1999*[1] | | |
| Overall average | 543 | 525 |
| State sector | 614 | 565 |
| Collective sector | 289 | 341 |
| Other sectors | 602 | 567 |
| *Average monthly income in the study areas in September/October 2000*[2] | | |
| Heads of households | 492 | 400 |
| Salary of those with a job | 652 | 617 |
| Workers | 423 | 373 |
| Cadres | 598 | 477 |
| Collective sector | 337 | 322 |
| State enterprise | 500 | 403 |
| Partners of heads of households | 284 | 297 |

Sources:
1  Based on Shenyang Municipal Statistics Bureau, 2000, and Chongqing Municipal Statistics Bureau, 2000.
2  Includes salary, pension, laid-off subsidy and other incomes.

The proportion of households claiming low-income support was between 3 and 5 per cent in these areas.

Lower income among residents was accompanied by the lack of other family assets. Since these areas were generally poor, most households did not own any valuables. About 60 per cent of households reported no savings at all. Among these who had, most of them only had a small amount of money in banks. The sample households in Chongqing seemed even poorer than those in Shenyang in terms of savings (Table 5.9). There were major changes in the salary system in the public sector and most government employees received substantial increases in their salary during the period of 1998 and 1999. Of those interviewed, less than 20 per cent of the households saw any increases in income, about half had no change, and over a quarter of households' income actually declined.

**Table 5.8** Income per capita: comparison with official surveys

| Income groups | Percentile | Average monthly income per person in 1999[1] (yuan) | | Average monthly income per person in 2000[2] (yuan) | |
|---|---|---|---|---|---|
| | | Shenyang | Chongqing | Shenyang | Chongqing |
| Overall mean | – | – | – | 295 | 258 |
| Median | – | – | – | 267 | 200 |
| Very low income | 0–10 | 190 | 242 | 63 | 43 |
| Of which the lowest | 0–5 | 166 | 216 | – | – |
| Low income | 11–20 | 258 | 309 | 124 | 93 |
| Low-middle income | 21–30 | 309 | 371 | 156 | 123 |
| | 31–40 | | | 200 | 158 |
| Middle income | 41–50 | 406 | 454 | 250 | 193 |
| | 51–60 | | | 292 | 233 |
| High-middle income | 61–70 | 529 | 565 | 326 | 270 |
| | 71–80 | | | 364 | 317 |
| Higher income I | 81–90 | 685 | 710 | 422 | 429 |
| Higher income II | 91–100 | 965 | 985 | 824 | 872 |
| Valid cases | – | 500 | 300 | 351 | 403 |

Source: Shenyang Municipal Statistics Bureau, 2000: 306–7; Chongqing Municipal Statistics Bureau, 2000: 133–5.

Notes
1 Survey of households in the cities in 1999 conducted by the Municipal Statistics Bureau. Sample sizes: Shenyang 500 households, Chongqing 300 households. These surveys include all social groups in these cities.
2 Data from the survey of this research calculated from responses about income last month.

**Table 5.9** Savings among the residents (unit: yuan)

|  | Shenyang | | Chongqing | |
|  | Respondents | % | Respondents | % |
| --- | --- | --- | --- | --- |
| Yes, have savings | 181 | 51 | 137 | 32 |
| Less than 5,000 | 47 | 26 | 64 | 48 |
| 5,000–10,000 | 50 | 28 | 34 | 26 |
| 10,000–20,000 | 43 | 24 | 18 | 14 |
| 20,000–30,000 | 23 | 13 | 8 | 6 |
| 30,000–40,000 | 6 | 3 | 1 | 1 |
| 40,000–50,000 | 6 | 3 | 1 | 1 |
| Over 50,000 | 6 | 3 | 7 | 4 |

## Institutional causes of poverty

The previous sections looked at the key features of households living in these poor residential areas and analysed employment and income levels of the main household members. In this section, correlation and regression analysis are used to establish the relationship between these household characteristics and poverty. Table 5.10 lists results from correlation coefficient tests (Spearman's $\rho$) of monthly income per person with variables on household characteristics, employment and income. Although only weak correlations were shown between most of the variables, the negative or positive signs of the correlation coefficient do give a good indication of which types of households had a very low income per capita and had experienced poverty. In terms of general household characteristics, it is clear that:

- low income is associated with the size of household. The bigger the house-hold and the more dependent persons in the household, the lower per capita income;
- lower educational level, poor health of head of household and partner also had a negative impact.

Although the influence of demographic characteristics is important, more significant relations exist between income and employment situations. This is shown by the higher coefficient values:

- the number of laid-off persons in a household is an important indication for low income;
- employment positions of the head of household and partner have an important impact on household income;
- low employment status (worker and cadre) and low grade have a negative impact on household income;

**Table 5.10** Relationship between monthly income per person and household characteristics, employment and income

| Variable | Spearman's $\rho$ correlation coefficient |
|---|---|
| *Household characteristics* | |
| Size of household | −0.256** |
| Number of employed persons in household | 0.285** |
| Number of laid–off persons in household | −0.394** |
| Number of school age children | −0.228** |
| Number of persons requiring support from the household | −0.138** |
| *Head of household* | |
| Educational level (from low to high) | 0.179** |
| Health (from good to poor) | −0.102** |
| Employment (1 never worked, 2 laid-off, 3 retired, 4 has a job) | 0.363** |
| Employer (1 private, 2 collective, 3 state enterprise, 4 other public) | 0.113** |
| Status in employment (1 worker, 2 cadre, 3 manager, 4 other) | 0.215** |
| If workers, grade (from low to high) | 0.162** |
| Contract (from long term to hourly work) | −0.038 |
| Years of employment | 0.081* |
| Job security (from secure to might be laid-off, already laid-off) | −0.271** |
| If laid-off, what is the hhd doing? (found another job, search, and at home) | −0.251** |
| *Partner of head of household* | |
| Educational level (from low to high) | 0.090* |
| Health (from good to poor) | −0.106** |
| Employment (1 never worked, 2 laid-off, 3 retired, 4 has a job) | 0.374** |
| Employer (1 private, 2 collective, 3 state enterprise, 4 other public) | 0.133** |
| Status in employment (1 worker, 2 cadre, 3 manager, 4 other) | 0.120** |
| If workers, grade (from low to high) | 0.096* |
| Contract (from long term to hourly work) | −0.128 |
| Years of employment | 0.136** |
| Job security (from secure to might be laid-off, already laid-off) | −0.255** |
| If laid-off, what is the hhd doing? (found another job, search, and at home) | −0.295** |

**Table 5.10** continued

| Variable | Spearman's ρ correlation coefficient |
| --- | --- |
| *Income* | |
| Have other income (1 yes, 2 no) | −0.147** |
| Income from other family members in household last month | 0.166** |
| Have bank saving (1 yes, 2 no) | −0.315** |

Notes
*     Correlation is significant at the 0.05 level (2-tailed).
**    Correlation is significant at the 0.01 level (2-tailed).

- the hierarchy of economic sectors (state, collective, private) which employed key household members is also an important factor in income.

The employment situations of the head of household and partner to a large extent were determined by the old urban economic organisation. In this sense, poverty among these people was mainly a result of institutional changes rather than individual personal quality.

Although the majority of residents in the study areas were poor, not necessarily every family there lived in absolute poverty. Regression analysis is used to identify and predict what type of household may fall below the poverty level in these areas. Two separate logistic regression analyses were carried out. Income per capita in household was re-coded into a binary dependent variable with values of either 1 or 0. In the first model, households with an income below the city's official poverty line (195 yuan in Shenyang and 169 yuan in Chongqing) were given the value 1 and others the value 0. In the second model, the World Bank poverty line ($1 per day) was used. Households with an income below 250 yuan per person per month (the same value for both cities) was given the value 1 and others the value 0. Independent variables include size of household, percentage of household members in employment and several other variables about the head of household (educational level, employment status, economic sector involved, work/office status). The analysis results (Table 5.11) are similar from the two models on most factors.

The probability of a household experiencing poverty in these areas increases with the total number of persons per household and decreases as the proportion of household members in employment becomes higher. In relation to the head of household, poor educational background, being unemployed (laid-off), working in the collective sector, and being a worker rather than cadre increase the probability of poverty. In another words, households headed by unemployed workers from the collective sector were the main social group that experienced severe poverty,

**Table 5.11** Logistic regression of poverty with household characteristics (per capita income below municipal/World Bank poverty line = 1, and other = 0)

| Household characteristics | Unstandardised regression coefficients | |
|---|---|---|
| | Municipal poverty line | World Bank poverty line |
| Number of persons in household | 0.311** | 0.344** |
| Percentage of household members in employment | −0.029** | −0.029** |
| Head of household education level: 1 primary or less, else 0 | 0.214 | 0.168 |
| *Employment status of head of household* | | |
| Laid-off or unemployed | 0.321* | 0.441** |
| Retired | −0.606** | 0.192 |
| Have a job | 0.285 | −0.633 |
| *Economic sector that employs head of household* | | |
| Private | −0.485 | −0.113 |
| Collective | 0.550** | 0.446** |
| State enterprise | −0.035 | −0.065 |
| Government or public institution | −0.030 | −0.268 |
| *Work or office status of head of household* | | |
| Worker | 0.520* | 0.439* |
| Cadre | −0.480 | −0.375 |
| Manager | −0.224 | −0.142 |
| Other | 0.184 | 0.078 |
| Constant | −1.822** | −0.758* |
| Model $\chi^2$ (df = 11) | 129.878** | 152.191** |
| Number of cases | 715 | 715 |

Notes
* Significant at 0.05 level.
** Significant at 0.01 level.
Deviation contrasts were used for category variables.

and households headed by cadres or enterprise managers were less likely to fall below the poverty line.

The main differences of the two models are the employment position of the head of household and the effect of private sector employment. In relation to the employment position of head of household, retirement and being in employment have the opposite effects in the two models. These results mean that households headed by retired people have a very critical income level. A slight raising of the poverty line could mean a substantial number of retired people being included in the poor group. They also show that, given the low and varied wages in the areas, a head of household in employment may not necessarily protect the family from falling below the poverty level, particularly when the poverty level is low as shown in the first model. This positive relationship between head of household who works and low income per capita also means that for residents in these areas, wages were less important than other sources of income. The employment of heads of households in the private sector in these areas could help families out of poverty only when the poverty level was low. This result indicates that in general wages of those who worked in the private sector were low. Like pensioners, households headed by employees of small private businesses were in a critical position. If the average wage in this sector does not increase with those in other sectors, these private-sector employees can easily fall into poverty in the future.

Although urban poverty is a new phenomenon in China, it shares many common features with that in other countries (Rakodi, 1995; World Bank, 2001). Musgrove (1980) believed that urban poverty was strongly associated with general household characteristics and poverty was associated much more strongly with large household size, low overall employment rates and high dependency ratios, rather than with low wages and unemployment. Poor households are not only in material deprivation, their members had low achievements in education and poorer health conditions; key household members are often employed in low-paid jobs in less important economic sectors such as small private businesses or collective enterprises. Their employment status was poor and they were often voiceless and powerless in work-related decision-making. They were vulnerable to changes and were more exposed to risk of unemployment.

Although the characteristics of individual households are important, the major causes of large areas of poverty are the historical legacy of these areas and the specific urban economic structure and employment pattern in these cities. Most of these areas, particularly the traditional housing areas, were poor areas before the communists came to power. During the socialist period, many had never integrated successfully with the planned economic system. The traditional informal private business was always an important source of income. Few residents from these areas found high-status jobs in the formal state sector. Many of them worked in the enterprises set up by the supplementary collective sector. The technologies and machinery used by these enterprises were generally poor, and the purpose of this sector was more about job creation than producing important products for the national economy. With lower consideration of efficiency, these enterprises and their employees can manage to exist; but when efficiency becomes an important issue, these enterprises and their employees were the first victims of the reform. Collective-sector employment has declined very rapidly since the middle of the 1990s; without a major change of policy and government support to this sector, we may see all collective employment being lost in the future.

# 6 Housing the urban poor

A poor housing area being demolished for redevelopment, Dadong District, Shenyang, November 2003.

## Urban housing reform

Housing and living conditions are important indicators of household poverty. Housing provision in Chinese cities and towns during the socialist planned economy period was dominated by the public sector. Along with job security, housing was the most important element of the welfare system. As a result of insufficient investment, housing conditions were generally very poor over the period from 1949–80. The overall average housing floor space per person was around 3 m$^2$ at both the beginning and the end of the period. Since the early 1980s, as part of the urban economic reform and the transition to a market economy, important changes had been made to urban housing provision system. During the 1990s a substantial proportion of the public housing was sold to sitting tenants. Commercial property developers emerged as the main housing providers. Official data show that, at the end of 2000, over 77 per cent of urban residents owned their homes. The average floor space per person had reached 20 m$^2$. Many urban families now live in purpose-built flats.

China has followed a pragmatic approach to housing reform. Urban housing reform in China had been a major research focus in recent years and many publications have been produced on this topic. (For details about housing reform please refer to works published by World Bank (1992), Bian and Logan (1996), Chen (1996), Chiu (1996), Leaf (1997), Li (2000a, 2000b), Logan and Bian (1993), Logan *et al.* (1999), Wang and Murie (1996, 1999, 2000), Wang (1992, 1995, 2001, 2003a, 2003b), Wu (1996, 2001), and Zhou and Logan (1996).) Throughout the 1980s, a series of reform policies were tested at various locations to commercialise the public sector dominated urban housing system. These included the sale of new housing to urban residents at construction cost (1979–81), subsidised sale of new housing (1982–5), and comprehensive housing reform (1986–8) (Wang, 1992). These experiments focused on increasing rents in the public sector, the introduction of housing subsidy and the promotion of sales of public sector housing to sitting tenants (Wang and Murie, 1996). The publication of the central government policy document, *Implementation Plan for a Gradual Housing System Reform in Cities and Towns* (State Council, 1988) marked the turning point of housing reform from pilot schemes to overall implementation in all urban areas. The objective of this plan was to 'realise housing commercialisation according to the principles of socialist planned market economy'. New policies included rent increases, issuing housing subsidies to offset rent increases, and sale of public housing. During the early stages of reform, the sale of flats involved the sale of the use rights only – changing the basis of payment for use and securing the family's right to use the property and pass it on through inheritance, but not securing the right to sell on the market. This plan was interrupted in 1989 by economic and political problems.

In October 1991, a major national housing reform conference was held in Beijing. The conference resolution, *On Comprehensive Reform of the Urban Housing System* compiled by the State Council's Housing Reform Steering Group, was issued in November, 1991 (General Office of the State Council, 1991). This document reinforced the 1988 resolution and required all urban authorities to carry out housing reform. It led to the large-scale sale of existing public housing at very low prices, particularly to their current occupiers. Because of concern

about the low-price sales, the government suspended the housing reform programme temporarily in 1993. New policies were issued in 1994 in the document
of *The Decision on Deepening the Urban Housing Reform* (Housing Reform
Steering Group of the State Council, 1994). This was an important and comprehensive policy document on housing reform. The new strategy included
comprehensive reform in housing investment, management and distribution
systems, which aimed to establish:

1    a dual housing provision system with
     a)    a social housing supply providing economic and comfortable housing
           for middle- and low-income households and
     b)    a commercial housing supply for high-income families
2    a public and private housing saving system
3    new housing insurance, finance and loan systems
4    a healthy, standardised and regulated market system of property exchange,
     repair and management.

Apart from rent changes and sale of public housing, this document formalised
several special arrangements to help ordinary urban households to participate in
the new housing market. The first important arrangement involved the establishment of a housing provident fund through which urban employers and employees
each made a contribution to the employee's housing saving fund. These savings
could only be used to purchase housing or for housing repairs. It could be used for
other purposes only when the employee retires. The rates of saving varied from
place to place between 5 per cent and 10 per cent of employee's monthly salary in
the public sector. The other important changes included the introduction of
subsidised commercial housing for low- and middle-income families. Central
government loans and free land allocations were used as the main mechanism for
the development of affordable housing (the *anju* – 'peaceful living' projects and
late *jingji shiyong fang* – 'economic and comfortable housing').

A key problem of urban housing reform was the material linkage between
housing and employment. To speed up the process of housing commercialisation
and monetary distribution, a major decision was made by central government in
1998 to stop public sector employers' role in direct housing allocation. A deadline
was set up to allow current housing building projects to finish. Thereafter, the
housing needs of all public-sector employees were to be met directly by property
developers or the housing market rather than by employers. Employers, however,
were allowed to issue housing subsidies to help employees to buy their house in
the market or through the government-supported affordable housing scheme (Wang,
2000).

Affordable housing was identified as a key source of new housing for low- and
middle-income groups. The government planned to make this type of housing
accessible to most urban residents (70–80 per cent). Higher-income households

in urban areas (10–15 per cent) were encouraged to obtain high standard housing through the market; and poor urban families (about 10–15 per cent) were to be given subsidised rented housing by their employers or the city government (State Council, 1998). These reform policies have brought important changes in urban housing provision. A few years ago, most new commercial housing was bought by employers and then distributed to their employees. By 2002, 80 per cent of public housing had been sold to the occupiers. About 95 per cent of new housing was sold directly to individual families.

The housing provident fund system was further regulated in 2001 with the publication of the Housing Provident Fund Management Ordinance. By November 2001, over 67 million urban employees (about half of all in employment) had joined the saving system. The fund helped 2.4 million families buy their home with low-interest mortgages (Liu, 2003). Home ownership became the most common form of tenure in cities, with over 82 per cent of urban families owning their home. Private home ownership also altered the distribution of urban assets. Official statistics showed that, in 2001, average household assets in urban areas were 228,300 yuan, of which 47 per cent was property (Liu, 2003).

Despite these successes, the impact of housing reform and development on different social and economic groups varied. First, it is important to recognise that housing reform was irrelevant to the large numbers of rural migrants found in the cities. Migrants had been excluded from the formal urban housing market. Most of them cannot afford to buy commercially built houses anyway. The only option for them was to rent in the informal sector. Housing reform also had limited direct impacts on people who were traditional home owners and not employed by the state sector. The people who benefited most from housing reform were senior employees in the public sector (Wang, F., 2003).

Although the objective of housing reform had been to improve housing conditions in general, the specific impact of housing reform depends upon the individual household's position in society. In the privatisation process what kind of housing a household had initially was crucial. Families in good-quality apartments would gradually secure their position through reform policies. People employed by work units, which did not perform well (such as the collective sector) and had not invested properly in housing, ended up living in poor-quality housing. While some urban families enjoyed a higher living standard than that experienced by ordinary Chinese before, a large number of poor urban families were stuck in poor-quality homes. In this sense housing reform had reinforced existing inequalities within China (Wang, 2000).

The Construction Ministry reported in 2003 that the main urban housing problems were no longer overcrowding, but those relating to the urban poor. The 2000 National Population Census revealed that:

- only 71 per cent of urban housing were purpose-built housing units
- on average, there was only 0.75 of a room per person in urban areas

- there were 15 million urban households with less than 8 m² of housing floor space per person (about 50 million residents)
- only 72 per cent urban families used electricity or gas as main fuels, the others still used coal or other natural materials for cooking and heating (Liu, 2003).

These figures, on the one hand, indicate the difficulties to meet the new housing target set at the Sixteenth National Congress of the Chinese Communist Party (one purpose-built housing unit per family, one room per person, and access to necessary facilities and equipment). On the other hand, they indicate the wide gap between the rich and the poor in terms of housing. Faced with the increasing problem of urban poverty, social rental (or cheap rent) housing was introduced in 1998 as a main element of social support in cities. Implementation however was very slow and remains in the testing and experiment stage in most cities.

While housing for the poor moved forward very slowly, high-standard and sometimes luxury commercial housing for the rich dominated housing developments in large cities, though there had been serious over-supply of this type of housing. In September 2003, five years after the 1998 policy document, the State Council issued new policies which aimed to rebalance the market development and provision system. Strict controls were to be imposed on the development of luxury villas and cottages. More emphasis would be given to the development of ordinary commercial housing, government-supported affordable housing and social-rental housing (State Council, 2003). Despite this policy change, affordable and social-rental housing required more government investment and effective regulation of the housing market. Under the liberal market economic philosophy and the continuous pursuit of commercialisation of housing provision, a large-scale increase in public housing investment and social housing stock in the near future are unlikely. The following sections of this chapter discuss housing conditions of official residents in poor areas of Shenyang and Chongqing.

## Housing conditions of the urban poor

Figure 6.1 shows the age of houses in the poor areas. It is very obvious that most houses were quite old. About 33 per cent of houses in Shenyang and 28 per cent in Chongqing were built before 1949; and 26 per cent in Shenyang and 36 per cent in Chongqing built during the first decade of the communist government. The 1960s was a period of strict control on house building, and only a small proportion of houses were built during this period. The 1970s saw some recovery of house building in these areas, and the activities slowed down again in the 1990s. Types of housing are presented in Table 6.1. In Shenyang, the dominant types of housing were traditional single-storey housing and multi-storey flats without lift. In Chongqing, the dominant styles were either single- or multi-storey traditional houses. The difference in building styles (single storey in Shenyang and multi-

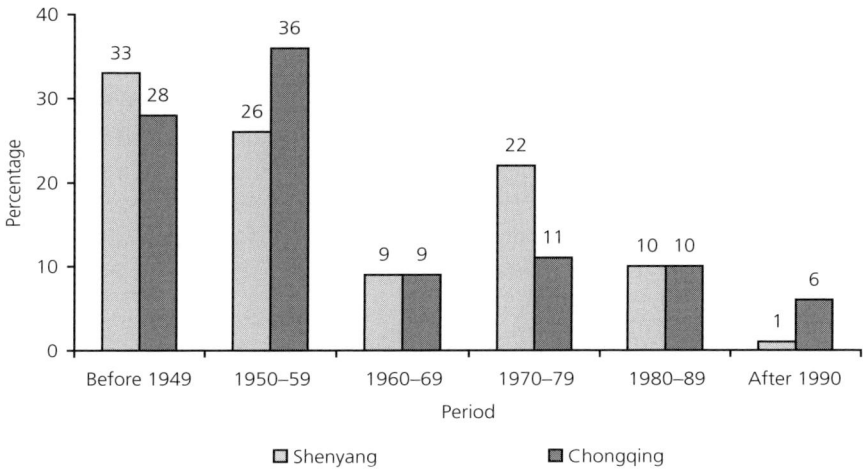

**6.1** When houses were built

**Table 6.1** Construction type of the houses

| Housing type | Shenyang | | Chongqing | | Total | |
|---|---|---|---|---|---|---|
| | No. of households | % | No. of households | % | No. of households | % |
| Traditional single storey | 200 | 55 | 158 | 37 | 358 | 45 |
| Traditional courtyard | 11 | 3 | 5 | 1 | 16 | 2 |
| Simple multi-storey | 20 | 6 | 181 | 41 | 201 | 25 |
| Multi-storey dormitory | 2 | 1 | 6 | 2 | 11 | 2 |
| Flat without lift | 122 | 34 | 70 | 16 | 192 | 24 |
| Other | 4 | 1 | 11 | 3 | 15 | 2 |

(mainly two) storey in Chongqing) reflected geographical differences in traditional housing construction between the north and the south. Over 70 per cent of simple single-storey houses and half of the multi-storey traditional houses were built before 1949 or during the 1950s. Over 62 per cent of courtyard houses were built before 1940; most dormitories and multi-storey flats were built either during the 1950s or the 1970s by the public sector.

Despite the reported improvement of housing conditions in cities in the recent years, housing in these areas was rather cramped. The average size of houses in the sample was only 33 m² of floor space – smaller in Shenyang (26 m²) and larger in Chongqing (39 m²). Since the 1980s, not many new houses were built in this size. The average housing floor space per person was only 8 m². The majority of these houses were not purpose-built apartments, but single rooms. Over 35 per cent of households lived either in one room or shared a room with another family. Of those purpose-built houses, some were shared by two or more families.

The overcrowding was accompanied by poor provision of facilities. As Table 6.2 shows, fewer than 70 per cent of households had exclusive use of a kitchen, 12 per cent shared a kitchen with other families, and over 18 per cent had no dedicated kitchen area and had to cook either in corridors or in a bedroom. Only about 20 per cent of households had exclusive use of an indoor toilet, while 63 per cent had to use public toilets in their neighbourhood.

These conditions caused widespread dissatisfaction among residents. Of the households surveyed, fewer than 20 per cent were satisfied with the size of their houses; only 13 per cent were satisfied with the internal structure of their houses. Despite this dissatisfaction with the housing conditions, residents were generally positive about other services and facilities at the district level. These included schools, transport, vegetable market, department stores/shops, and health services. Residents also enjoyed good relationships with their neighbours although there were some concerns about security and safety in their areas.

The age distribution of the residents identified in the last chapter is reflected by the length of residence of these people in the areas. Over 60 per cent of households moved into their current house more than 20 years ago (before urban reform began), of which 12 per cent actually moved into their housing 50 years ago. Many new residents moved into these areas during the 1980s and the 1990s (Figure 6.2).

## Ownership

The main form of housing tenure was traditional private family ownership (Table 6.3), which accounts for 41 per cent. The other main form of tenure was public housing, which included houses provided by the municipal government and the work unit (including those recently privatised ones). The number of households renting their houses from other families (the private rental market) was very small.

The relationship between head of household's employment status and type of tenure was interesting. Traditional home ownership was the most important source for housing across all employment sectors in these areas, but the head of household employed in either private or collective sectors depended more on the traditional home ownership (Table 6.4). More private and collective sector employees also relied on municipal housing provision while state-sector employees relied more on their work unit. Over 45 per cent of state factory employees lived in work unit housing (currently renting or bought through privatisation).

As well as their current home, a small number of households owned other properties in either their own city (6 per cent), other cities/towns (1 per cent), or in

**Table 6.2** Availability of indoor facilities (%)

|  | Indoor and exclusive use | Indoor sharing | Facility lacking |
|---|---|---|---|
| Tapped water | 93 | 6 | 1[1] |
| Kitchen | 70 | 12 | 18 |
| Telephone | 54 | 2 | 44 |
| Bottled gas | 43 | 1 | 56 |
| Piped gas supply | 40 | 1 | 59 |
| Toilet | 20 | 18 | 62[2] |
| Heating system | 24 | 1 | 75 |
| Shower | 16 | 1 | 83 |
| Balcony | 12 | 3 | 85 |
| Bath | 3 | – | 97 |

Notes
1     Outdoor sharing.
2     Public toilet located in the neighbourhood.

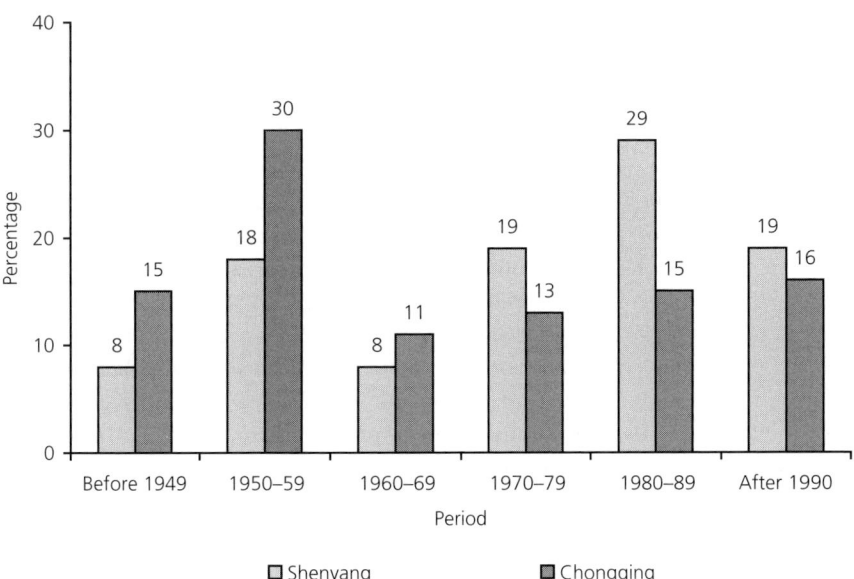

**6.2** When households moved into their current house

**Table 6.3** Housing ownership (tenure)

| Ownership/tenure | Number of households | % |
|---|---|---|
| Traditional home owners | 328 | 41 |
| Inherited | 137 | 17 |
| Bought from another family | 185 | 23 |
| Bought relocation housing | 6 | 1 |
| Rented privately from other families | 26 | 3 |
| Rented from government | 131 | 17 |
| Rented from work unit | 120 | 15 |
| Bought through privatisation | 140 | 18 |
| Work unit built with contribution | 25 | 3 |
| Bought use rights | 12 | 2 |
| Bought full rights | 81 | 10 |
| Bought affordable housing | 22 | 3 |
| Other | 50 | 6 |

rural areas (2 per cent). Of those with other properties in the city, about half of them were rented out to other families and the rest was either used by relatives or left empty. Properties in other cities/towns or rural areas were mainly used by relatives. Over 7 per cent of the sample received some rental income from their properties, with an average of 250 yuan per month. For these households, rental income was an important resource. Over 5 per cent of households used part of their current home for business purposes (e.g. shops). In Chongqing, some houses (about a quarter) in the study areas were rented to rural migrants. However, most rental properties were owned not by local residents, but by landlords who lived elsewhere. Better-off families had moved out from these poor areas, but kept their house in order to secure cash compensation when the area was redeveloped.

Before moving to their current homes, 26 per cent of households interviewed lived in houses provided by the same work unit, 22 per cent by a different work unit, 27 per cent lived in non-work unit houses; the rest lived in either suburban villages or town, or came from the outside of the city. Most moves actually happened within either the public sector or private sector, and the proportion of movements across sectors was relatively small: of the 550 households which provided information about their previous housing tenure (most of the others had not moved house), 35 per cent moved within the public sector; 18 per cent moved from the private sector to the public sector; 31 per cent moved within the private sector; and 13 per cent moved out of the public sector to the private sector.

## Housing costs

Because the quality of these houses was poor and most residents were owners as well, housing costs as a proportion of family income was not very high. Over 62

**Table 6.4** Relation between employment sector and tenure

| Current housing tenure | Head of household's employment sector | | | | | |
|---|---|---|---|---|---|---|
| | Private | | Collective | | State | |
| | No. of households | % | No. of households | % | No. of households | % |
| Owner: traditional | 43 | 53 | 95 | 50 | 163 | 38 |
| Rented private | 5 | 6 | 5 | 3 | 13 | 3 |
| Rented from municipal | 16 | 20 | 50 | 27 | 58 | 13 |
| Rented from work unit | 7 | 9 | 20 | 11 | 86 | 20 |
| Owner: privatised | 10 | 12 | 17 | 9 | 112 | 26 |
| Total | 81 | 100 | 187 | 100 | 432 | 100 |

**Table 6.5** Household expenditure (percentage)

| | Shenyang | | | Chongqing | | |
|---|---|---|---|---|---|---|
| | *Highest expenditure* | *Second highest expenditure* | *Third highest expenditure* | *Highest expenditure* | *Second highest expenditure* | *Third highest expenditure* |
| Food | 56 | 33 | 9 | 62 | 31 | 7 |
| Education of children | 24 | 17 | 3 | 23 | 17 | 7 |
| Healthcare | 13 | 12 | 16 | 11 | 11 | 12 |
| Fuel and water bills | 3 | 25 | 41 | 2 | 24 | 46 |
| Housing | 2 | 3 | 9 | 1 | 6 | 9 |
| Clothes | 1 | 8 | 18 | 1 | 10 | 14 |
| Holidays, recreation | 1 | 1 | 2 | – | 1 | 2 |
| Transport | – | 1 | 2 | – | – | 3 |
| Total | 100 | 100 | 100 | 100 | 100 | 100 |

per cent of households spent three per cent or less of their total household income on housing, another 28 per cent spent between three to ten per cent income on housing. Less than five per cent spent more than 20 per cent of their income on housing. Housing costs were ranked not high among household expenditures. Food expediture was the largest spending for the majority of households, followed by education of children and healthcare (Table 6.5).

Households renting from the private market spent a higher proportion of their income on housing. Those with lowest spending on housing were the homeowners. In the public rental sector, over 60 per cent of households spent less than five per cent of their income on housing. Comparing housing spending in 1995, 1997 and 2000, the results show no major changes over the period. Low rents in the public sector indicated a continuation of government subsidy for those having access to public housing. There was a tendency for households with higher incomes actually to spend less on housing (Figure 6.3).

## Impact of housing reform

Apart from the continuation of low rents in the public sector, other housing benefits were distributed through the implementation of housing reform policies. Of the 390 public sector tenants, 140 households participated in various housing purchase schemes and became home owners or partial owners. The average house price

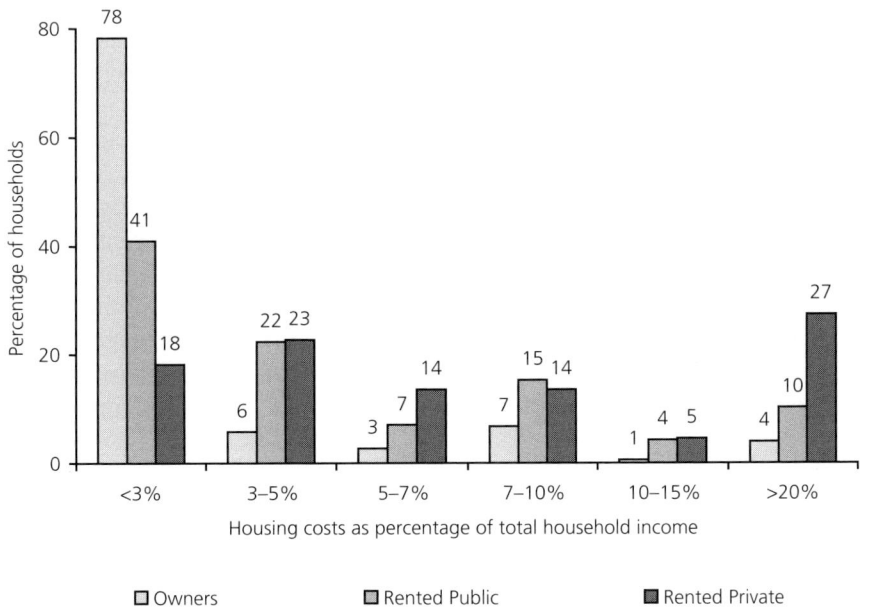

**6.3** Housing costs in different sectors

was about 12,800 yuan and the average amount paid by these families was 8,690 yuan. The difference was covered by employers' subsidies or discounts. The sources of money these families drew on to purchase these houses were mainly from their own savings. A few also received or borrowed money from parents or children, other relatives or friends. The use of the new housing finance arrangement such as the housing provident fund, bank loan/mortgage or relocation compensation was extremely low, less than one per cent.

Over 31 per cent of households were still public-sector tenants in these areas. The reasons for remaining so include:

- house not for sale (42 per cent)
- too poor and could not afford to pay the price (39 per cent)
- had other house (2 per cent)
- did not like the area or the quality of the house (10 per cent)
- other reasons (7 per cent).

This list shows that the two most important reasons for remaining in the public sector was not the choice of these families.

Housing reform had introduced several financial measures to help urban residents to improve their housing conditions. The most important one was the housing provident fund system. Among the households interviewed, only 16 per cent had participated in the provident fund and made monthly contributions (including contribution made by partners). Because the size of provident funds saved was very small, no family had borrowed from the fund to buy a house. There were also important disparities in the amount held by workers and cadres; the average saving among workers was only 1,134 yuan while that among cadres it was 2,177 yuan.

More than half (55 per cent) of households felt the 1998 policy on abolishing work unit housing allocation had no implication for them at all; about 23 per cent supported the policy and another 22 per cent felt the policy had a negative impact on them. The difference in support for this policy across sectors is very interesting. Households living in privatised housing and in municipally-owned rental housing showed stronger support for the policy, while a higher proportion of traditional home owners and those renting from private and/or work units were against this policy. The main reason for supporting the policy was more cash to improve housing conditions and the main reason for not supporting it was the loss of opportunity for housing allocation.

For families living in these poor traditional areas, another opportunity for housing improvement was through the urban renewal process, in which municipal governments set up a policy framework and commercial property developers carried out the redevelopment (see Chapter 8 for more discussion). Local politicians and planners preferred redevelopment of poor housing areas and to quickly eliminate the image of poverty and backwardness of their cities. Property developers were encouraged to build multi-storey flats and to allocate parts of them to the original residents with a subsidy and sell the remaining flats at market prices. This process and cross-subsidy sounds favourable to the local residents, but the families involved normally had to pay a large sum of money to the developer for moving back to the area. The new flats were larger in terms of floor space than the original demolished houses, but did not necessarily offer a larger useable floor space. Most new flats allocated to original families were poor quality and in difficult locations. In Chongqing for example, because of the hilly landscape, flats on the first few floors had limited access to natural light and were often very damp. These flats had a low market value and were often allocated to the returning local residents, who had little bargaining power. With low income and little savings, many families could not afford to move back. This type of renewal could actually force many poor residents out of these areas or to spend all their savings on poor-quality housing when many other household expenses (such as healthcare, education and even food) were also increasing rapidly.

Another option for traditional home owners was to sell their old houses and use the money to buy a new flat. These households were asked to estimate the market value of their houses. The median value was only 30,000 yuan. This was far below the average commercial property price in the two cities (house prices in Shenyang in 2000 were between 1,500–5,000 yuan/ m² according quality and location; in Chongqing it was between 1,600–2,500 yuan/m².) Theoretically speaking, those households could take out a mortgage from a bank to finance house purchase. But without a job or stable income, no financial institutions would lend money to them.

Despite the lack of financial resources, most households (over 80 per cent) welcomed redevelopment of their area, and preferred to move back to the original area with housing compensation rather than be relocated to the suburban areas. (This was not the option given to the residents in the two areas redeveloped in 2003. Families were offered cash compensation only to find their own housing.) About half of the households interviewed would like to move away from their current houses if there was a choice. Most of them (over 65 per cent), however, only had the wish, but did not have a clear plan or the financial resources. The most important reason for wishing to leave was to improve living conditions or due to scheduled redevelopment. The common reasons for moving house, such as nearness to work, relatives, or good schools, were not major concerns for most of them. Of those who had no plan to move, the most important reason was lack of money (79 per cent).

The housing aspiration of these residents was interesting. Residents were asked about their preferred housing under different financial circumstances. Under their existing financial situation, 58 per cent of residents felt their current house was the only affordable one. The next largest group preferred subsidised rental housing from the public sector. The least preferred housing was private rental. The rest could afford commercial or private market housing (old and new) with some government support or subsidy. This group was most likely to stay in the area if redevelopment was carried out. If the economic situation of these households improved, their preferences for housing could change substantially. Their preferred housing was commercially built new housing. In terms of housing types, most popular choices were multi-storey housing with no lift (33.2 per cent), single-storey courtyards (21.8 per cent) and cottages with garages (19.2 per cent). Tower blocks with lifts (12.7 per cent) and self-built housing (9 per cent) were less favoured choices. These results show that most urban poor residents in China (even the poorest ones) had their trust in the formal housing sectors (either public housing or commercially built housing estates) rather than the informal housing sector. Price was the most important factor that influenced housing choice among the poor. Estate environment, size (floor space), location and internal structure of houses were also important factors. Age of housing, safety of the area, distance to work and local employment opportunities were considered less important.

## Housing as a cause of poverty

There is a strong association between household income, housing and poverty. Discussion in previous sections has shown that both residents and their housing conditions were generally very poor. However, housing conditions, employment and income situations were not the same for all households living in these areas. Despite there being no rich households, not every household was in poverty. Table 6.6 shows results from some correlation analysis. Although most results show a weak correlation, they are significant and the general patterns of the relationship are very clear:

- Households with a longer residency (1) and with smaller floor space per person (2) and residents of rented housing (3), particularly that rented from the private sector, tend to have a lower income.
- Households with exclusive use of a toilet, kitchen, shower, gas and telephone tend to have a higher income (4–8).
- High-income households tend to spend proportionately less on housing than low-income households (9–12).
- High-income households were more likely to have improvement in living conditions in the previous five years (13).

Low income and poor living conditions were the most important indicators of poverty in Chinese cities. Theoretically speaking, insecure jobs and poor pay were the main causes of poverty. However, low income alone could not explain the problems faced by the urban poor. Apart from other factors, such as education, health and family structure, housing was a very important issue. Poor housing conditions inherited from the previous economic system and the associated weak

**Table 6.6** Relationship between household per capita income (yuan) and housing

| Housing-related variables | Spearman's $\rho$ correlation coefficient | Valid cases |
|---|---|---|
| 1 Year family moved into the house: 1900–2000 | 0.124** | 742 |
| 2 Floor space per person (m²): 2–90 | 0.216** | 748 |
| 3 Tenure/ownership: from ownership to private rental 1–5 | −0.144** | 795 |
| 4 Toilet: from exclusive use to no provision 1–4 | −0.140** | 746 |
| 5 Kitchen: from exclusive use to no provision 1–4 | −0.064 | 738 |
| 6 Shower: from exclusive use to no provision 1–4 | −0.036 | 730 |
| 7 Piped gas: from exclusive use to no provision 1–4 | −0.158** | 690 |
| 8 Telephone: from exclusive use to no provision 1–4 | −0.152** | 732 |
| 9 Total monthly housing cost in 2000: yuan | −0.068 | 623 |
| 10 Housing cost as % of household income in 2000 | −0.222** | 543 |
| 11 Housing cost as % of household income in 1997 | −0.147** | 506 |
| 12 Housing cost as % of household income in 1995 | −0.143** | 502 |
| 13 Housing change in last 5 years: major improvement to decline 1–5 | −0.097** | 747 |

Note
** Significant at 0.01 level.

financial position could cause poverty as well. Both employment status and housing assets inherited from the previous system were important factors that determined a family's chance of surviving in the new economic system. With large-scale income increases among affluent groups in cities, the unemployed and the laid-off workers became increasingly poor; and with large-scale increases in commercial housing prices, the value of poor-quality houses occupied by the low-income residents became more and more insignificant. The hope for major housing improvement became remote for many of the families living in the poor areas. It was very easy for low-income households to fall into a cycle of poverty as presented in Figure 6.4. The two possible ways out offer hope for some families, but many do not have the skills and resources required.

**Employment and income**          **Housing conditions**

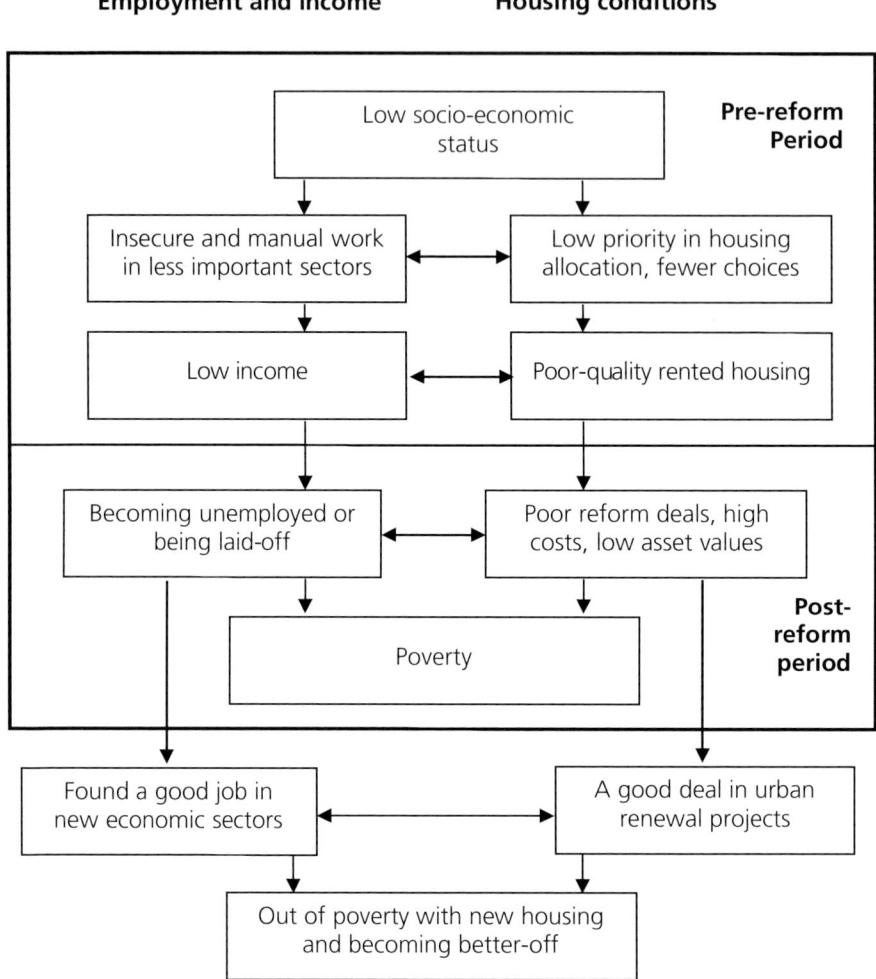

**6.4** Relationship between employment, income, housing and poverty

In both cities, there were strong linkages between housing quality and the history of the areas. Traditional style, low-quality housing is the dominant type of shelter for the urban poor. Apart from the 'new workers' villages' in the Shenyang and the Tuwan areas in Chongqing, the other areas had been established during the first half of the twentieth century before the communist government. In Shenyang they were the poor workers' districts during the Japanese occupation of the 1930s and 1940s; and in Chongqing they were poor areas during the 1930s and the 1940s when the city served as the national wartime capital. This historical association with poverty had been a problem for these areas during the planned economic period when industrial factories and government institutions were set up in other locations. Only qualified residents from these poor areas had found jobs in the public sector and they had also gradually moved out. The remaining population was engaged in the peripheral support industries and services (mainly in the collective sector) in poor employment conditions. In this way these areas had never actually been fully integrated into the socialist cities before the economic reform. They were at the margins of the socialist urban production system though some of them were located near to the centre of these cities. The movement of residents from these areas based on political criteria in the earlier period was followed by another wave of selective outward migration based on household economic power. Families, which made money in new private businesses, were also able to purchase commercial housing in the open market, though the number belonging to this category was small.

The housing conditions found in some of these low-income areas in the two cities were not as bad as those found in the slums in many developing countries before the take-off of the urban economy and the property boom. They had provided reasonable living conditions for the residents. Conditions had degenerated during the reform period and this became more obvious when major improvements were made in other areas. Urban renewal had replaced many old houses with new modern multi-storey buildings. Those demolished often included those located in central districts where demand for commercial property was higher and where the redevelopment provided developers with higher returns on their investments. The areas left were those in more peripheral locations with a lower land value. In Shenyang, many smaller areas of older housing located either along railway lines, or near to large industrial factories could still be found. In Chongqing, all the areas identified were located at peripheral locations on steep slopes. The names of these areas, such as Wangjiapo (Wang's slope), Shibapo (slope of stone plank), Shibati (18 stairs), give a good indication of the physical conditions on which these houses were built. Their peripheral location and difficult physical settings also affected their land value. Private ownership, poor residents and a very high population density were other factors which made these places less attractive for large-scale redevelopment. Because of the poor physical and social profiles of these areas, they had become areas of social exclusion in cities and the first destination of rural-to-urban migrants.

There has been significant and continuous improvement in housing conditions in Chinese cities over the last 20 years, but the improvement was very uneven between areas and social and economic groups. For the majority of the low-income households living in traditional areas, housing conditions remain poor and basic. Many households live in overcrowded rooms with poor facilities. Most houses are old and some were built during the first half of the last century, long before the communists came to power in 1949. These areas were at the margins of the planned socialist economic system. The residents tend to be those either employed by the non-state sector – the collective and private sectors – or low-status manual workers employed by the state factories. This group had a low priority in housing allocation in the past and many of them relied on the poor-quality traditional private housing or housing provided by the municipal government.

Urban housing reform involved the privatisation of public housing to the sitting tenants. However, the impact of reform in the low-income areas was very marginal. Traditional home owners and families renting privately had not benefited from housing privatisation. Even those renting from the public sector did not buy their houses. The majority of households experienced either no change in their living conditions or found their living standard had declined over the last five years. The social and financial profiles of the poor households made any significant housing improvement (e.g. to purchase a purpose-built flat) very difficult.

Although poverty is a new phenomenon in Chinese cities, it has begun to show its many faces. Housing conditions of the poor are important factors. Although employment and income are the important factors which could cause poverty, reliance on assessing household income level alone will not solve the poverty problem faced by the urban poor. There is a very strong relationship between housing and urban poverty among official urban residents. Poor inherited housing conditions were the result of the housing allocation system based on socialist social and political rank established during the planned economic period. When housing reform policies were implemented, the poor were either excluded or were given a poor deal as a result of privatisation. When the privileged bought purpose-built houses from the public sector with large subsidies, they put themselves in a better position on the housing ladder. Low-income groups who had not secured suitable houses in the allocation system gained very little from housing reform. They were left at the bottom of the housing ladder and remained as potential first-time buyers all the time. At the same time, their jobs were at risk and their income declined while other living costs increased. The lack of a proper house is now a major indicator of household poverty and a major obstacle for the poor to participate effectively in the new market economy. Past reform policies were not directed at the low-income groups. More support for the poor is required to reduce the gap between the rich and the poor, and to eliminate poverty in cities.

# 7 Poverty among migrants

New housing replacing the old, Huanggu District, Shenyang, November 2003.

Rural to urban migration has been a major feature of urbanisation in most developing countries since World War II. China, as a special case, had effectively limited this population flow during the early years of the communist government through the residence registration (*hukou*) system (see Chapter 3). Since the early 1980s, agricultural reform and the demand for cheap labour in towns and cities had resulted in an increasing number of people moving from rural areas to cities.

Rural to urban migration has since become a very important part of the development process. Literature on migration in China has increased steadily over the last few years (see, for example, Christiansen, 1990 and 1992; Day and Xia, 1994; Davin, 1999; Fan, 1996, 1999 and 2001; Kirkby *et al.*, 2000; Ma and Xiang, 1998; Shen, 1995 and 2002; Solinger, 1999; Yang, 2000; Xu, 2001). These publications have made important contributions to the understanding of the recent urbanisation process in China. However, most of them focused on the general features of migrants and process of migration found in the eastern coastal regions and major national cities such as Beijing, Shanghai and Guangzhou. This chapter continues the discussion from the previous chapters and discusses the living conditions of migrant households in Shenyang and Chongqing. As well as looking at the demographic features of migrants, it focuses on the relationship between housing, employment and income of the migrants. Some comparisons with poor official residents will be made to assess poverty problems among the migrants.

## Age and marital status of migrants

Gugler (1995) observed that young unmarried adults predominate among migrants in search of employment in developing countries. Early research on China revealed a similar pattern (Davin, 1999; Yu and Day, 1994; Goldstein and Goldstein, 1994). In terms of age, the migrant population in Shenyang and Chongqing showed a similar pattern. The age of the heads of migrant households and their partners in the sample ranged from 15 to 76 with an average age of 35. The dominant age groups were the late twenties and early thirties. Most heads of households and their partners were at the peak of their working ages at the time of interview, with 75 per cent of them under 40. While a small proportion of these heads of households and their partners came to the cities at a very young age with their parents, the average age when they first arrived at the city was 30 for the heads of households and 29 for the partners.

In terms of marital status, a different pattern from earlier findings was found. Of the 318 households surveyed, less than 11 per cent heads of households were single, 85 per cent married and 4 per cent divorced or partner had died. Of the married ones, 88 per cent of partners stayed in the city with their husband or wife. In contrary to the common belief that most migrants were single, the majority of these people travelled to the city after getting married, not before. The most popular time for migration was in the first six years of marriage. Over 67 per cent of couples arrived in the city together or within a month of each other. Among these interviewed, only about 23 per cent of males and 16 per cent of females migrated to the city as single. About 91 per cent of the married or divorced families had dependent children; and 38 per cent brought their dependent children to the city. A high proportion of heads of households reported that they had siblings in the same city.

## Education level of migrants

Research on migration in other developing countries found that there tends to be a positive correlation between income/educational level and distance travelled. The poorest urban inward migrants tend to come from nearby rural areas (Connell, 1976). Yu and Day found that people with less education were less likely to migrate in China (1994). Mallee noted that the majority of rural migrants have had at least junior middle school education (1996). Davin (1999) also indicated that the proportion of migrants who had completed junior middle school was higher than the proportion in their communities of origin. While data collected from these two cities supports these general observations, it also shows that there were a large proportion of migrants with very low educational achievement (Table 7.1). Among the heads of households and their partners, 44 per cent had either primary education or no education at all. Less than half were educated to junior middle school level. Only about 11 per cent had education beyond junior middle school level. This could be similar to the general pattern of education level in rural areas, where the proportion of senior middle school leavers was significantly lower than that in urban areas. A small number of heads of households in the sample had an urban registration (from other towns or small cities). Of these with senior school or above education, nearly half actually came from an urban background. There was no sign of improvement or decline in migrant education level over the last 15 years.

## Where do they come from?

The 2000 population census found that 65 per cent of migration (79 million) in China was within the same province, and cross-province long-distance migration accounted for 35 per cent (42 million). The majority of heads of migrant households (87 per cent) in the study areas came from the countryside; 13 per cent of them had an urban *hukou* registration, but not from the city itself. Most of the partners

**Table 7.1** Educational levels of migrants (percentage)

| Educational Level | Heads of households | Partners | National average |
|---|---|---|---|
| No formal education or partially finished primary school | 13 | 9 | 9 |
| Primary school | 30 | 37 | 33 |
| Junior middle school | 46 | 44 | 39 |
| Senior middle school (high) | 7 | 8 | 11 |
| Technical school | 1 | 1 | 8 |
| College and above | 3 | | |

Source for national average: State Statistics Bureau, 2003.

**Table 7.2** Origins of migrants

| Location of origin | Shenyang | | Chongqing | |
|---|---|---|---|---|
| | Number of households | % | Number of households | % |
| Suburban towns of this city | 7 | 4 | 15 | 10 |
| Suburban village of this city | 8 | 5 | 62 | 40 |
| Towns or cities of this province | 14 | 9 | 16 | 10 |
| Rural areas of this province | 35 | 22 | 11 | 7 |
| Towns or cities of other provinces | 14 | 9 | 5 | 3 |
| Rural areas of other provinces | 81 | 51 | 46 | 29 |
| Other | | | 3 | 1 |
| Total | 159 | 100 | 158 | 100 |

also came from rural areas, though a higher proportion of them had an urban registration (17.4 per cent), with 7 per cent of them actually from the city itself. Poor migrants were mainly from nearby rural areas (Table 7.2). In Shenyang, 37 per cent of migrants in the sample were from Liaoning Province which has Shenyang as its provincial capital city. The other main areas were the nearby north-eastern provinces – Jilin and Heilongjiang – each accounting for 13 per cent and 12 per cent respectively. There were no migrants in the sample from either the prosperous southern coastal provinces such as Guangdong and Fujian or border regions in the far west such as Xinjiang and Tibet. In Chongqing, the majority migrants interviewed came from the Sichuan Basin, with 63 per cent from the rural hinterland of the city itself and 31 per cent from the neighbouring Sichuan province. Very few of them came from far-away provinces. This confirms the pattern found by earlier studies of other developing countries that migrants tend to come in proportionately larger numbers from densely populated areas that are in frequent contact with the city (Friedmann and Wulff, 1975).

The general demographic characteristics of the particular group of migrants discussed above cast some doubt over the common belief that rural to urban migration in China was temporary. The majority of migrants found in these locations tended to be long-term residents rather than temporary visitors. Figure 7.1 shows the percentage of sample migrants (heads of households only) which arrived at the two cities in each year since 1980. Although they were still referred to as temporary residents by the urban authorities, nearly a quarter of them (23.4 per cent) had come to the city before 1991. Only 24 per cent stayed in the city for less than a year.

Figure 7.1 is also interesting as it shows a very similar tread in immigration in these two cities, though they are over one thousand kilometres apart and each located in a different region in the country. The ups and downs in the immigration

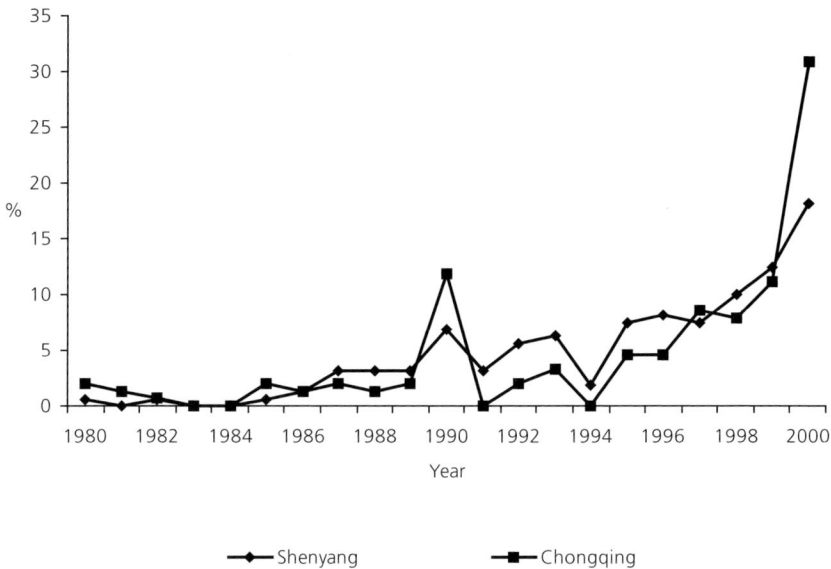

**7.1** Percentage of sample migrants arriving in the city in each year

levels also correlated with the general national trend of urban economic development and political events. The Tiananmen Square students' demonstration in 1989 attracted a large number of migrants into cities. This was followed by a sharp decline caused by subsequent strict political control. In 1992 Deng Xiaoping made his famous tour of the south. Urban economic development was once again speeded up. This led to large-scale property development in cities, which attracted many migrant labourers. Late 1993 and 1994 was a period of adjustment that resulted in the decline of immigration. A steady increase has been observed since 1997 in both cities. The recent sharp increase in Chongqing was a result of its designation as the fourth city directly under the control of central government, which provided the city with more investment for the development of basic infrastructures and other facilities.

## Housing and living conditions

Very little direct evidence was found from migration surveys in developing countries to support the idea that the availability of housing or community facilities other than schools attracts migrants to urban areas independently of economic incentives. Housing left behind in the place of origin was of better physical and environmental quality and with a much higher level of security of tenure than migrants' first urban housing. In Chinese cities, housing for migrants was generally poor quality. Shen (2002) identified three main housing types used by rural migrants: company quarters, construction sites and rented housing. If migrants had no association with large urban employers, which provided housing as a package of the employment, they tended to live mainly in traditional old urban areas or in suburban villages. The main tenure in the study areas was private rented housing, which accounted for over 80 per cent in both cities, though the location of housing areas in the two cities differed, as did the landlords, suburban farmers in Shenyang and poor urban households in Chongqing. The proportion of other tenures, such as ownership, renting from employers, staying with relatives or friends, was very small.

The types of accommodation for migrants found in these cities were predominantly simple and single-storey traditional style shelters (82 per cent). Only about 16 per cent of accommodation was in modern structures such as flats or privately-built multi-storey private houses. Half of the migrants interviewed lived in one room; 7 per cent shared a room with another person or family; another 29 per cent occupied two rooms; and only 7 per cent had exclusive use of a purpose-built flat. The average floor space per household was only 23 m². Floor space per person varied from less than 1 m² to 100 m² and the average was about 10 m² (inflated by a few very large houses). Most migrant families experienced overcrowding problems. About 5 per cent of households had less than 2 m² of floor space per person; 17 per cent 2–4 m²; and another 21 per cent 4–6 m² (the general average floor space per person in urban areas in China was about 20 m² in 2000). The poor quality of housing used by migrants was reflected in their dissatisfaction with living conditions (Table 7.3).

**Table 7.3** Satisfaction level with housing and living environment

|  | *Percentage of the very satisfied and satisfied* |
| --- | --- |
| Internal facilities | 12 |
| House and room structure | 18 |
| Neighbourhood services | 21 |
| Housing floor space available | 31 |
| Area security | 37 |
| Healthcare services | 39 |
| Middle/high school | 40 |
| Primary school | 41 |
| Transport | 41 |
| The district | 41 |
| Local shops | 50 |
| Vegetable and food market | 71 |
| Relationship with neighbours | 77 |

**Table 7.4** Provision of facilities

|                   | Exclusive use | Shared indoors | Shared outdoors | Not available |
|-------------------|---------------|----------------|-----------------|---------------|
| Shower            | 4             | 2              | 2               | 92            |
| Bath              | 4             | –              | –               | 95            |
| Piped gas supply  | 7             | 1              | –               | 92            |
| Toilet            | 8             | 5              | 87              | –             |
| Telephone         | 11            | –              | –               | 89            |
| Central heating   | 11            | –              | –               | 89            |
| Bottled gas       | 50            | 1              | –               | 49            |
| Kitchen           | 63            | 9              | –               | 28            |
| Water tap         | 81            | 4              | 7               | 8             |

Table 7.3 also shows that migrants were less concerned about the neighbourhood environment. The facilities available in areas used by migrants were poorer than the local urban residents (see also Chapter 6). Of the basic amenities, only 4 per cent had exclusive use of a shower or a bath; 8 per cent had exclusive use of a toilet. There were a large number of families who shared kitchen and water supply (Table 7.4).

Although housing conditions for migrants were very poor, rent in the private sector was high in all Chinese cities. Of those interviewed, apart from 11 households that did not pay any rent for various reasons, rent was a major part of household spending. The average monthly rent per square metre of floor space was 8 yuan in Shenyang and 11 yuan in Chongqing. Rent in Chongqing was higher and more variable than that in Shenyang because of the central location. In comparison with official residents living under similar conditions, migrants paid a much higher proportion of their income on housing (Figure 7.2). Only about 20 per cent of migrant households spent less than 10 per cent of their income each month on housing, and another 10 per cent spent more than 40 per cent of their income on housing. Of the official urban residents interviewed, more than 80 per cent paid less than 5 per cent of their income on housing.

The majority of migrants interviewed (86 per cent) kept their houses in their original home town or village. The possibility of keeping a house in their original place of residence between the urban-to-urban and rural-to-urban migrants was similar. How long they had been in the city was an important factor as to whether migrant families kept their houses in the original place of residence. The shorter their stay in the city, the more likely they kept their original home. About 80 per cent of original homes owned by migrants were used by other family members or relatives; 5 per cent were rented out and 15 per cent left empty. The size of houses at original places of residence ranged from 12 to 500 m², and was generally bigger than their current urban homes. The quality was also better, with 55 per cent built

113

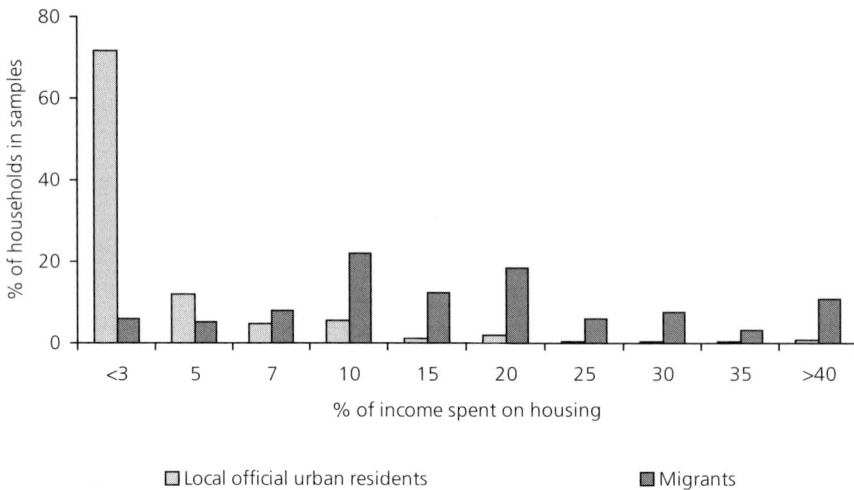

% of households in samples

% of income spent on housing

☐ Local official urban residents    ■ Migrants

**7.2** Housing costs: a comparison with local urban residents

in the 1980s and 1990s. Only 20 per cent of migrants thought their urban accommodation was better than their house back home. For most of them, migration resulted
in a drop in living conditions.

Most migrants were not satisfied with the house they lived in. To endure poor
living standards in cities was a strategy for them to reduce costs and to save more
money. About 40 per cent of households interviewed had changed accommodation
at least once since they arrived in the city. Of the most recent moves, only a quarter
was to improve living conditions; 20 per cent was for a reduction in rent and other
living costs; 15 per cent to be near work; and 5 per cent to avoid problems with
landlords. Moving near to friends or relatives was not listed as a main reason.

## Employment and income

It is important to look at the employment and income situation of migrants to
understand why most of them lived under poor conditions. Economic reasons and
job opportunities were always thought to be the most important factor for migration
in developing countries. The trend of migration discussed above supports this
view. The number of migrants increased when urban economy expanded. More
migrants were found in the large coastal cities where economy grew faster than in
inland cities.

Shenyang and Chongqing both had a large share of the traditional state-owned
enterprises. Since 1996, economic restructuring resulted in the closure of many
unprofitable factories in the cities and large numbers of urban industrial workers
had been laid-off. Unemployment rates in these cities were quite high and social
instability was already a problem. Why does the number of migrants in these

cities continue to increase? The explanation seems to be that migration was influenced more by the growth rates of the local economy and the expansion of the construction and service industries than by the amount of unemployment found in the old state-owned enterprise sector. While the traditional industrial sector was in decline, other new economic sectors (e.g. informal and small businesses) were created which attracted migrants from rural areas.

The majority of adult migrants interviewed were working. Of the heads of migrant households, nearly half (49 per cent) were engaged in family businesses, another 28 per cent worked for other private businesses. The proportion of those working in the traditional urban collective and state sectors was very small, 2 and 4 per cent respectively. About 12 per cent of heads of households had no jobs at the time of interview (a third of them were over 60 and the others were looking for jobs). Of the partners of heads of households, 37 per cent worked in family businesses, 19 per cent worked for other private businesses and 37 per cent had no jobs. The proportion in the traditional urban sectors was even smaller. The proportion of households having no one in work was very small (less than 3 per cent), while the proportion of both head of household and partner engaged in family business was quite large (20 per cent).

Private and family-based businesses made important contributiosn to urban economic development in China in the last decade. In Chongqing, for example, most employment was in the state and collective sectors in 1990. Only 4 per cent of urban work force was in the private or family-based business sector. By the end of 1999, over 20 per cent of urban employment was found in these sector. Most restaurants and shops were run by individual families. Vegetables, fruit and other agricultural product trades were dominated by family-based businesses, and many of these families came from rural areas.

Employment conditions for migrants were generally very poor. Among the 318 heads of households, only one had unemployment insurance, three had joined a pension scheme, seven had medical and health insurance, and eight had other unspecified insurance. Within the group who worked for others, very few had a long-term or permanent contract. Over 75 per cent did not know how long they could stay in their job. Despite short contracts and uncertainty, employment among migrants was relatively stable as well, at least among this particular sample. The length of the heads of households' current employment varied substantially from less than a month to more than 20 years, with an average length of 5 years.

The majority of households (87 per cent) provided information about their income in the previous month. Individual income varied substantially among migrants in both cities. The lowest monthly income in the sample was only 50 yuan and the highest was 3,500 yuan. The average monthly income was 713 yuan among heads of households who worked and 517 yuan among their partners. The average income of heads of households was higher than the average income of the poor official residents. A comparison of head of household incomes was made between the two cities. In Shenyang the average income of heads of households was 819 yuan, which was 37 per cent higher than that in Chongqing. The difference in the partners' income between the two cities was much smaller (542 yuan in Shenyang and 479 yuan in Chongqing).

In comparison with overall average salaries in these cities, the income of heads of migrant households in October 2000 was higher than the average salary in the city in 1999, while the average income of the partners was similar to the city average. In 1999, the average salary was 543 yuan/month in Shenyang and 525 yuan/month in Chongqing (Shenyang Statistics Bureau, 2000; Chongqing Statistics Bureau, 2000). Taking into consideration salary increases in 2000, the average income of heads of migrant households was similar to the overall average in the city. This level of income among the migrants was the result of a higher proportion of them being engaged in business rather than working for others. Among the heads of households who ran a family business, the monthly income (748 yuan) was 10 per cent higher than those working for others (678 yuan).

This income level does not necessarily mean that the migrant families had a better living standard than the official urban residents. For migrants, wages were their only source of income and all expenditure needed to be covered by it. The composition of income among urban residents was, however, much more complicated. The official salary was only part of the whole package; they received various bonuses, subsidies, benefits, and for some, the so-called 'grey incomes'. The per capita disposable income is a better indication of migrant living standards. The published monthly per capita disposable income of urban households was 447 yuan in Shenyang and 491 yuan in Chongqing in 1999. For migrants, if we only include the dependent family members living in the city, the monthly per capita disposable income was 363 yuan (405 in Shenyang and 307 in Chongqing). If we include family members (parents or children) back at home who required support from the migrant, the income per person would be reduced substantially. Many migrants had between one and seven persons to support. One of the main objectives of most migrants was to send money home each month. Of those interviewed half of them did so regularly. On average about 190 yuan was sent home by each household. This reduced the disposable income among the family members living in the city and made their general living standards much lower in comparison with official urban residents. Measured by the World Bank US$1 a day benchmark, most migrants actually lived around or under the poverty line.

Low income and policy restrictions are the main reasons for poor living conditions among the migrants. When asked with their current income level, what type of housing was most suitable for them, over 65 per cent preferred their current house or private rental. When asked if the restrictions on migration were removed and income levels increased in the future, the current home become the least favourable choice. Table 7.5 also indicates that some migrants would welcome government support for housing. Over 15 per cent felt subsidised rented housing would be best for them with their current income. In both cities, such government support was not on the policy agenda at all. Most migrants knew very little about major housing policies in the city they lived. The majority of them did not know about the housing provident fund or the housing subsidy which most urban residents were entitled to.

## Other costs of living

Low income had limited the choice for housing among migrants in Shenyang and Chongqing. Other living costs were important factors as well. Migrants ranked their major expenditures during the interview. Buying food was at the top of the list, which was followed by housing (Table 7.6). Official statistics indicated that

**Table 7.5** Housing preferences  (numbers in brackets are % of respondents)

| Rank order | With the current income, what type of housing suits you best? | If income is increased and the restrictions on migrants removed, what type of housing will be ideal for you? |
|---|---|---|
| 1 | Current housing (45) | Affordable housing (20) |
| 2 | Private rental (20) | Cheap commercial housing (19) |
| 3 | Subsidised rental (16) | Good commercial housing (15) |
| 4 | Affordable housing (6) | Private rental (13) |
| 5 | Secondary market housing (5) | Secondary market housing (9) |
| 6 | Cheap commercial (4) | Cottage (8) |
| 7 | Suburban farmer house (3) | Suburban farmer house (7) |
| 8 | Good commercial (1) | Subsidised rental (5) |
| 9 | | Current housing (3) |

**Table 7.6** Expenditure pattern of migrants (% of respondents in brackets)

| Rank order | Largest expenditure | Second largest expenditure | Third largest expenditure |
|---|---|---|---|
| 1 | Food (61) | Housing (45) | Water/electricity  (40) |
| 2 | Housing (24) | Food (28) | Housing (17) |
| 3 | Childcare/ education (11) | Childcare/ education (11) | Clothing (14) |
| 4 | Healthcare (2) | Clothing (7) | Food (8) |
| 5 | Clothing (1) | Water/electricity (5) | Healthcare (8) |
| 6 | Recreation (1) | Healthcare (3) | Childcare/ education (6) |
| 7 | | Recreation (1) | Transport (5) |
| 8 | | | Recreation (2) |

average food consumption each month was between 160 and 180 yuan per person in these two cities in 1999. This was about half of the average disposable income per capita among migrants.

The expenditure patterns of migrants and the poor official residents were very similar (see Chapter 6). Food was ranked the largest household expenditure by most residents in both groups. Fuel costs and children's education were the other main spending. The difference between the two groups was housing and healthcare. Nearly 24 per cent of migrants ranked housing as their largest expenditure, another 45 per cent ranked it second and 17 per cent ranked it third. Of the poor official residents, less than 15 per cent ranked housing as their first, second or third largest expenditure. The costs of healthcare was ranked very low by the migrants. Childcare and education were not ranked high. This may not be their own choice, but a reality within their budget. After food and housing, there was not much left for other activities. Of those interviewed, only 36 per cent of migrant households had a bank account. Others carried their savings in cash with them all the time. About a third provided information on their savings, of which 43 per cent had less than 5,000 yuan saved.

Transport could be another major expenditure for migrants because of the peripheral location where they lived. Daily travel patterns differed between the two cities. Heads of migrant households travelled a longer distance to work in Shenyang than in Chongqing. In Shenyang, most migrants travelled more than 1.5 kilometres to work, with over 40 per cent working over 4 kilometres away from where they lived. In Chongqing over 50 per cent of migrants travelled less than 1.5 kilometres to work. This reflects the differences in location of the migrants found in the two cities. The most popular way of travelling to work in Shenyang was by bicycle, while in Chongqing walking to work was the main mode of travel (Figure 7.3). Bicycles were not used in Chongqing because of the hilly terrain. In both cities, the use of buses was relatively low (though bus fares were relatively low in both cities) and migrants avoided the cost of daily travel.

Finding a job, housing and child education were major problems most migrants identified. Without government support, their life was much more difficult than that of ordinary official residents. At the same time, the very lack of official residence made migrants most vulnerable to labour abuse and other social injustices.

## Migration to earn a living

Rural to urban migration was an important part of economic development in China over the last two decades. Migrants made a great contribution to the construction and maintenance of Chinese cities. Without their hard work, the urban landscape must be very different from the prosperity shown today. Some migrants themselves also benefited from this migration process. When asked to compare their situation before and after the move to the city, over 60 per cent in the sample thought their

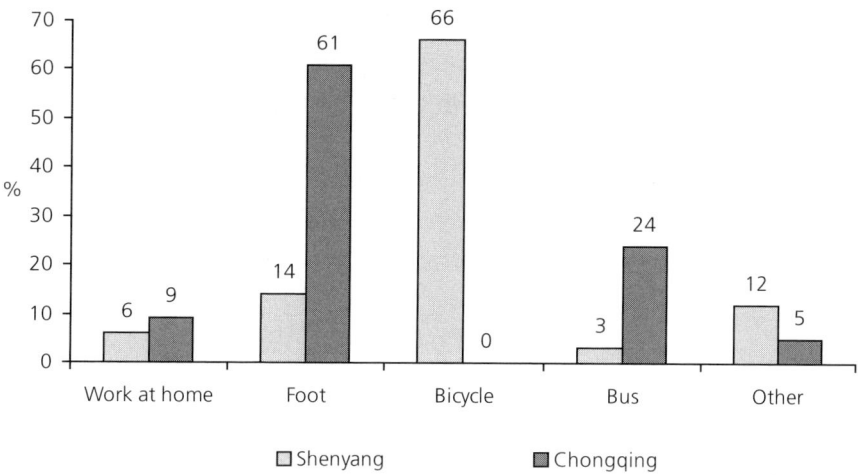

**7.3** Methods of travelling to work

quality of life had either improved a lot (14 per cent) or improved a bit (46 per cent). Nearly half of them also thought the quality of life of their families back at home had either improved a lot (13 per cent) or a bit (37 per cent) as a result of migration.

Compared with staying in the villages, any income from urban employment would be a benefit to migrant households. However, employment and living conditions revealed in this study cast some doubt on the very popular belief that rural labourers can become rich if they can find a job in city. There was a saying that migrants earned money in cities and returned home to build new houses or even set up factories (*jingcheng dagong, huixiang jianfan bangongchang*). This may have worked for a few migrants during the early years of the open-door policy and when urban wages for migrants were relatively high and the price of building materials was cheap in rural areas. This optimistic outcome looked very unlikely for most migrants found in these two cities. Migration had become a way to earn a living rather than to become rich.

Not all migrants in Chinese cities were floating or temporary residents. Many of them had been in these cities for many years. Analysis was carried out to assess whether the time spent in the city had any effect on the quality of life among migrants. Correlations between the number of months in the city and several variables on income and housing show that quality of life did not improve much over the time. Early arrivals not necessarily had a higher income or better standard of living (Table 7.7). Without official recognition, the life of all migrants was poor however long they had stayed in the cities.

As we saw in Chapter 3, 121 million people in China were living away from their registered place of residence in 2000. The wellbeing of this huge group of people is

**Table 7.7** Improvement of living condition over time (Kendall's $\tau_b$ correlation analysis results)

|  | Total number of months a migrant has stayed in the city[1] |
|---|---|
| Income of head of household | 0.079 |
| Income of partner | 0.072 |
| Total income of household | 0.108** |
| Income per person | −0.032 |
| Have a bank account | 0.096* |
| Amount of money in bank account | 0.113 |
| Size of house (m² of floor space) | 0.161** |
| m² of floor space per person | 0.030 |
| Distance between home and work | −0.011 |
| Housing costs as percentage of family income | −0.042 |
| Self assessment: 1–5 (from declined a lot to improved a lot) | 0.186** |

Notes
1    Number of months range from 0 to 784, average 67.7 (5.5 years).
*    Significant at 0.05 level; ** significant at 0.01 level.

a very important issue in both policy development and academic research. It has been widely acknowledged that rural to urban migration had made a major contribution to the development of Chinese cities and the urban economy. This chapter demonstrated that not all migrants found in Chinese cities were temporary or seasonal workers. Many of them had stayed in the city for many years and they were not planning to leave. When asked about their future plans, 58 per cent preferred to stay in the city; only 28 per cent would like to go back to their original homes.

In comparison with most urban residents, their living conditions remained very poor, and they were found mainly in poor areas of the cities. The main reasons for the low quality of life were poor employment conditions and low income. Most migrants interviewed worked hard to earn a living, but their income remained low and they had no access to government support or social benefits. The average disposable income per person among the migrants was much lower than the average in the city. Most of them actually stayed just above the poverty line. Costs of living among migrants were much higher than for urban residents who had a similar level of income. Comparison shows a distinct difference in the amount of income spent on housing by the migrants and other urban low-income families. Some may argue that migrants prefer poor quality housing in order to save more money to send home. For most migrants included in this study, poor quality housing was not a choice. With their income level and the cost of food, the only way to stay in the city was to reduce the cost of housing.

The migrant population in Chinese cities was a very diverse group of people. Comprehensive research on such a large group of people is very difficult. Migrants interviewed in these two cities included those who had established their own 'homes' in the city; and did not include workers living in building sites or with urban families as domestic workers. In some sense, the people included in the sample were at an advanced stage of the migration process and were long-term migrants. Compared with those staying temporarily at construction sites, this group could have a more important influence over long-term population changes in cities and levels of urbanisation.

## Not a one-way journey

In his study of Latin America housing and urbanisation, John Turner identified three levels of housing and household life cycle among migrants:

> ... the lowest is that of the 'bridgeheader' seeking a toehold in the urban system and hoping to achieve the intermediate level of the 'consolidator', who has obtained a relatively firm foothold but is in danger of losing it unless he can consolidate his newly achieved socio-economic status; the third level is that of the higher income (insured or professionally secure) 'status seekers'.
> (Turner, 1968: 358)

In comparison with Turner's analysis, rural to urban migration demonstrated some very different characteristics (Figure 7.4). The most important feature of the

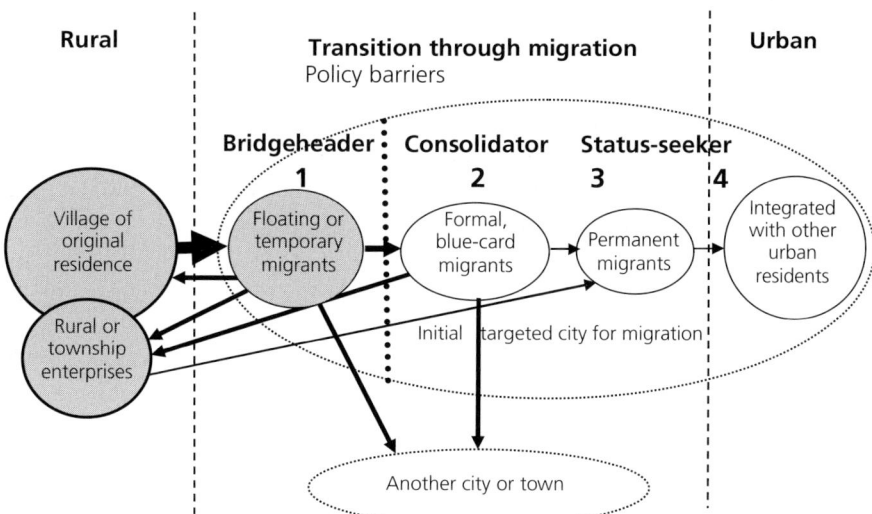

**7.4** The process of rural to urban migration in China

121

migration in China was that it was not a simple one-way process. For some migrants, it involved a return journey. They go to cities to work for a few years, and then return to their home village. For others, government policies prevented them from settling down in cities and integrating with urban residents. They were allowed to 'float' in cities as 'temporary' residents. As a result, poor employment conditions and living environment prolonged the 'bridgeheader' stage of the migration process. The only route to becoming an official urban resident was through the 'blue-stamped residence card' system. This was applied to a few successful businessmen who had made a lot of money and could offer to pay the full price of a commercial house in the city. Even for those who had a residence card, to acquire the normal urban resident registration and to be treated as same as other urban residents could take several years (Figure 7.4). This arrangement was not fair to migrants and their families and was in contradiction to the government policy to promote urbanisation and sustainable urban development.

The very lack of official residence made migrants more vulnerable to labour abuse and other social injustices. With the continuing growth of the urban economy and the increasing concern about inequality, the problems of migrants should be addressed in a more sympathetic way. The least the government can do is to set a time limit (e.g. two years' full employment, which could be different in different cities). Once a migrant meets this requirement, he or she should be granted proper urban resident status. This may increase their morale and promote good citizenship. Otherwise, as Yang (2000) has indicated, because of the lack of official recognition of their residency, and related entitlement to government-provided employment, housing and other social services, temporary migrants are unlikely to identify themselves with the city in which they currently live and work – the city is simply viewed as location of employment, and can change as the job changes. This may also result in an increase of crime and social malaise.

# 8   The elimination of poverty

Building with Chinese characteristics in the historic town of Xi'an, October 2003.

The widening gap between the rich and the poor has caused some concern among the party leaders and government officials. As early as the middle 1980s, social security systems independent of the work units were introduced to deal with problems in urban employment. In the 1990s, more policies were developed to reduce and eliminate urban poverty. Some of the new policies were based on existing practice while others modelled on other countries' practice. Though these social support systems were still in their infancy, they had made some important contributions to maintaining social stability and reducing the extent of urban poverty. This chapter reviews some of these new social support systems and highlights their main characteristics.

## Social support and welfare policies

Under the planned economic system, over 98 per cent of urban residents were employed by either the state or the collective sectors. All work units owned by the state also provided comprehensive welfare services, including job security, health-care and child education. Under this arrangement, government had effectively decentralised the social welfare services to employers. The functions of local government were more related to production management than service provision. Only in cases of natural disasters, such as flood, drought or earthquake, did the government organise and fund large-scale relief programmes.

With the introduction of the market economy, welfare provision by work units was reduced substantially in order to improve production efficiency. From the middle of the 1980s, new social support policies were introduced to fill some of the gaps between the old and the new systems. These included policies aimed at creating more job opportunities to reduce urban unemployment, and several social security systems established to protect the weak and unemployed in the cities. The new system included:

1  Social insurance systems: as an alternative to the work unit welfare provision, new social insurance systems were established to provide help to employed people. These include five different elements:
    - retirement insurance – pensions
    - health insurance
    - unemployment insurance
    - employment accident insurance
    - maternity leave insurance.
2  Social relief systems which targeted poor groups or those affected by natural disasters:
    - natural disaster relief
    - special target relief
    - rural poverty relief
    - urban poverty relief – urban minimum living standard scheme.
3  Social welfare systems
    - collective welfare offered by employers
    - special welfare targeted at different groups, retired, disabled, children, etc.
    - neighbourhood services.
4  Social preferential treatment and compensation.

**Table 8.1** Key features of the new social security systems

| Scheme | Year in which reform began | Year of major associated changes and legislation | Contributions and fund accumulation | Benefits | Coverage |
|---|---|---|---|---|---|
| Retirement insurance – pension | 1984 | Decisions on the establishment of the Unified Enterprise Pension Scheme (1997).<br><br>Main sector: enterprise employees, gradually enlarging to include other sectors. | Overall Pension Fund from budget subsidy, enterprise contribution.<br><br>Individual Pension Fund from individual and employer's contribution.<br><br>Enterprise contributes about 20% of total salary, split between individual and overall fund; Individual contributes 8% of salary into individual fund. | Basic pension from overall fund determined by the local authority; plus 1 yuan from every 120 yuan of individual fund accumulated. | Coverage increased every year. By 2002, 99.4% of enterprise employees were in the scheme.<br><br>About 111.3 million employees and 36.1 million pensioners were in this new scheme at end of 2002. |
| Health insurance | 1988 | Decision on the establishment of basic health insurance scheme in urban areas (1998). | Overall Fund and Individual Fund: Work units contribute 6% of total salary, split | Overall fund for large hospital costs and long-term illness; Individual fund | 2001: 76 million individuals participated; 2002: increased to 94 million, of<br>continued... |

**Table 8.1** continued

| Scheme | Year in which reform began | Year of major associated changes and legislation | Contributions and fund accumulation | Benefits | Coverage |
|---|---|---|---|---|---|
| | | Sector: all urban work units. | between individual and overall fund; individual contributes 2% of salary into individual fund. | for small and general medical costs. | which 26% were pensioners. |
| Unemployment insurance | 1986 | Unemployment Insurance Ordinance (1999).<br><br>Sector: all work unit employees, excluding rural migrant workers. | Contribution: work unit: 2% of total salary; individual: 1% of salary<br><br>Conditions for benefits:<br>a) over 1 year of contributions;<br>b) lost job involuntarily;<br>c) registered with unemployment benefit authority;<br>d) wish to find a new job. | a) Monthly benefit (maximum 24 months) depends on length of contribution;<br>b) medical care during unemployment;<br>c) funeral costs if died during unemployment;<br>d) help with job training and searching. | 2001: 103.5 million persons in the scheme and 3.1 million persons received benefits. 2002: 101.8 million persons in the scheme; 4.4 million receive benefits. |

**Table 8.1** continued

| Scheme | Year in which reform began | Year of major associated changes and legislation | Contributions and fund accumulation | Benefits | Coverage |
|---|---|---|---|---|---|
| Employment accident insurance | | Temporary regulations on work accident involve enterprise employees (1996). Sector: enterprise. | Employer contributes about 1% of total salary in 2001. | Medical costs, disability compensation and care costs. | About 44.1 million employees insured in 2002. |
| Maternity leave insurance | 1988 | Temporary regulations on child birth by enterprise employees (1994). Sector: female employees in enterprise. | Employer contributes about 0.7% of total salary in 2001. | Medical costs and maternity leave payment. | About 34.9 million persons insured in 2002. |

Sources: Compiled from several short reports on Labour and Social Security in China, published by the State Council News Office in April 2002 and Ministry of Labour and Social Security, State Statistics Bureau, 2003.

Much of the social relief, social welfare, social preferential treatment and compensation systems were based on early practice and aimed at those with special needs. Table 8.1 summarises the main features of the new social security systems.

## Anti-poverty policies: the three defence lines

Of these new social protection schemes, the most important ones related to poverty reduction and elimination are unemployment insurance and the urban minimum living standard scheme. As discussed in Chapter 4, industrial restructuring during the late 1990s resulted in massive redundancies of workers in state-owned enterprises. While the new unemployment benefit system was unable to cope with this problem, a special scheme – Basic Living Allowance for Laid-off Workers – was introduced. This scheme together with unemployment benefit and the urban minimum living standard were referred as the three defence lines against urban poverty.

### Basic Living Allowance for Laid-Off Workers

The Ministry of Labour and Social Security (1999) identified many factors which led to large number of workers being laid-off in the state-owned factories. The pursuit of full employment under the planned economy resulted in more people being employed by state factories than necessary. The lack of market competition and information and irrational planning led to repetitive construction of industries, and each factory was unable to function to its full capacity. Poor management and corruption also led many state factories into debt or bankruptcy. To compete with the new economic sector such as the foreign and joint-venture companies, state factories needed to restructure and reduce their work force. Laying off workers was seen as necessary and an unavoidable price to pay.

State-owned enterprises began to lay-off surplus labour in the early 1990s. Initial measures included: no salary but maintaining employment relationship for possible future return, early retirement, long holidays, taking or waiting for internal rearrangement, or leaving voluntarily. The scale of these early lay-offs was relatively small and redundancy was made mainly on a voluntary basis. Some middle-tier managers and more adventurous workers took these opportunities and left the relatively poorly paid jobs in the state sector and started their own business (the so-called *xiahai* – down to sea). Some of them did become rich. These early redundancies did not cause serious social problems in cities.

By the middle of the 1990s, with increasing competition from products made by new private or joint-venture companies, many state and collective enterprises ran into problems. Laid-off staff became widespread and most people were laid-off unwillingly. By the late 1990s, redundancy became a very serious social and political problem in most cities. A survey in Shenyang revealed that about 29 per cent of industrial workers were laid-off in 1997. In the country as a whole, official estimates of laid-off workers were 10 million in 1998. Others gave a much higher estimate, at 20 to 30 million (Zhang, 1998; Zhu, 1998). The disparity over the scale of redundancy was caused, on the one hand, by the size of the country and the complex structure of the data collection process; on the other hand, the different definitions of redundancy also resulted in different figures. Many different kinds of redundancy could occur, and the main types include:

a)   permanent workers in state-owned enterprises (before the introduction of the labour contract system in 1986, all workers in state-owned enterprises were employed on permanent contract and were supposed to work in the factory for their whole life)

b)   contract workers in state-owned enterprise before the end of their contract (all post-1986 industrial workers were employed on contract basis)

c)   contract workers at the end of their contract in state-owned enterprises

d)   temporary workers in state-owned enterprises (most of them were rural migrants without any formal contract)

e)   workers in collectively owned enterprises

f)   staff in institutions and government organisations.

Most official statistics on laid-off workers only included a) permanent workers, part of b) contracted workers before the end of their contract and f) staff in institutions and government organisations. These were people the state still had a legal responsibility for. In practice, all industrial workers who lost their jobs referred to themselves as laid-off workers. Data collected through surveys always give a higher redundancy rate than the official statistics, because many people who lost their jobs thought they were laid-off workers, but they were not included in these categories defined by the government. The official definition is important to laid-off workers, because those who were recognised officially could register with a re-employment service centre for help, while the un-recognised ones did not have this benefit. They become unemployed straight away.

Because the new unemployment benefit system only had a short life and most industrial workers had either just joined the scheme or were yet to join, a transitional arrangement was introduced to deal with the official laid-off workers. The government demanded that all large state-owned enterprises set up a re-employment service centre (RESC) to help those who were laid-off. Small enterprises with fewer laid-off workers were required to appoint special personnel to handle laid-off workers. The responsibilities of the RESCs include:

•    paying basic living allowance to laid-off workers each month

•    making pension, unemployment and health insurance contributions on behalf of the laid-off workers

•    training laid-off workers in new skills and help them to find new jobs.

A laid-off worker also retained some rights in relation to housing allocation and subsidies when registered at the RESC. RESCs and municipal government's labour and employment service authorities gave incentives to local small businesses to employ laid-off workers. Laid-off workers were also encouraged to start their own businesses; measures normally included simplified registration, waiving of business tax, personal income tax and other administrative charges for a certain period. Normally, the maximum period for these benefits for each laid-off worker was three years. At the end of this period, employment relationship ended whether the worker had found a job or not. Once a laid-off worker had found a new job, he or she left the RESC and ended his or her employment relationship with the employer.

Funds required to run the RESCs and to pay the basic living allowances for laid-off workers came from three sources: a third from the enterprise itself, a third from government budget (central government for centrally owned enterprises and local government for locally owned enterprises) and a third from social funds (such as the local unemployment benefit funds). This financial arrangement did not work in some areas with more serious redundancy problems. In Chongqing, for example, 80 per cent of state-owned enterprises either had already suspended production or were near to suspension. Not a small proportion of their employees, but a large proportion of them needed help. Local authorities found it difficult to pay the cost of running the re-employment service centres. Social contributions should come from the local unemployment insurance fund, but the system itself was only at an early stage of development and funds accumulated were still very small. In some cases local government became the sole source for laid-off allowances, which created a serious financial problem. In some areas, many laid-off workers had not received any allowance at all (Yu *et al.*, 2000).

Laid-off benefits and the RESC were innovative measures to deal with the unemployment problems created by the transition to a market economy. Although the system had a limited scope and covered only those who lost their jobs as a result of industrial restructuring in the state sector, the government saw it as an important way to make progress in enterprise reforms and maintain social stability at the same time.

## Unemployment insurance

As unemployment became a main cause of urban poverty, unemployment insurance and benefits were seen as the second defence line against poverty. Along with labour and employment reform, the unemployment insurance system was introduced in 1986 with various experiments in the following years. In 1993, unemployment insurance became compulsory for all workers in state-owned enterprises. Contributions to the socialised enterprise unemployment benefit fund were made by employers with only a fixed percentage of the total salaries of the enterprise. The main objectives of this system were to: a) ensure a minimum living standard during unemployment; b) help in training in new skills and job seeking; c) support the reform of state-owned enterprises.

Based on early experiments, an Unemployment Insurance Ordinance was issued in January 1999 by the State Council. This ordinance extended the coverage of unemployment insurance from state-owned enterprises to all work units including public institutions, state owned enterprises, collective owned enterprises, foreign companies, and private companies. The new regulation also required both employer and employee to make contributions. The employer's contribution was set by the central government at 2 per cent of total salary payments and individual's contribution was 1 per cent of salary (State Council, 1999a). There were, however, variations in contributions from province to province. Shaanxi province, for example, set the employer's contribution at 2.5 per cent in 2003.

The management of the unemployment fund was at municipal government level, including decisions about levels for contribution and benefit. An adjustment fund was also established at the provincial level to balance differences between municipalities. The main sources of unemployment benefit funds were contributions from employers and employees, and bank interest. In case there was a shortage, government support could be made through budget allocation. This means the system is essentially a mutual help system.

The main unemployment benefit is the monthly allowance paid over a fixed period depending on the length of contribution made by the individual before becoming unemployed. National guidelines on benefit were:

- Less than 1 year's contribution: none
- 1 to 5 years' contribution: 12 months
- 5 to 10 years' contribution: 18 months
- Over 10 years' contribution: 24 months (State Council, 1999a).

The actual length and level of benefit were decided by local government. Unemployment benefit is normally slightly lower than the local minimum wages (between 70 to 90 per cent of the local minimum wages), but higher than the local minimum living standard. Other benefits during the qualified period include healthcare allowances and training costs. If a person dies during the qualified period, benefits will also include funeral costs and compensation to dependents.

Although the new regulation required that all work units participate in the new unemployment insurance system, the main participants were state-owned enterprises. Most enterprises owned by other sectors and public institutions largely stayed out. In 1998 before the new regulation, there were 79 million employees covered by the scheme. There was some increase in the following three years. By the end of 2001, it had reached 105.7 million. Since then, the number of employees covered began to decline. By June 2003, it had declined to 100.8 million.

There were steady increases in the registered unemployment and those claiming unemployment benefits over recent years. Officially registered unemployment increased from 5.7 million in 1998 to 8 million in June 2003. Together with the registered laid-off workers, over 12 million urban employees were out of work. Those who claimed unemployment benefits increased even faster. In June 2003, about 4.4 million persons were claiming unemployment benefits (see Figure 8.1).

## Urban minimum living standard

Laid-off workers' allowances and unemployment benefits were aimed at people who were of working age but who had lost their jobs, particularly from state-owned enterprises. They provided transitional help for people moving to new jobs. These arrangements had some general effects on poverty prevention, but they could not prevent some families from falling into poverty. Payment of the benefits was only to these persons concerned and had no consideration of their dependents. There was also a time limit for the entitlements. Some poor families did not qualify for these benefits. To deal with these problems, the urban minimum living standard scheme was introduced. This was also referred to as the third defence line against poverty in urban areas. (Hussain, 2003)

The city of Shanghai first tested the minimum urban living standard in 1992. It was introduced to all other cities in the following years. In 1997, when laid-off workers became a serious problem, the State Council required the establishment of the urban minimum living standard throughout the country by 2000. Central government saw this system as an important part of urban social protection system, because it a) 'reflects the advantages of the socialist system'; b) is an important support to the establishment of market economy; c) is essential

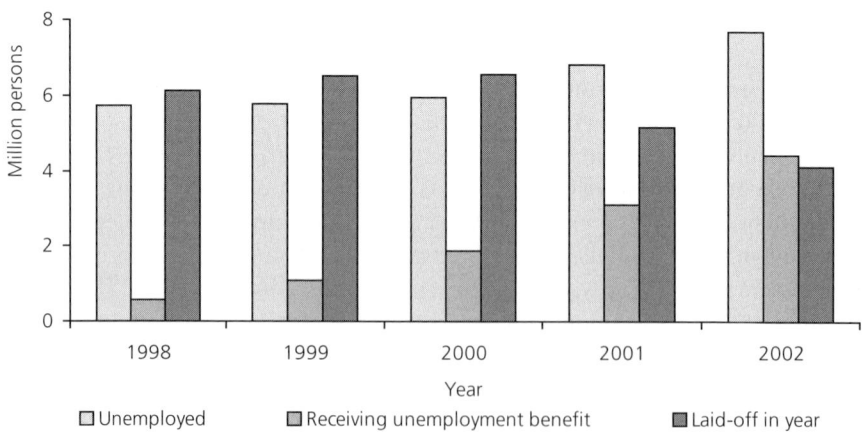

**8.1** Unemployment benefits receivers and laid-off workers

Source: Ministry of Labour and Social Security and State Statistics Bureau, 2003.

to maintain social stability and the successful reform of state owned enterprises (State Council, 1997).

The central instruction required municipal civil affairs authorities to provide help to those 'non-agricultural urban residents' whose gross monthly income fell below the local minimum living standard. Target groups include:

- the traditional 'three no' people;
- unemployed people and their families;
- low-paid employees or laid-off workers and their families.

These policies were further enforced by the Urban Minimum Living Standard Ordinance (State Council, 1999b) in October 1999.

The main feature of the minimum living standard is the locally decided poverty line based on costs of *basic* clothing and food, also taking into consideration fuel costs and education of children. Heads of households can apply for support to the local authority. They have to fill an application form and submit it to the street committee office or township office for assessment. The local authority may investigate the financial situation of these families through home visits, personal or written enquiries. Lists of qualifying families are published; any objections (including those from neighbours) can lead to disqualification. Changes in family income should be reported and authorities can check the family's income level periodically to ensure fairness. The amount of support varies: a) for the 'three no' households or individuals, the full amount (up to the poverty line) is payable; b) for other low-income households and individuals, the difference between actual income per capita and the local poverty line is paid. Working-age adults receiving income support were required to participate in local voluntary work. They should also actively cooperate with local labour and employment authorities in searching for a job. The funds required for this income support would come from government budgets.

Although this system was set up recently, its coverage expanded very quickly. Central government put much pressure on local authorities to provide help to all qualifying families. In 1997, about 2 million urban residents were covered by these schemes. Three years later, it had reached 4 million. At the end of March 2003, 21.4 million urban residents received this support (Wu, 2003). By November 2003, about 5 per cent of official urban residents (22 million individuals in 8.8 million households) were receiving financial support under the urban minimum living standard scheme (Ministry of Civil Affairs, 2003a) (Figure 8.2). By then the government claimed that all poor families had been included in the scheme. Of the 21 million individuals covered by the scheme, 20 per cent were either in full employment or laid-off; about 30 per cent were unemployed; 9 per cent were either the 'three no' individuals or retired; the rest were dependents.

In early 2003, the minimum living standard (the local poverty line) ranged from 143 yuan per person per month at the inland city of Nanchang to 344 yuan in the special economic zone city of Shenzhen. Average payment across the whole

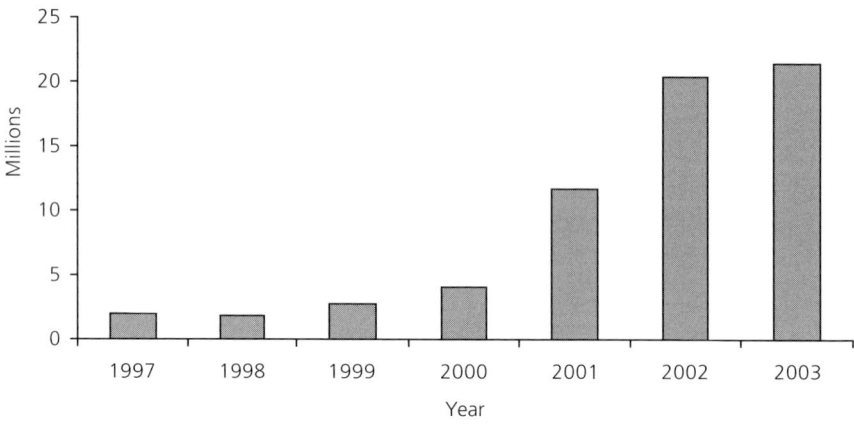

**8.2** Number of urban residents receiving government support

Source: State Statistics Bureau, 2003; Ministry of Civil Affairs, 2003b.

country during January to May 2003 was only 55 yuan per person per month (Table 8.2). This varied from city to city; in Beijing the average support was the highest at 79 per cent of the amount defined by the poverty line, while in Shenyang it was only 23 per cent. This may indicate that in the prosperous cities, poverty could be a serious problem as well. Since most of these locally decided poverty lines were very low, the support could only solve these families' food problems. Consideration of other problems such as health, education, housing and trans-portation were not included. Despite these problems, the introduction of this urban minimum living standard represents major progress in urban poverty elimination. Without this support, 21 million urban residents could experience more difficulties.

## Integration of the three defence lines

Laid-off workers' benefits were aimed at permanent employees made redundant by state-owned enterprises. The government felt it had a responsibility to help these people to find new ways of living after having lost the socialist 'iron rice bowls'. Although being laid-off was a crisis for these workers in comparison to those remaining in work, officially recognised laid-off workers also had some advantages in comparison with other unemployed persons. The laid-off workers' allowance paid by the re-employment service centres, under normal conditions, was higher than unemployment benefit. Because of an existing relationship with their employers, laid-off workers could get some other benefits, such as healthcare, child education and housing. There was also flexibility in the amount paid as an allowance, depending on the financial situation of the employers. Well-performing enterprises could pay a higher allowance than poorly performing ones. People

**Table 8.2** Urban minimum living standard practice in selected cities in 2003

| City | Minimum standard from July 2002 (yuan/person/month) | Number of persons receiving support ('000s) | Number of households receiving support ('000s) | Average support during January to May 2003 (yuan/person/month) | Average benefit as % of minimum standard |
|------|------|------|------|------|------|
| Beijing | 290 | 147 | 66 | 229 | 79 |
| Urumqi | 156 | 282 | 11 | 83 | 53 |
| Guangzhou | 300 | 32 | 13 | 153 | 51 |
| Shanghai | 280 | 444 | 204 | 138 | 49 |
| Nanjing | 220 | 62 | 29 | 96 | 44 |
| Chongqing | 185 | 706 | 344 | 75 | 41 |
| Xi'an | 180 | 179 | 69 | 63 | 35 |
| Fuzhou | 220 | 24 | 10 | 70 | 32 |
| Wuhan | 210 | 267 | 102 | 65 | 31 |
| Tianjin | 241 | 277 | 110 | 72 | 30 |
| Shenyang | 205 | 200 | 80 | 48 | 23 |

Source: Ministry of Civil Affairs, 2003a, 2003b.

laid-off early also were allowed to stay longer in the RESC. Only recently have new regulations begun to limit the time spent at the RESC.

The initial unemployment insurance system had a similar aim in dealing with surplus labour in state-owned enterprises. Recent improvement, particularly the enlargement in coverage, made this a universal system under the market economy. Laid-off workers from state-owned enterprises spent a period at the RESC first. If they failed to find a new job in three years, they were normally transferred to the unemployment benefits system. In this way, it was hoped that the two systems would eventually merge and the RESC could be phased out. From 2001, the government began to phase out the laid-off workers arrangement. Employees were given the option to take cash compensation for their services (*maiduan*) and end their employment relation with the current employer. People who choose this option can register with the unemployment office straight away. Though this is not a good option, many employees agreed with the settlement, particularly if the enterprise was not doing very well. Continuing the employment relationship may mean they end up with nothing.

For employees laid-off by non-state sectors, unemployment offices were their first destination. Unemployed persons' relationship with their employers was cut. They no longer had any claim to social benefits offered by the employers. Unemployment benefit payments were normally lower than laid-off workers' allowance. For the official laid-off workers, failure to find a new job within the time limit and being transferred to the unemployment benefit system meant a further decline in income and living standard.

The urban minimum living standard had a wider coverage than the laid-off workers' allowance and unemployment benefit. Households receiving any of the other two benefits could still apply for this support if their income fell below the poverty level. For people who had used up their unemployment benefit entitlements, but had not found a job, the support from the urban minimum living standard became the only source of income. Local poverty levels (income per person) were set below the level of unemployment benefit payment. People who had exhausted their unemployment benefit entitlements and lived on the minimum living standard would see another decline in their overall income and standard of living. The relationships between the three defence lines are shown in Figure 8.3.

One of the most recent developments in poverty elimination were re-employment services targeted at specific groups. Re-employment service centres were instructed to help the so-called '4050' group – unemployed males in their fifties and females in their forties. The '4050' group was born during the economic crisis period of the 1950s and 1960s, and normally had a relatively poor educational achievement during the Cultural Revolution period. Most of them spent their valuable youth in the countryside through the 'sending down' movement. When returning to cities, they were assigned mainly to non-skilled posts in either state or collectively owned enterprises. They became the prime targets for being

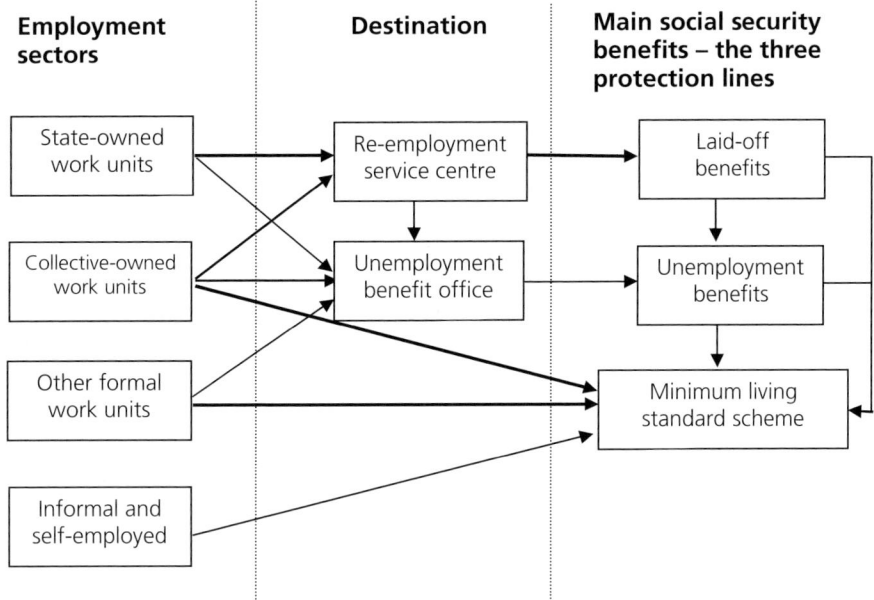

**Employment sectors**

**Destination**

**Main social security benefits – the three protection lines**

State-owned work units

Collective-owned work units

Other formal work units

Informal and self-employed

Re-employment service centre

Unemployment benefit office

Laid-off benefits

Unemployment benefits

Minimum living standard scheme

**8.3** Relationship between three defence lines against poverty

laid-off during the industrial restructuring. With both school-age children to support and elderly parents to look after, this group had the heaviest burden of family responsibilities. Most new enterprises and businesses were reluctant to employ them. It was also very common for both husband and wife to belong to this category. According to a survey of 66 cities carried out by the Ministry of Labour and Social Security in 2003, about 29 per cent of urban laid-off workers and other unemployed persons were in this group. The total of them were estimated at 3 million (Liu, 2003).

## New social housing policies

Housing commercialisation and privatisation in urban areas over the last 20 years has substantially changed the nature of housing distribution (see Chapter 6). Much public housing has been sold to sitting tenants. New employees had to buy their housing in the market. Because of high house prices in cities, more and more laid-off workers and other unemployed persons found it difficult to acquire suitable housing. There were calls to include new social housing in the reformed social security system.

Housing policies published in 1998 proposed three different ways of housing provision in urban areas: high standard commercial housing, low-cost affordable housing, and cheap rental social housing. When these new policies were issued, central government officials anticipated that 15 per cent of high-income families would buy good-quality commercial housing directly from the market; 70 per cent of the middle-income families would purchase affordable commercial housing (*jingji shiyong fang*); and 15 per cent of low-income families would rent social housing from the municipal government (*lianzu fang*). During the last five years, policy emphasis has shifted a bit. More households were encouraged to buy ordinary commercial housing. The social values of affordable housing were redefined to offer help to the low-income families only.

Although the reintroduction of the social housing (*lianzu fang*) idea reflects an improved understanding of the urban housing market, its provision developed very slowly in most cities. By 2003, the practice of social housing was still at an experimental stage, with only a few provinces producing local regulations aimed at introducing this system. Local policies have moved away from the originally anticipated 15 per cent coverage to focus on a very small group of extremely poor families. There was also diversification in practice, including free or low-rent housing provided by the local government, to rent allowance and cash subsidies. In 2000, Beijing municipal government carried out a housing survey. It identified 32,000 households (about 1.4 per cent of the total households in the city) which required government help in housing (Yang, 2003). The number of households actually benefiting from social housing was very small. By the end of 2002, the municipal authority only paid rent allowances to 998 households (Xie, 2003).

Shanghai, one of the frontrunners in social housing provision in the country, had issued rent allowances to 3,366 households in 2003. Based on early experiments in two districts, Shanghai Housing and Land Resources Management Bureau produced a policy document to guide the development of social housing in the city. The document made provision for households that meet *all* the following conditions to apply for government support for housing:

- monthly per capita income is below the municipal poverty level, and has received income support from the Civil Affairs authority for more than six months;
- living floor space per person is less than 5 m²;
- all household members have Shanghai residence registration for over two years;
- at least one member of the household had local permanent non-agricultural *hukou* registration for more than five years; and
- family members have legal care or foster relationship between them.

According to the above rules, the number of households qualifying for social housing was very small. In Changning District, of the 220,000 households, 3,651 (1.7 per cent) had an income under the poverty line, only 121 households actually qualified for social housing (Ying, 2001). In Zabei District, 8,153 out of 261,000 households were below the poverty line and 184 of them met the conditions for housing support (Liu, 2001).

The maximum limit for housing support was set at 7 m$^2$ floor space per person in the city. Households meeting the above conditions could apply to the District Social Housing Office (*lianzuban*) for support. If a household was assessed and qualified for support, rent allowances would be given to cover the cost of renting the difference between 7 m$^2$ and the current per capita floor space used by the family. Rent levels were set according to the location in the city, with 40 yuan/m$^2$/ month (2001 standard) in central areas, 30 yuan suburban districts close to the centre and 20 yuan in counties and outlying districts. For example, if a family of three live in the central area in a house with only 10 m$^2$ of floor space and meet conditions for social housing support, they would be entitled to a rent allowance of 11 m$^2$ or 440 yuan per month.

To ensure rent allowances are used for housing purposes, the Social Housing Office pays the allowance directly to the landlord, rather than to the family itself. This means that a family can only get this support when it improves its living conditions by moving to larger accommodation. For special households of elderly or disabled people, direct housing allocation can be made. Those households are required to pay 5 per cent of their income as rent.

Funds required by this social housing programme are split half and half between the district and municipal authorities. Because of limitation of funds and availability of housing, applications from households were queued based on the date of application. Lists of successful households would be published in local media, and objections from the general public or neighbours could lead to disqualification. Households securing support will have their income and housing situation checked every half-year. If a household no longer meets the conditions, the rent allowance payment will be stopped. In case of direct housing allocation the household will be asked to move out of the social housing within six months. If housing and income conditions of the household get worse, there is no automatic increase in the allowance. The family has to apply for an increase and wait in the queue for its turn (Shanghai Property and Land Resource Management Bureau, 2001).

Social housing provision was seen as an important part of social protection system by the central government. However, the progress of this policy was slowed down by lack of stable funds in most cities. As a result, coverage by this support was very narrow. As in Shanghai, most other cities also linked social housing provision with the local minimum living standard and have only provided help to families falling below the poverty level. Households with per capita income above the poverty level but living under poor conditions were not included. For convenience in operation, most local authorities preferred rent allowances or cash subsidy rather than direct provision of low-rent public housing. Rent subsidies would avoid the concentration of the poor into specific areas. When direct allocation was necessary, only old empty public housing was used. In a few cities local housing authorities purchased difficult-to-sell commercial housing for this purpose.

Subsidised rental housing was seen by many local officials as a temporary measure to solve a short-term problem. Authorities had to evaluate the financial situation of the families each year to make sure only those still illegible stayed in the social housing provision system. However, most of these families' situations were determined by their educational background and personal qualities, which may not change very much. With increasing numbers of unemployed and laid-off workers, there were signs that the number of households actually requiring help was increasing rather than declining.

## Effects of urban redevelopment

As discussed earlier, traditional housing areas and suburban villages are the prime locations for the urban poor in Chinese cities. Recent reports show that many urban households living below the poverty level were in old housing areas. Therefore, government policies on redevelopment of these areas have important implications to poverty elimination.

Redevelopment of old urban areas has been a well-established practice in cities since 1949. In the early 1950s, most of the ordinary housing stock was very old and in poor condition. There were many incidents of sudden collapse of buildings in the rainy season and loss of life. The government organised small-scale rehabilitation programmes in large cities to eliminate dangerous housing and build new ones on land freed. During the 1960s, because of increases in urban population and under-investment in housing, general living conditions in cities got worse, particularly in poor areas. The problems were not only related to dangerous housing, but also to overcrowding. In response to these problems, municipal governments began to build new housing to release the pressure. In the 1970s, large cities, such as Beijing, tested the idea of redevelopment of whole poor housing areas. Residents were moved to temporary accommodation nearby or to empty local government-owned housing. The entire areas were rebuilt and the original residents moved back to new houses. The scales of these early redevelopments were relatively small, and the sole purpose was to improve the living conditions of the poor. The negative social and economic impacts on the residents of these schemes was very limited, and preserved established local communities.

More urban redevelopment was carried out during the 1980s. Larger housing estates were built by government-owned property developers, first in nearby suburban areas; residents in old areas relocated to these new estates permanently. Land freed was redeveloped, and new houses were sold to well-off families or work units at market prices. The main objectives of these redevelopments was still to improve housing conditions and the urban living environment in general. Since the distance moved by original residents was relatively small, this approach was acceptable to the old residents as well. The social costs of this type of redevelopment were small and could be compensated by the improved living environment. There were also economic benefits to the local government and the publicly owned development companies, but their profits were kept a small margin.

During the property boom years of the 1990s, urban redevelopment happened at record speed. The measures used were also very different from the previous decades. The organisation and implementation of redevelopment had shifted from the government-owned developers to a variety of private and joint-venture companies. The government identified poor areas first and outlined favourable tax and policies on land-use fees as an incentive to developers. The responsibility for compensation and relocation of original residents was also transferred to commercial operators. With this approach the emphasis of redevelopment had shifted from the removal or repair of dangerous housing to large-scale area-based redevelopment. Apart from residential areas, redevelopments could include major commercial streets.

There was a diversification of investment in the redevelopment process as well. Public investment was replaced by bank loans, private and international investments. The higher prices of new commercial property and the central land prices became the most important motivations for redevelopment projects. Development companies often increased the approved building densities in their projects and limited the rate of return by poor local residents by offering cheap accommodation at long distance in suburban areas (Li, 2000).

In Beijing, the Municipal Housing and Property Bureau and several other authorities carried out a housing survey in 1991. They identified 202 areas of poor and dangerous housing in the city. This included a construction floor area of 10 million $m^2$ and housed 240,000 families with nearly 1 million residents. In the following years, many of these areas were earmarked by developers for renewal (Li, 2000). By the end of 1999, redevelopment started in 150 areas and 48 of them were completed. Over 4 million $m^2$ of old housing were demolished and 12 million $m^2$ floor area of new housing was built. The process affected 160,000 families, of which 119,000 households were re-housed with only 48,000 families moving back to the original area (Shun, 2000).

In the whole country, a total of 1.5 million urban homes were demolished between 1992 and 1994, but many development companies later ran into financial problems and some projects were left half completed for a very long time. About 1 million households stayed in temporary accommodation or with relatives. In every large city, there were several thousand households staying in temporary accommodation for many years. In Shenyang, over 130,000 households stayed in temporary accommodation at one time. After 1995, because of overheating in the real estate market, profits from redevelopment began to decline. Demolition and redevelopment slowed down a bit. This did not mean the end of redevelopment. In Shanghai, for example, about 70,000 households were relocated each year during the late 1990s. The second stage of the Minzhu underground rail project alone affected more than 7,000 households. During the Ninth Five-year Plan period (1996–2000), a total of 330 million $m^2$ of floor area in old property and housing was demolished, twice that in the previous five years (Xie, 2001).

Wuhan Municipal Demolition and Relocation Management Office reported that some developers secured the land from the government and demolished existing houses, then sold the land to other developers to make a profit without compensating residents or transferring compensation costs to the new developer. An overseas developer demolished over 500 houses in the central district of Hankou in 1994, and by 2001 the relocation housing was still not completed; over 400 households were left in a transitional state. Another developer cleared an area with 2,000 families in 1993 in the same district. Two 30-storey buildings were planned for relocation housing which were left at basic structure stage. About 1,500 households had no formal housing arrangements. These relocation problems caused several demonstrations in the city. The Office recognised that government regulations and laws at the time treated the parties involved differently. For example, developers could sue residents in court and relied on legal and administrative measures to force residents to move. The regulations did not give much power to residents to protect their own interests in case the developer failed to pay the compensation or fulfil the promised relocation arrangements. The regulation only allowed the local authority to fine the developer if it failed to implement their relocation arrangements. Because relocation and compensation usually involved a huge amount of money, a fine by the local authority (if they could get it) could hardly pay monthly costs of the temporary accommodation arrangement. It was far from enough to solve the housing problems of those who had lost their homes (Wuhan Municipal Demolition and Relocation Management Office, 2001).

Reviewing the residential area redevelopment practice in Beijing in the 1990s, Li (2000) identified several major problems. The redevelopment process was poorly managed and government lost control to the real estate companies. Instead of improving poor people's housing, the main objectives of developers were to maximise their profits. Developers competed for good locations and areas that involved lower compensation and fewer relocations, and were less interested in redeveloping the poor or high-density areas. Some developers took over large areas but did not have the financial resources to complete the project. Redevelopment cycles were extended to four to five years, some even seven to eight years. In areas identified for redevelopment, normal social and economic activities were disrupted. No changes in residence registration were allowed; separation of households (where more than one individual and/or family shared accommodation) and housing exchanges were also banned. Because of the uncertainty, residents spent little money on their houses. Local shops were seriously affected as well with no refurbishment of shops and frontage, low stock-keeping, and insecurity for employees. All these caused local and wider social and political problems.

Redevelopments in the 1990s also had a limited effect on poverty reduction. The process relied entirely on the real estate development market, and resulted in less policy and market interests in the poorest areas which required the redevelopment most urgently. In many cities redevelopment actually destroyed many reasonable good housing areas which could be used by the poor. For residents engaged in informal sectors of the economy, (e.g. repairing, rubbish and waste collection, street trading) the redevelopment cut them off from their income sources.

Some of these problems were also identified by the Ministry of Construction. In his speech at the National Conference of Urban Housing and Property Demolition and Residents Relocation in 2000, Vice Minister Liu Zhifeng reported that in some cities, local authorities and developers did not have sufficient financial resources, but carried out large scale demolition and redevelopment. Some developers illegally reduced the compensation standards and used force to relocate poor residents. This practice resulted in many complaints from residents. Between January and August 2000, the ministry received 1,350 letters of complaint about unfair compensation; and 103 individuals or groups appealed to the ministry about problems relating to demolition and relocation. He also outlined some related political problems. There was no certainty in urban planning on redevelopment. Each change of leadership in municipal government resulted in changes in land-use plans and unnecessary demolition. Those redevelopment projects were not aimed at solving urban housing problems, but as face-lift projects to demonstrate the 'achievements' of the local leaders (Liu, 2000).

The Ministry also recognised that urban housing demolition and residents' relocation in some sense was a government compulsory action. Once the process started, whether the owners or residents were happy or not, their houses had to be demolished by the end. The owners and the users of old housing were the relatively weak and not an organised socio-economic group. They were drawn into the redevelopment activities. All those characteristics mean that the interests of this group could be easily hurt. Evidence from all cities demonstrated this clearly. The ministry urged all local authorities to pay particular attention to the interests of the residents and owners (Liu, 2000). Minster Liu called for more low-price housing to increase the choice for relocated residents. He also encouraged local governments to pay more attention to those low-income families that could not solve their housing problems using the small amount of compensation.

In response to these problems, new policies on redevelopment were issued by the State Council in 2001 in a revised Ordinance of Urban Housing and Property Demolition and Compensation. Major new policies include:

- compensation of original owners at market values for existing properties
- market values to be assessed by professional valuation
- more powers to owners to protect their rights
- more choices for compensation, e.g. prefer cash compensation to housing replacement
- require the demolition/development companies to put a proportion of their planned compensation fund into a special bank account with spending examined and approved by the local housing authorities

- new roles assigned to local government with emphasis on management and maintaining a legal balance between the developers and the residents, rather than carrying out demolition and compensation themselves directly.

These policies aimed at regulating the redevelopment market and providing an important framework for local authorities to produce detailed implementation guidelines. They aimed at solving some of the problems identified above, such as long periods of temporary accommodation. However, in terms of poverty elimination, the new policies could create more problems in the future. In comparison with old practices, the new regulation gives more protection to owners rather than users of existing houses. In the previous system, it was the responsibility of the developers to re-house the rental tenants and compensate the owners. The new regulation required owners to either end the rental contract with their tenants or find alternative arrangements for them. Most families that rented housing in the poor areas were extremely poor. Their interests were not well protected by the new regulation. Reasonable compensation to the owners according to the market principles is major progress. However, some of the owners may not be poor and do not live in the area at all. Redevelopment will benefit the relatively richer landlords rather than the poor who live in these areas.

The living conditions of most of the remaining owner-occupiers in run-down areas were very poor. In determining compensation, the old practice emphasised re-housing and material compensation based both on the original size of the houses and the number of registered residents. Most poor households always chose relocation. Redevelopment would result in some improvement of their living conditions, though they might be moved to a less favourable location. The new regulation made the provision of compensation based on market values of the property. It sounds as though it was giving more advantage to owners rather than the developers. In reality, it takes the number of residents in the household out of the calculation. A small run-down house, even evaluated at market value before redeveloping the area, will not give the family enough money to buy new housing in the same area. The only option for them is to move to other relatively poor locations. The preference of cash compensation over re-housing, in the long term, is an advantage to the developers rather than the original residents. The developers will make compensation at the price fixed at the beginning of the development stage once for all; the residents will be dispersed from the area and later organised protest or demonstrations could be avoided. For the original residents, inflation will eat away at the compensation and housing price increases may prevent them from entering the housing market. The evaluation of market values of the old house does not include the loss of established communities, social relationships, and local economic opportunities, particularly these related to the informal sectors. In this sense, the redevelopment may create more poor people or relocate urban poor from the central areas to peripheral districts.

Most local politicians were very keen to see the disappearance of old areas from their cities. The construction of new infrastructure such as road and underground systems, and the drive to create a better living environment for the rich by enlarging gardens and open spaces, will mean more redevelopment in the next few years. More traditional housing areas have been replaced by modern concrete flats in the last couple of years. The price of this 'success' will be the loss of low-cost housing for the poor. There will be no place for existing poor families and rural migrants in the central area, and suburban slums and low-income housing estates hidden away from the modern image of urban landscape will bring new problems.

Since the publication of the new regulations, many local housing officers realised that the market approach to redevelopment alone will not solve the problems of poor people's housing. Some social supports are necessary in areas where redevelopment is not the choice of the residents. Very poor residents who could not afford the redevelopment and relocation should be helped. In Beijing, new policies were issued in 2000 to encourage the cooperation and participation of individual households, local government and work units in organising redevelopment. Redevelopment and relocation were combined with the housing reform programme, which involved price controls, work unit cash subsidies and low-interest loans from housing provident funds. Municipal government gives residents the right to decide whether redevelopment is necessary; residents were also involved in the discussion about redevelopment plans, stages of implementation, financial arrangements and compensation levels, relocation and return ratios, and resolving disputes, etc. Resident committees and street offices were used as the main channels to communicate with residents. The objectives of these new measures were 'to eliminate dangerous housing; reduce overcrowding; improve the living condition and the capital's general environment. This re-emphasis of social values is a very positive sign of development, which could have some impact on poverty reduction in the city.

## Limitations and future challenges

Increasing inequalities and the emergence of poverty in cities during the 1990s caused serious concerns among the leaders of the Communist Party. To maintain both economic growth and social stability were the two top priorities of the party. As part of the market system, social security policies were introduced to ensure smooth transition and reduce tensions between different groups. As we saw in previous sections, some of the new policies introduced did play an important role in achieving the aims of economic growth and social stability. However, these anti-poverty policies have several limitations. First of all, social support was kept at the very minimum level. There was no intention of achieving a more equal society. The urban minimum living standard, for example, only provided poor families with the most basic level of support for survival rather than for relative comfort. The support can only protect these families from hunger or cold. Keeping the support level low may force poor families to search for other ways to improve their living conditions; the system underestimates the difficulties those families faced during the special period. Most of the poor people would like to work rather than to be unemployed. Job opportunities are just too few for such large groups.

The new systems tried to be open and fair. To obtain urban minimum living standard income support and social housing, households had to reveal their problems, not only to the authorities, but to the public as well. Names of households qualifying for support were publicised. This does not help the poor families to maintain their confidence and morale. A few years ago, everyone was more or less the same, now some were publicly declared as poor and requiring government support. This could be considered as public humiliation to these adults and their children. Unless they were really desperate, many families may prefer to stay away from the problems of the application process and the intrusive investigation for such a small amount of cash each month.

So far these social policies were all aimed at solving the problems among the official urban residents, with a focus on the existing state-sector employees in particular. Rural migrants were excluded from any of these government support systems. If measured according to the same standard, most rural migrants will belong to the poor category. There is a huge demand for social support among this group. They were even excluded from making contributions to some of the social security systems. These arrangements are understandable if rural migrants only work in cities temporarily. In reality most of them stayed in cities for many years. Demands to respect their citizenship and give them equal rights in cities are getting stronger. There were recent moves to relax the policy controls imposed on them.

Future urbanisation and particularly the ongoing reform of population registration pose the main challenge to the practice of these social support systems. Increasing migration to urban areas and the inevitable recognition of their existence could change the established social groups in cities and enlarge the poor groups substantially. It is unlikely and impossible for municipal authorities to extend the new social housing and minimum living standard to cover the migrants over a short period; migrants may be allowed to compete in job-hunting with local residents on more equal terms, but they could be excluded from various social and financial supports for years to come.

Although the urban renewal programme seems not to directly affect the lives of migrants in cities, it does destroy the rental accommodation which suits their needs in terms of cost and location. In the future less and less of this housing will be found in the central areas; migrants will have to move further and further away from the central areas and rely on the suburban villages for living. The increased commuter costs and the cultural contrasts will mean further marginalisation of rural people in cities. This will also have important implications for government policy for further urbanisation and *hukou* system reform. Not many migrants could afford to buy purpose-built housing in cities. Unless a wide range of different qualities of housing is allowed to exist, suburban slums could become a main feature of future urbanisation.

# 9 Conclusion

Modernisation? High-rise housing, offices and open spaces in central Guangzhou, October 2003.

Successful reform and sustained economic growth has made China different from other former socialist countries, but the recent emergence of urban poverty represents some of the common problems of transitional economies. Previous chapters have revealed that the urban poor in China are not isolated cases in cities and have become a serious problem. The proportion of urban poor and the extent of poverty are now critical issues to the future development. They could lead to social instability that the Communist Party has tried hard to avoid. In this concluding chapter the different experiences in transition and poverty between eastern European countries and China will be highlighted first. I will then discuss the future prospects for the urban poor in China in relation to the possible effects of further market reform, urbanisation and globalisation. Finally, the chapter will discuss policy options for a more balanced and equal society.

## Different experiences of transition and poverty

Almost all former socialist states have experienced some sort of transition from planned economy toward market economy. The routes of such transition have, however, differed. We noted in Chapter 2 that an important difference existed between transition process in the central and eastern European countries and China. The eastern European countries were thought to follow a 'big bang' approach. Fundamental changes in different areas of the society happened simultaneously in a short period. There was also a clear destination for transition – toward a market economy and western-style democratic system.

China was thought to have followed a gradualist approach. Changes from planned to market economy happened at a slower pace. In each policy area, experiments were normally carried out in various locations, then revised and tested at a larger scale in more places. If successful, the new policy was finally adopted at the national level. The term 'gradualism' does catch the main feature of this cautious reform policy process. In relation to the society as a whole, the word 'gradualism' however may not be the best description about changes in China. In economic terms, some of the policies adopted were comparable to the 'big bang' approach. The abolition of people's communes in rural areas and the introduction of the family responsibility system over a couple of years affected several hundred million people. Industrial restructuring in the state sector in the last few years which laid-off many million workers was another dramatic change. In political terms, maybe not much change could be referred to as a transition. Some minor adjustments were made, but they were not as 'gradual' as they happened in the economic sphere. Reform in China did not have such a clear objective as that in European countries, or China had not been forced on to such a pass. So far the Chinese Communist Party leadership has no desire to introduce western-style democracy into the Chinese political system.

In some other areas, China also experienced more change than eastern European countries. Examples include reduction of rural poverty, changing relations between town and country, rural to urban migration, opening up the country to the outside world, improvements in urban living condition. Housing reform in cities affected a large proportion of urban residents and changed the state-dominated urban housing provision, and private home ownership was re-established over a period of 15 years. Real estate development has changed the urban landscape completely and some of the best architectural projects were carried out in central areas of many big cities. All these are evidence of a major transition from a traditional society into a modern society, but not necessarily from socialism to capitalism. In this sense, Chinese transition is only a special way of development in which a relatively poor country tries to catch up with the developed world. This transition has not followed a well-designed straightforward path. Transition was a bumpy ride with ups and downs, stops and starts and a spiral progress. This is a 'progressive reform' rather than a gradualist transition (Figure 9.1). Gradual transition implies the move to the same destination as the eastern European countries, but only at a slower pace. Under the current political, social and economic settings, we have no idea what a 'modern' society China will be in the future. We know that political, economic and social changes will continue, probably along 'the route' set by the country's then paramount leader, Deng Xiaoping, that is, 'cross the river by feeling the stones using your feet'. We have no clear idea about what the 'other side of the river' will be like. Nevertheless, we can speculate that this progressive reform process will last for a long period (Table 9.1).

Differences in the pace and content of transition has important implications for the social structure of previously socialist cities. In eastern Europe, since the old system collapsed and was replaced by a new one, urban social structures experienced a major re-organisation. Personal assets (social and economic) built up during the socialist period were important factors, but almost everyone had to find their position in the new system in a relatively short period (Figure 9.2). In China, the existing socialist political and socio-economic structure was not replaced in cities entirely by a new one. New social groups had been added onto the existing structure and existing groups had to adjust themselves into the reformed system. The co-existence of both old and new systems and the overlapping between the two had important implications for urban social and economic development (Figure 9.3). For some, particularly those in the top social and political hierarchy (at all administrative levels),

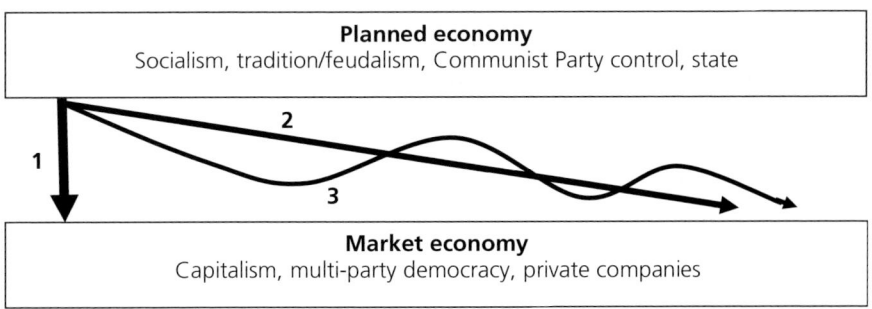

1 'Big-bang' transition; 2 Gradualist transition; 3 Progressive reform

**9.1** Different modes of transition

# Conclusion

**Table 9.1** Future prospect of Chinese reform

| Main areas | Possible state to be reached | Estimated time required |
|---|---|---|
| Economic reform | Economic reform is called off officially. Unlikely in the next decade or so, because there many changes need to be made | Not before 2020 |
| Economic organisation | The market begins to play the dominant role, with state-owned sectors becoming less dominant and functioning within a market framework, and most old style work units being transformed into modern firms | At least another 10–15 years |
| Social organisation | Sustained socialised benefits and security systems set up and covering the majority of the population, both urban and rural | At least another 10–15 years |
| Housing | Urban housing reform process completed and housing provision for the majority through the market. Housing subsidies merged with normal salaries. Social housing for the poor covers about 10 to 15 per cent of the urban population | 10–15 years |
| Urban landscape and development | All old areas have been redeveloped and no poor quality traditional buildings left. Large-scale urban expansion slowdown and urban environment improvement and maintenance become the main aspects of development | Urbanisation process will continue for at least another 30 years |
| Urbanisation | Urbanisation has reached a higher level and a balanced urban and rural relationship established. Official restriction of population movement removed | 30–50 years |
| Growth and development | Policy shifted from economic growth to more comprehensive development approaches | In 5 years |

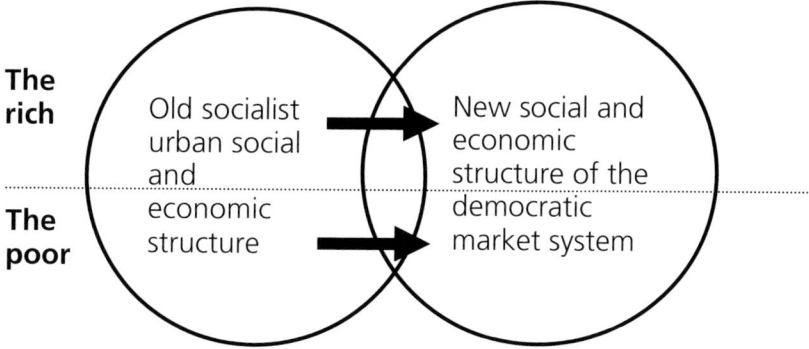

**The rich**

**The poor**

Old socialist urban social and economic structure

New social and economic structure of the democratic market system

**9.2** Social and economic changes under the 'big bang'

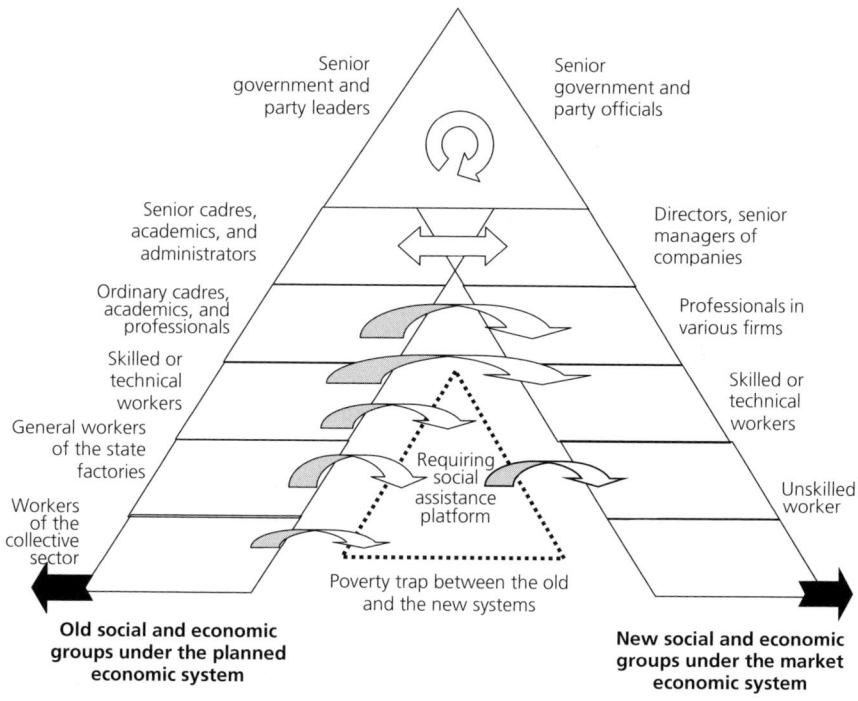

Senior government and party leaders

Senior government and party officials

Senior cadres, academics, and administrators

Directors, senior managers of companies

Ordinary cadres, academics, and professionals

Professionals in various firms

Skilled or technical workers

Skilled or technical workers

General workers of the state factories

Requiring social assistance platform

Unskilled worker

Workers of the collective sector

Poverty trap between the old and the new systems

**Old social and economic groups under the planned economic system**

**New social and economic groups under the market economic system**

**9.3** Social and economic changes under progressive reform

there was no dramatic transition. Reform brought them the opportunity to benefit from both systems. Erosion of the old communist disciplines combined with the incomplete and improper market regulations created easy opportunities for mismanagement of state property into private assets and corruption. For the middle groups, such as those with technical and professional skills and the right social and political connections, transition means a small leap from an old economic sector to the new market system. Once they have completed this transition, they can begin to benefit from the new urban economy by selling their skills and knowledge at 'market' values. For the social and economic groups at the lower end of the system, economic reform brings many negative impacts, such as job insecurity, loss of social benefits, stagnating incomes and high costs of living. These people did not have the energy, skills, assets or connections to complete the transfer. Many of them have become unemployed and demand support from the government. The gap between the planned economic system and the new market economic system is also much wider for low-status workers. This gap can be a poverty trap if one has left or is pushed out of the old system but failed to find a proper role in the new market economy.

Reviewing transition in eastern European countries, Ferreira (1997) concluded that

> ... even an efficient privatisation designed to be egalitarian may lead to increases in inequality (and possibly poverty), both during transition and in the new steady-state. Creation of new markets in services supplied by the public sector may also contribute to an increase in equality, as can labour market reforms that lead to a decompression of the earnings structure and to greater flexibility in employment. The results underline the importance of retaining government provision of basic public goods and services; of removing barriers that prevent the participation of the poor in the new private sector; and of ensuring that suitable safety nets are in place.
>
> (Ferreira, 1997: 1)

China achieved very good results in terms of economic development. However, Chinese cities have not entirely avoided the problems of poverty. Benefits of economic growth were not shared equally in urban society. There were limited effects of the trickle down of benefits to disadvantaged social groups. Market reforms have led to very uneven distributions of income and huge income gaps between the rich and the poor. Taking the official social assistant level as an indicator, over 22 million non-agricultural urban residents have an income below the official poverty line. If the poverty line is raised slightly to the level of US$1 a day, a lot more urban residents will be classified as poor.

The fading away of socialist principles and the introduction of market economy will lead to an increasing gap between the rich and the poor and to growing urban poverty. Countries which followed the 'big bang' approach had to face a sudden explosion of poverty and had to quickly develop new measures before they were out of control. Countries carrying out progressive reforms will slow down or delay the emergence of urban poverty. This also allowed these countries to develop new anti-poverty policies and social security systems, which may reduce the number of the poor and the extent of poverty. Anti-poverty measures were not always readily available under the 'big bang' approach because of the low priority given to the poor by the new administrative and political elites. In this sense, Chinese progressive reform could reduce the degree and length of suffering by the poor.

This analysis highlights the differences in transition and poverty between China and eastern European countries in the last 20 years. These differences pointed to some positive aspects of the Chinese progressive reform experience in dealing with urban poverty. Twenty years was a long period for the narrowly defined transition from planned to market economy; however, it is a short period for social transition, e.g. from a backward agricultural society towards a modern economy. Twenty years of reform in China may only mark the first stage of such a fundamental transition. Urban poverty will not be something which appeared briefly and then disappeared. It will accompany this long-term transition.

## The future of urban poverty

Historical and inherited problems such as the 'three no' individuals and disabled people, the pursuit of full employment in urban areas and overstaffing in the public sector, were important causes for urban poverty. However, these historical problems did not result in serious poverty under the planned economic system. The number of poor people inherited from the previous period was also relatively small. Reform and the marketisation of the urban economy, particularly the reduction of universal benefits and rising unemployment, are new causes of increased incidents of urban poverty. Adult unemployment, laid-off workers and poverty among pensioners were all related to the process of marketisation and the reform in the old state-owned public sectors. To project the future of urban poverty, we need to focus on the main factors, which determine the future course of urban development in China.

### Impact from market reform

Eastern European cities experienced serious problems of poverty because of drops in income caused by stagnation of the urban economy and increased inequality. Chinese cities experienced poverty, though the urban economy was developing at a pace unmatched in history. The structural adjustment policies of neo-liberal theory followed by many other countries throughout the world since the 1980s had all led to some degree of increased inequality. Even in the advanced market economies of the USA and the UK, urban poverty is still a major problem. There is no 'perfect market' which will lead to a rational distribution. There are always powerful forces, and motives exist in private as well as public sectors to control or frustrate the market. Such forces may be beneficial for growth, but not for poverty elimination.

Urban poverty under a market economy, as seen by radical neo-Marxist social and political theory, could be understood only as a result of conflicts between classes which were a direct outcome of the operation of the capitalist mode of production; urban forms, urban issues, urban government, urban ideology could be understood only in terms of the dynamic of the capitalist system. Urban 'problems' arose not by chance or through mismanagement but because the interests of one or other social class faction had been served by the emergence of such problems (Gilbert and Gugler, 1992). 'Urban disorder was not in fact disorder at all; it represented the spatial organisation created by the market, and derived from the absence of social control of the industrial activity' (Castells, 1977: 14–15). Rich and poor are the two sides of the capitalist-style economic growth. The successful development of Chinese cities was to a certain extent sustained by the large number of urban poor. Large-scale real estate and infrastructure development could not happen without the exploitation of low-paid labour, particularly rural migrants. During this initial stage of so-called capital accumulation, the rich rely on the poor to build up their wealth. In other words, some people are getting richer because most of the others are poor. Inequality and poverty are key features of the market economy and are unavoidable problems of market transition. Although China has made important progress in privatisation and marketisation over the last 25 years, the core elements of the economic system were still in the socialist format. In terms of GDP contribution and employment, the state is still the dominant sector. This economic structure ensures a long process of reform. With the overall objective of reform to improve economic efficiency, equality in distribution will have a lower priority. More and more people will be forced out of the old welfare support system and many of them could become new groups of urban poor.

The 'development state' has been a leading paradigm for the study of capitalist economies in eastern Asia countries (Chan et al., 1998; Woo-Cumings, 1999). As an alternative to liberal and Stalinist states, the development state does not retreat to play a minimal role in the face of market forces, and the state intervenes actively in the market to coordinate economic development. The developmental state is equally essential in the domain of social welfare provision. During the transition, escalation of tensions among social groups is likely to ensue from rapid social and economic changes. Threatening social crises require extensive social and political coordination in the distribution of resources, for social stability is built upon social equality. The market itself does not have a mechanism to stabilise a society, which is under tension caused by widening income gaps. Urban development in the transition from the centrally-controlled system to market-oriented economy needs the state to play its roles. There is evidence that China had based some of its reform strategies on the experiences of other East Asia countries. At the same time of introducing market mechanism into the economic system, the state has paid some attention to the reform of old welfare provision and introducing new social support system. In this way, the negative impacts of reform can be reduced. In future reform, we may see the continuing increase in inequality and poverty and more government efforts to reduce poverty in cities.

## Impact from urbanisation

Marxist researchers on poverty in western Europe trace the current development of poverty and poverty policies from the period of the gradual replacement of feudalism by capitalism as the modern economy began to develop in the seventeenth and eighteenth centuries. Novak (1988) argues that it is only at this point that poverty is created. This is because at this time the majority of people are separated from the land and become workers, and thus they lose control over the means of producing material support and become dependent upon wages from paid labour. After this, those who cannot work for wages cannot support themselves and thus are impoverished. For Novak, therefore, poverty is caused by the logic of the capitalist wage labour market (Alcock, 1987, 1993).

China is changing from a traditional, agricultural-based society toward a modern urban society. Combined with the liberal economic reform policies, much of the change represents a shift described by Novak. The process of urbanisation is accompanied by large numbers of farmers losing or giving up their land and becoming workers and losing control over the means of producing material support and becoming dependent upon wages from paid labour. The suburban landless farmers and rural migrants are exactly these groups of which some cannot find work for wages and cannot support themselves. We may argue that current urban poverty was a direct result of the success of early rural reform. If the strong control of the commune system remained in villages, most of the rural migrants found in cities would be tied to the land. Urban unemployment created by the restructuring of the old state factories could be easily absorbed by the expansion of the new private sector. Without 100 million migrants competing for jobs, adults among the 22 million low-income urban residents could all be employed one way or another. On the other hand, we can also argue that urban poverty was a direct result of government policies. First, it allowed rural people to take up jobs in cities which led to the unemployment among the official residents. Second, it had refused full urban citizens' rights to millions of rural people. They were allowed to 'float' in cities and towns, but were not 'urbanised'. They were treated as outsiders subordinate to the official urban residents, and working machines which could be shifted around. These unjustified policies created a favourable business environment in which migrants were crudely exploited by the new class of entrepreneurs. Government policies excluded migrants from new social security systems and paid no attention to the poverty problem among them. In comparison with the number of migrants, the official urban poor group helped by the new social security support currently is only the tip of a big iceberg.

Urbanisation will have a major impact on urban poverty. When urbanisation levels increased, urban poverty became a more serious issue in many developing countries. China's urbanisation level is still relatively low and the next few decades will see more people moving from rural villages to urban areas. Apart from the 100 million rural migrants, there is still a huge reservoir of extra rural labour in China. The Agricultural Ministry indicated (at a meeting in Chongqing on rural labourer training on 1 April 2003) that there were 480 million rural labourers in China in 2003, of whom 320 million were farmers. Under the current production system, agriculture only requires 170,000,000 labourers. This means there were about 150,000,000 surplus rural labourers. Improvement in agricultural technologies may reduce the need for farming labourers even further and double the number of migrant workers in cities. This will create even more pressure on the urban physical, social and economic system.

The physical development of cities has also had very important implications for poverty. Current housing developments and urban renewal projects, in particular, have some negative impacts on the urban poor. With increasing income distribution, cities should offer a wide range of housing to suit all social classes including the poor. The commercial properties developed over the last decades were aimed at the rich or the new middle classes. The majority of low-income households found it more and more difficult to buy new housing without government or employer support. For poor families and migrants, low-quality, simple and traditional housing offered the best option for living, but most of this type of house in central areas had been demolished and land freed for other purposes. There is serious mismatch in the range of housing available in urban areas to the range of income distribution. Housing for the poor disappeared quickly in central areas, and poor families were relocated to other less profitable places, often in remote suburban areas. The choice of accommodation for future migrants will be very limited and the most probable destinations will be temporary shelters around construction sites and slums in distant suburban areas. Formalisation of urban landscape and housing will also eliminate the informal employment opportunities in cities, which will in turn affect the income and welfare of the urban poor and rural migrants. Unless special government policies are developed and implemented quickly, this process of *urbanisation of poverty* will continue.

## Impact of globalisation

Open-door policies and globalisation had been seen as a major driving force in urban development in China over the last twenty years. As much as in western market societies, China's urban development depends upon (and its development options are limited by) the country's global connections. This is not a new phenomenon; indeed, most of China's major coastal cities developed under foreign influence after the mid-nineteenth century (Logan, 2002). In its first thirty years, the communist government was isolated in the world. Reform and the open-door policies since 1978 were to a large extent to rebuild this global connection. After many years of negotiation, China is now a member of the WTO, which demonstrates the country's successful integration with the world economic system. An important indicator of recent global connections is foreign direct investment, which grew exponentially after 1991 (Wu, 2000). As a result many cities along the coastal areas had been 'globalised'. Cities such as Beijing and Shanghai are favourable locations for many international organisations and business headquarters. The successful bid to host the 2008 Olympics by Beijing will speed up this globalisation process.

Globalisation, however, has both positive and negative impacts on the national and local economies. Many people argue that globalisation is necessary and in the long run beneficial, especially to developing countries. By opening up economies to market forces and world trade, it allows countries to specialise in areas where they have a comparative advantage; and through trade with the rest of the world, they can achieve economic growth, employment and increased living standards. Increased exports from developing countries allow them to buy imports from the developed world. It is, then, a process that is of benefit to both. Other gains include increased access to the latest technology and capital, and to networks and markets (Martinussen, 1997). Critics of these economic strategies argue that, while some groups of workers have benefited from globalisation, large sections of the workforce throughout the world have experienced unemployment, poverty and inequality. Developing countries and those of the former Eastern Bloc and Soviet Union undergoing structural adjustment programmes have witnessed increased poverty as their economies were opened up to market forces and their welfare spending was slashed as a condition of adjustment loans. Even the developed countries suffered

> whereas the macro-economic therapies (under the jurisdiction of national governments) tends to be less brutal than those imposed on the South and East, the theoretical and ideological underpinnings are broadly similar ... The consequences are unemployment, low wages and the marginalisation of large sectors of the population.
>
> (Chussodovsky, 1996, quoted from SPIU, 2001: 1)

Industries and workers in both developed and developing countries are being forced into unprecedented competition (SPIU, 2001).

Although the globalisation process had helped China to develop its urban economy, its effects on the poor varied. It was widely believed that the open-door policies had resulted in fast economic growth and contributed to the reduction of poverty in the country in general, particularly in the rural areas. However, the negative impacts on the urban social structure began to show. International competition had led to the closure or restructuring of state-sector industries which brought about large-scale unemployment in cities. The urban redevelopment process provides the necessary office space for international business and a luxury living environment for the rich at the expense of the traditional poor residents who occupied central locations. Increased competition in cities resulted in poor working conditions among the disadvantaged groups such as the rural migrants.

Assessing the impact of China's entry into the WTO, Guan (2003) predicted that as the biggest developing country, China's economic competition with other countries will become stronger simultaneously in two directions. One direction will be to compete with developed countries in high-tech industries – a 'race to the top'. The other competition will be with other developing countries in the international market for a larger share of international investment and trade in labour-intensive industries – a 'race to the bottom'. As a result of stronger competition in both these directions, an increase in inequality would seem inevitable. Considering its ambitious economic strategy to catch up with developed countries, maintaining a high level of economic efficiency will be the first priority of government. As a result, social justice may be consigned to a secondary position for some time. Even if government social policy were to be based merely on considerations of social stability rather than social justice, the intensity of pressure from international economic competition may not allow it enough room to balance its economic and social goals (Guan, 2003).

This analysis points to a future increase rather than decrease in inequality in China. Without appropriate policy interventions, China could return to the pre-communist dichotomous urban system, in which areas with greater global influence were distinct from the indigenous body of poor areas. The benefits from globalisation will be reaped by a few rather than shared by many. Considering the level of urbanisation and the degree of exposure of the population to the external forces, globalisation will have a significant and long-term impact on the urban poor in China.

## Policy options

The approach to reducing poverty in the world has evolved over the past 50 years in response to a deepening understanding of the complexity of development. In the 1950s and 1960s many viewed large investments in physical capital and infrastructure as the primary means of development. In the 1970s awareness grew that physical capital was not enough and that health and education were at least as important. The 1980s saw another shift of emphasis to improving economic management and allowing greater play for market forces. In the 1990s, governance and institutions moved toward a centre stage. New conceptualisations of poverty also emerged, which recognised that poverty is not just about income or expenditure levels but is multifaceted, covering a wide range of aspects: prospects for earning a living; deprivation and exclusion; basic needs; social aspects; psychological aspects; etc. (Gordon and Townsend, 2000). New approaches to the assessment of poverty emphasise: a) vulnerability – a dynamic concept referring to negative outcomes on the well-being of individuals, households, or communities from environmental changes; b) asset ownership – individuals', households' and communities' ability to resist negative impacts relates to their ability to mobilise assets in the face of hardship; c) livelihood: comprises the capabilities, assets (both natural and social) and activities required for a means of living (Moser *et al.*, 1997). Based on these strategies and in the light of changed global contexts, the World Bank in 2001 proposed a new strategy for attacking poverty in three ways: promoting opportunity, facilitating empowerment and enhancing security (World Bank, 2001).

Since urban poverty is a relatively new problem in China, understanding of the urban poor is limited. Current policies had a strong emphasis on the capital investment and infrastructure development approach (1950s–1960s) and economic management and marketisation (1980s). Less effort was given to equal distribution, basic needs, education and health. There was also a limited understanding of the most recent theoretical developments since the 1990s, such as good governance and institutions, and local and individual vulnerability. Government anti-poverty policies and support given to the urban poor based on a minimum poverty level were very inadequate and some new social benefits available in cities were only transitional arrangements. Resources allocated for such schemes were not adequate. Large financial support sometimes was offered to the middle-income groups rather than the poor. Considerable amounts of housing subsidies, for example, were given to a large number of highly paid government officials and professionals, while there was no money to fund a small social housing programme.

Past development policies often had very negative impact on the poor. The most obvious include:

- Housing and real estate development policies had ignored the serious consequences of social segregation. Most large housing estates became either gated communities for the rich or the so-called affordable housing for the middle-income groups. There were also other housing areas dedicated to the low-income families displaced from the central redevelopment areas. This pattern of development may solve the short-term housing problems, but has created a very uneven social structure.
- Large-scale, in some places, entire central area redevelopment, destroyed homes and informal job opportunities for low-income families and removed affordable housing for the future urban poor and rural migrants. It had destroyed much of the traditional landscape and created a uniform of 'modern' architectural styles. All cities, particularly the central areas became more and more similar across all regions.

# Conclusion

- The half open policies on migration have damaged the interests of the new urban poor. They provided a legal basis for the exploitation of rural population by urban establishment. Allowing migrants to enter the cities, but denying them the equal labour protection resulted in inhuman working conditions.

Since Deng Xiaoping introduced the policy to 'let some people get rich first' in the early 1980s, the overall economic development attitude and trend seem to be pro-rich and pro-growth. Most economic policies aimed at high GDP growth and major social policies aimed at maintaining social stability rather than to achieve equality. Productivity and efficiency were given higher priority over fairness and equality. To change this pro-rich and pro-growth development mentality is a very important option for the government. In future reforms, more consideration should be given to the development of pro-poor production or service sectors. All profound economic and social change produces winners and losers. The role of government in these circumstances is to help manage the process of change – to maximise economic opportunities for all, and to equip people, through education and active market policies, to take advantage of these opportunities.

> Pro-poor development requires growth and equity. Poverty reduction is faster where growth is combined with declining inequality, and poverty reduction is also more easily achieved in less unequal countries – the lower the level of inequality, the larger the share of the benefits of growth that accrue to the poor.
> (UK Government, 2000: 18)

Inequalities in China (both between rural and urban areas and within them) have reached an alarming level. It is time for the government to take action now. Equality is not necessarily a trade-off to growth. The fundamental task of social policy should aim to balance the need for redistribution of income that underpins human dignity and equality of opportunity, high labour market participation and low unemployment, and the dynamism of the market economy. The best social policy is full employment. However, the kind of full employment that existed under the old regime is incompatible with the goals of the transformation process. The challenge to policymakers is to recognize their responsibility to devise policies that generate sufficient numbers of real jobs to combine low unemployment with transformation.

In terms of immediate policy changes to promote the pro-poor strategy, several areas could be considered, such as reconsidering urban development strategies and putting a brake on the current trend of urban sprawl by developing new high-class housing estates. After so many years expansion, the shortage of housing, particularly modern high-rise flats, is not a major problem any more. A diversification of housing styles, size and ownership should be promoted, and more affordable housing for the poor should be developed or protected. Urban development should shift its focus from the official urban residents to a dynamic population through migration. The most serious poverty problems currently in cities are not those related to official residents, which the government policies are currently focused on. Rural migrants are the bigger group of the poor and their numbers are set to increase as well. City-based social support, however well-funded, will not solve this problem. Legal labour protection should be extended to cover the migrant population to ensure they are paid equally and properly. Only in this way can they be kept out of poverty.

The extent of future urban poverty also depends much on the rural areas. Integration of the cities and their rural hinterland will be the only long-term option. Development priorities and major investments should be put into improving transport and other physical, social and economic infrastructure in suburban regions. New policies should promote integration of urban and rural health and education systems and encourage the outflow of the urban population to live in towns and villages. Efforts should be made to increase employment opportunities in suburban areas and provide the necessary facilities for commuting between the rural hinterland and the cities. Urbanisation does not mean an endless spread of concrete covering the land and everyone coming to a built-up area to live in a modern flat. Good living environment consists of better integration of rural and urban areas.

Face-lifting urban renewal projects should be stopped. Rather than demolishing the traditional buildings and relocating the established urban communities, priority should be given to the improvement of infrastructure in traditional areas. New policies should help individual households to improve or rebuild their own houses according to their ability and assets. They should encourage diversification of housing design and use of traditional styles and materials. This approach may also preserve some of the traditional landscapes in Chinese cities and avoid uniform modern landscapes. It is also more sustainable than the large-scale redevelopments, which could lead to more expensive renewal in the future. The aspect on which city governments can often have the greatest impact on poverty reduction is through the direct provision of infrastructure and services, and ensuring access to land for housing and economic activities (Devas, 2001).

The current *hukou* system may help the municipal governments to keep the official urban poor at a manageable level, it is however the most damaging institutional constraints imposed on the poor, particularly rural migrants. This *hukou* system should be reformed as soon as possible and everyone allowed to compete under the same conditions. At the same time as developing new labour regulations to protect the civil rights of migrants, the political rights of migrants should be protected either through existing local community networks or special representative organisations. Only in this way, can the source for future poverty be controlled and rural migrants gradually build up their normal life in cities.

Although China did well in institutional building in comparison with many other transitional countries, reform of the municipal government fell back in relation to economic changes. The functions of local government have changed over the years, but are far from those suitable to a market economy. Local government officials to a large extent are not responsible to the local population, but to their superiors. Many of them still work according to the rules under the planned economy and are not familiar with the new functions as coordinators, negotiators and interests balancers in the market. Most of them were good at managing production, investment and spending, and learnt a lot by collecting money through various tax, fees and charges, but were not very good at provision of services. Government officials' income has increased substantially over the last few years, which was also a factor in the increased gap between party and government officials and ordinary workers. A fundamental reform of municipal government aimed at improving accountability and services is essential.

The Third Session of the Sixteenth National Congress of the Chinese Communist Party passed an important document – *Decision on Improving and Dealing With Some Problems of the Socialist Market Economic System*, in which the Central Committee of the CCP put forward five overall consideration development strategies: a) overall consideration of urban and rural areas, b) overall consideration of different regions, c) overall consideration of economic development and social development, d) overall consideration of human needs and environmental protection, and e) overall consideration of China's internal development and the demands of the global market. These policies marked a major change from previous practice and provide some scope for social justice and poverty elimination. Their effects will be tested in the next few years.

# References

Alcock, P. (1987) *Poverty and State Support*, Harlow: Longman.

Alcock, P. (1993) *Understanding Poverty*, London: Macmillan Press.

Andrusz, G., Harloe, M. and Szelenyi, I. (eds) (1996) *Cities After Socialism: Urban and Regional Change and Conflict in Post-socialist Societies*, Oxford: Blackwell.

Bachtler, J., Downes, R. and Gorzelak, G. (2000) *Transition, Cohesion and Regional Policy in Central and Eastern Europe*, Aldershot: Ashgate.

Berliner, J.S. (1994) 'Perestroika and the Chinese model', in R.W. Campbell (ed.) *The Post-Communist Economic Transformation*, Boulder, CO: Westview.

Bian, Y.J. (1994) *Work and Inequality in Urban China*. Albany, NY: State University of New York Press.

Bian Y.J. (2002) 'Chinese social stratification and social mobility', *Annual Review of Sociology*, 28: 91–116.

Bian, Y.J. and Logan, L.J. (1996) 'Market transformation and the persistence of power: the changing stratification system in urban China', *American Sociological Review*, 61(5): 739–58.

Bradshaw, M. and Stenning, A. (2000) 'The progress of transition in East Central Europe', in J. Bachtler, R. Downes and G. Gorzelak (eds) *Transition, Cohesion and Regional Policy in Central and Eastern Europe*, Aldershot: Ashgate.

Burawoy, M. and Krotov, P. (1992) 'The Soviet transition from socialism to capitalism: worker control and economic bargaining in the wood industry', *American Sociological Review*, 57(1): 16–38.

Cannon, T. (2000) *China's Economic Growth: The Impact on Regions, Migration and the Environment*, Basingstoke: Macmillan.

Cannon, T. and Jenkins, A. (1990) *The Geography of Contemporary China: The Impact of Deng Xiaoping's Decade*, London and New York: Routledge.

Castells, M. (1977) *The Urban Question: A Marxist Approach*, London: Edward Arnold.

Central Committee of the CCP (2003) *Decision on Improving and Dealing With Some Problems of the Socialist Market Economic System*, Beijing: People's Press.

Chan, K.W. (1992) 'Economic growth strategy and urbanisation policies in China, 1949–1982', *International Journal of Urban and Regional Research*, 16(2): 275–305.

Chan, K.W. (1996) 'Post-Mao China: a two-class urban society in the making', *International Journal of Urban and Regional Research*, 20(1): 134–50.

# References

Chan, K.W. and Tsui, K.Y. (1992) '"Agricultural" and "non-agricultural" population statistics of the People's Republic of China: definitions, findings and comparisons', Occasional Paper, No. 1, Hong Hong: University of Hong Kong, Department of Geography and Geology.

Chan, S., Clark, C. and Lam, D. (1998) *Beyond the Developmental State: East Asia's Political Economies Reconsidered*, International Political Economy Series, Basingstoke: Palgrave Macmillan.

Chen, A.M. (1996) 'China's urban housing reform: price–rent ratio and market equilibrium', *Urban Studies*, 33(7): 1077–92.

Chen, J.Y. and Chen, J.J. (1993) *Socio-economic Changes of China's Rural Areas: 1949– 1989*, Shanxi: Shanxi Economic Press.

Cheng, T. and Selden, M. (1994) 'The origins and social consequences of China's *hukou* system', *The China Quarterly*, 139: 644–68.

*China Daily* (2004) 'Income gaps have to be closed', http://news.xinhuanet.com/english/ 2004–02/25/content_1331147.htm.

Chiu, R. (1996) 'Housing affordability in Shenzhen Special Economic Zone: a forerunner of China's housing reform', *Housing Studies*, 11(4): 561–80.

Chongqing Master Planning Office and Chongqing Urban Planning and Design Institute (1998) *Chongqing City Master Plan 1996–2020* (Internal planning document).

Chongqing Statistics Bureau (2000) *Chongqing Statistical Yearbook 2000*, Beijing: China Statistics Press.

Christiansen, F. (1990) 'Social division and peasant mobility in Mainland China: the implications of *hukou* system', *Issues and Studies*, 26(4): 78–91.

Christiansen, F. (1992) 'Market transition in China: the case of Jiangsu labour market, 1978–1990', *Modern China* 18(1): 72–93.

Chung. J.H. (1999) *Cities in China, Recipes for Economic Development in the Reform Era*, London and New York: Routledge.

Chussodovsky, M. (1996) *The Globalisation of Poverty*, London: Zed Books.

Connell, J.B. (1976) *Migration from Rural Areas: The Evidence from Village Studies, Delhi*, Oxford: Oxford University Press.

Cook, I.G. (2000) 'Pressures of development on China's cities and regions', in T. Cannon (ed.) *China's Economic Growth: The Impact on Regions, Migration and the Environment*, London: Macmillan.

Cook, S. and Holly, S. (2001) *Unemployment, Poverty and Gender in Urban China: Perceptions and Experiences of Laid Off Workers in Three Chinese Cities*, IDS Research Report No. 50, Brighton: University of Sussex.

Cook, S. and White, G. (1998) *The Changing Pattern of Poverty in China: Issues for Research and Policy*, IDS Working Paper 67, Brighton: University of Sussex, Institute of Development Studies (IDS).

Croll, E. (1994) *From Heaven to Earth: Images and Experiences of Development in China*, London and New York: Routledge.

Davin, D. (1999) *Internal Migration in Contemporary China*, Basingstoke: Macmillan.

Davis, D.S. (2000) *The Consumer Revolution in Urban China*, Berkeley, CA: University of California Press.

Davis, D.S., Kraus, R., Naughton, B. and Perry, E. (1995) *Urban Spaces in Contemporary China: The Potential for Autonomy and Community in Post-Mao China*, Cambridge: Woodrow Wilson Center Press and Cambridge University Press.

Day, L.H. and Xia, M. (1994) *Migration and Urbanisation in China*, Armonk, NY: M.E. Sharpe.

de Melo, M. and Ofer, G. (1999) *The Russian City in Transition: The First Six Years in 10 Volga Capitals*, Washington, DC: World Bank, Country Economics Department.

de Melo, M., Denizer, C. and Gelb, A. (1996) 'Patterns of transition from plan to market', *The World Bank Economic Review*, 10(3): 397–424.

Devas, N. (2001) *Who Runs Cities? The Relationship Between Urban Governance, Service Delivery and Poverty*, Working Paper No. 4 for the Urban Governance, Partnerships Poverty Research, Birmingham: The School of Public Policy, University of Birmingham.

Egedy, T. and Kovacs, Z. (1999) 'Social exclusion and the future of high-rise housing estates: the case of Budapest', paper presented at the XIII AESOP Congress, 7–11 July, Bergen.

Enyedi, G. and Szirmai, V. (1992) *Budapest: A Central European Capital*, London: Belhaven Press.

Fan, C.C. (1996) 'Economic opportunities and internal migration: a case study of Guangdong Province, China', *Professional Geographer*, 48(1): 28–45.

Fan, C.C. (1999) 'Migration in a socialist transitional economy: heterogeneity, socio-economic and spatial characteristics of migrants in China and Guangdong Province', *International Migration Review*, 33(4): 493–515.

Fan, C.C. (2001) 'Migration and labour market returns in urban China: results from a recent survey in Guangzhou', *Environment and Planning A*, 33(1): 479–508.

Fei, M.P. (1999) *Introduction to Social Security*, Shanghai: Huadong Science and Technology University Press.

Ferreira, F.H.G. (1997) *Economic Transition and the Distributions of Income and Wealth*, Policy Research Working Paper 1808, Washington, DC: The World Bank.

Friedmann, J. and Wulff, R. (1975) *The Urban Transition*, London: Edward Arnold.

Gao, S.S. (1998) *20-Year Reform of China's Labour and Employment System*, Zhengzhou: Zhongzhou Guji Publishing House.

Gaubatz, P.R. (1995) 'Urban transformation in post-Mao China: impacts of the reform era on China's urban form', in D.S. Davis, R. Kraus, B. Naughton and E.J. Perry (eds) *Urban Spaces in Contemporary China: The Potential for Autonomy and Community in Post-Mao China*, Cambridge: Woodrow Wilson Center Press and Cambridge University Press.

Gaubatz, P.R. (1996) *Beyond the Great Wall: Urban Form and Transformation on the Chinese Frontiers*, Stanford, CA: Stanford University Press.

Ge, R.J., Pan, H.P. and Wang, X.Y. (2003) *Study of Landless Farmers: A New Weak Social Group Created by Urbanisation*, available online at http://news.xinhuanet.com/newscenter/2003–05/08/content_862395.htm.

General Office of the State Council (1991) 'On comprehensive reform of urban housing system (General Office of the State Council document No. 73) in Z.M. Qu (eds) (1992) *Housing Reform Handbook*, Xi'an: Xi'an Housing Reform Office.

Ghanbari-Parsa, A. and Moatazed-Keivani, R. (1999) 'Development of real estate markets in central Europe', *Environment and Planning A*, 31(8): 1389–99.

Giddens, A. (1996) *Sociology*, Cambridge: Polity Press.

Gilbert, A. and Gugler, J. (1992) *Cities, Poverty and Development: Urbanization in the Third World* (2nd edn), Oxford and New York: Oxford University Press.

# References

Goldstein, A. and Goldstein, S. (1994) 'Permanent and temporary migration differentials', in L.H. Day and M. Xia (eds) *Migration and Urbanization in China*, Armonk, NY: M.E. Sharpe.

Goldstein, A. and Goldstein, S. (1996) 'Migration motivations and outcomes: permanent and temporary migrants compared', in A. Goldstein and W. Feng (eds) *China: The Many Faces of Demographic Change*, Boulder, CO: Westview.

Goodman, D.S.G. (1989) *China's Regional Development*, London and New York: Routledge.

Gordon, D. and Townsend, P. (2000) *Breadline Europe: The Measurement of Poverty*, Bristol: The Polity Press.

Gregory, F and Brooke, G. (2000) 'Policing economic transition and increasing revenue: a case study of the Federal Tax Police Service of the Russian Federation 1992–1998', *Europe-Asia Studies*, 52(3): 433–55.

Guan, X. (2003) 'Policies geared to tackling social inequality and poverty in China', in C.J. Finer (ed.) *Social Policy Reform in China: Views from Home and Abroad*, Aldershot: Ashgate.

Guangzhou Municipal Statistics Bureau (2003) *Guangzhou Statistical Yearbook 2003*, Beijing: China Statistics Press.

Gugler, J. (1995) 'The urban-rural interface and migration', in A. Gilbert and J. Gugler (eds) *Cities, Poverty and Development: Urbanization in the Third World* (2nd edn), Oxford: Oxford University Press.

Harloe M. (1996) 'Cities in transition', in G. Andrusz, M. Harloe and I. Szelenyi (eds) *Cities After Socialism: Urban and Regional Change and Conflict in Post-socialist Societies*, Oxford: Blackwell.

Hare, P.G. (2001) 'Institutional change and economic performance in the transitional economies', *UNECE Economic Survey of Europe in 2001*, Issue 2: 77–99.

Harvie, C. (1998) *Economic Transition: What Can Be Learned from China's Experience*, Research Paper, Wollongong: Department of Economics, University of Wollongong.

Hou, X. (1997) 'A tentative study on guiding housing consumption and promoting new economic growth', *Beijing Real Estate*, No. 1: 21–23.

Housing Reform Steering Group of the State Council (1994) 'The decision on deepening urban housing reform', in Housing Reform Steering Group of the State Council (eds) *Urban Housing System Reform*, Beijing: Reform Press.

Hubai Province Urban Surveying and Research Team (2002) *A Worrying Student Poverty Problem in Hubai*, available online at http://www.stats.gov.cn.

Hussain, A. (1994) 'The Chinese economic reforms: an assessment', in D. Dwyer (ed.) *China: The Next Decades*, Harlow: Addison Wesley Longman.

Hussain, A. (2003) 'Urban poverty in PRC', unpublished research report, (TAR: PRC 33448).

Jiang, Z.M. (2002) 'Build a well-off society in an all-round way and create a new situation in building socialism with Chinese characteristics', Report to the 16th National Congress of Chinese Communist Party, *People's Daily, Overseas Edition*, 18 November 2002: 1–3.

Johnson, D.G. (1988) 'Economic reforms in the PRC', *Economic Development and Cultural Change*, 36(3): 225–45.

Keivani, R., Parsa, A. and McGreat, S. (2001) 'Globalisation, institutional structures and real estate markets in Central European countries', *Urban Studies*, 38(13): 2457–76.

Khan, A.R. and Riskin, C. (2001) *Inequality and Poverty in China in the Age of Globalization*, New York: Oxford University Press.

Kirkby, R.J.R. (1985) *Urbanisation in China: Town and Country in a Developing Economy 1949–2000AD*, London: Croom Helm.

Kirkby, R., Bradbury, I. and Shen, G. (2000) *Small Town China, Governance: Economy, Environment and Lifestyle in Three Zhen*, Aldershot: Ashgate.

Knight, J. and Song, L. (1999) *The Rural–Urban Divide: Economic Disparities and Interactions in China*, Oxford: Oxford University Press.

Kolodko, G.W. (1998) *Ten Years of Post-socialist Transition: The Lessons for Policy Reforms*, Washington, DC: The World Bank Development Economics Research Group.

Kornai, J. (1990) *The Road to a Free Market Economy: Shifting from a Socialist System – The Example of Hungary*, New York: W.W. Norton.

Leaf, M. (1997) 'Urban social impacts of China's economic reforms', *Cities*, 14(2): v–vii.

Li, L. (2000) 'History of old housing renewal in Beijing and policy suggestions', *Beijing Real Estate*, 122(December): 33–6.

Li, S.M. (2000a) 'Housing consumption in urban China: a comparative study of Beijing and Guangzhou', *Environment and Planning A*, 32(6): 1115–34.

Li. S.M. (2000b) 'The housing market and tenure decisions in Chinese cities: a multivariate analysis of the case of Guangzhou', *Housing Studies*, 15(2): 213–36.

Li, Z.L and Chen, F. (2003) 'Xi'an Luanzheng farmers are not happy to lose their land', *People's Daily Overseas Edition*, 1 July 2003: 6.

Liu, C.J. (Deputy Governor of Zabei District, Shanghai) (2001) 'Ensuring the successful experiment of social housing provision', in Housing Reform and Real Estate Work Circular, Nos 24–26, 2001 (unpublished internal circular), Housing and Real Estate Industry Department, Ministry of Construction.

Liu, J. (2003) 'The Ministry of Labour and Social Security planned to re-employ one million '4050' persons in 2003', *People's Daily, Overseas Edition*, 15 August: 1.

Liu, X. and W. Liang (1997) 'Zhejiangcun: social and spatial implications of informal urbanization on the periphery of Beijing', *Cities*, 14(2): 95–108.

Liu, Z.F. (2000) Speech at the National Informal Discussion Conference of Urban Housing and Property Demolition and Residents Relocation, Beijing, 17 September.

Liu, Z.F. (2003) 'Promote healthy and sustained development of housing and real estate', speech at the 2003 Annual Housing and Property Conference, 13 January, Wuhan.

Logan, J.L. (2001) 'Housing reform, neighbourhoods and the work unit system in urban China', Paper presented at the International Conference on Managing Housing and Social Change: Building Social Cohesion, Accommodating Diversity, City University of Hong Kong, 16–18 April 2001.

Logan, J.R. (2002) *The New Chinese Cities: Globalisation and Market Reform*, Oxford: Blackwell.

Logan, J.R., Bian, Y.J. and Bian, F.Q. (1993) 'Inequalities in access to community resources in a Chinese city', *Social Forces*, 72(3): 555–76.

Logan, J.R., Bian, Y.J. and Bian, F.Q. (1999) 'Housing inequality in urban China in the 1990s', *International Journal of Urban and Regional Research*, 23(1): 7–25.

Lu, J.H. (1998) 'Beijing's old and dilapidated housing renewal', *Cities*, 14(2): 59–69.

Ma, H. (1990) *Modern China's Economic and Management*, Beijing: Foreign Languages Press.

# References

Ma, L.J.C. (2002) 'Urban transformation in China, 1949–2000: a review and research agenda', *Environment and Planning A*, 34(9): 1545–69.

Ma, L.J.C. and Hanten, E.W. (1981) *Urban Development in Modern China*, Boulder, CO: Westview.

Ma, L.J.C. and Xiang, B. (1998) 'Native place, migration and the emergence of peasant enclaves in Beijing', *China Quarterly*, 155: 546–81.

Ma, S. and He, X.M. (2003) *Problems of Urban Village Redevelopment, Xi'an Produced New Policies*, available on line at http://www.realestate.cei.gov.cn/gg00/J030507A. htm.

Mallee, H. (1996) 'In defence of migration: recent Chinese studies of rural population mobility, *China Information*, X(3–4): 108–40.

Mandic, S. (1997) 'Making housing policy during transition', in B.C. Mali, K.D. Andrews and B. Turner (eds) *Proceedings of the International Conference on Housing in Transition*, 3–5 September, Piran, Slovenia. Ljubljana: Urban Planning Institute of the Republic of Slovenia and European Network for Housing Research.

Mandic, S. and Stanovick, T. (1996) 'Slovenia: fast privatisation of stock, slow reform of housing policy', in R.J. Struyk (ed.) *Economic Restructuring of the Former Soviet Bloc: The Case of Housing*, Aldershot: Avebury, published in association with the Urban Institute Press.

Marcuse, P. (1996) 'Privatization and its discontents: property rights in land and housing in the transition in Eastern Europe', in G. Andrusz, M. Harloe and I. Szelenyi (eds) *Cities after Socialism: Urban and Regional Change and Conflict in Post-Socialist Societies*, Oxford: Blackwell.

Marshell, T.H. (1973) *Class, Citizenship and Social Development*, Westport: Greenwood Press.

Martinussen, J. (1997) *State, Society and the Market*, London: Zed Books.

McMillan, J. (1997) 'Markets in transition', in D.M. Kreps and K.F. Wallis (eds) *Advances in Economics and Econometrics: Theory and Applications*, Cambridge: Cambridge University Press.

McMillan, J. and Naughton, B. (1992) 'How to reform a planned economy: lessons from China', *Oxford Review of Economic Policy*, 8(1)(Spring): 134–43.

Ministry of Civil Affairs (2003a) *Urban Minimum Living Standard Situation in November 2003*, available online at http://www.mca.gov.cn/news/content/recent/20041590824. html.

Ministry of Civil Affairs (2003b) *The Urban Minimum Living Standard Situation in Cities at Prefecture Level or Above, January–May, 2003*, available online at http://www.mca. gov.cn/news/dibao.htm.

Ministry of Labour and Social Security (1999) *Who Are the Unemployed? How to See our Unemployment Problem?* available online at http://www.molss.gov.cn/column/ sy/sygn.htm#4.

Ministry of Labour and Social Security and State Statistics Bureau (2002) *Statistics Report of the 2001 Labour and Social Security Development*, available online at http:// www.stats.gov.cn/tjgb/qttjgb/qgqttjgb/200206110029.htm.

Ministry of Labour and Social Security and State Statistical Bureau (2003) *Report on Labour and Social Security Development in 2002*, available online at http:// www.molss.gov.cn/news/2003/04301.htm.

Moser, C., Gatehouse, M. and Garcia, H. (1996) *Urban Poverty Research Sourcebook: Module II: Indicators of Urban Poverty*, UMP Working Paper Series 5, Washington, DC: UNDP/UNCHS(Habitat)/World Bank.

Murphey, R. (1980) *The Fading of the Maoist Vision*, New York: Methuen.

Musgrove, P. (1980) 'Household size and composition, employment and poverty in urban Latin America', *Economic Development and Cultural Change*, 28(2): 249–60.

Naughton, B. (1996) *Growing Out of the Plan: Chinese Economic Reform, 1978–1993*, New York: Cambridge University Press .

Naughton, B. (1999) 'China's transition in economic perspective', in M. Goldman and R. MacFarquhar (eds) *The Paradox of China's Post-Mao Reforms*, Cambridge, MA: Harvard University Press.

Nee, V. (1989) 'A theory of market transition: from redistribution to markets in state socialism', *American Sociological Review*, 54(5)(October): 663–81.

Nee, V. (1996) 'The emergence of a market society: changing mechanisms of stratification in China', *American Journal of Sociology*, 101(4): 908–49.

Nee, V. (2000) 'The role of the state in making a market economy', *Journal of Institutional and Theoretical Economics*, 156(1): 64–88.

Nee, V. and Matthews, R. (1996) 'Market transition and societal transformation in reforming state socialism', *Annual Review of Sociology*, 22: 401–35.

Nee, V. and Stark, D. (1989) *Remaking the Economic Institutions of Socialism: China and Eastern Europe*, Stanford, CA: Stanford University Press.

Novak, T. (1988) *Poverty and the State: A Historical Sociology*, Milton Keynes: Open University Press.

Pannell, C.W. (1990) 'China's urban geography', *Progress in Human Geography*, 14(2): 214–36.

Pannell, C.W. (2002) 'China's continuing urban transition', *Environment and Planning A*, 34(9): 1571–89.

Perkins, D. (1991) 'The transition from central planning: East Asia's experience', *Korea Development Institute, IDEP Forum*, 9(2): 3–20.

Population and Labour Department of State Statistics Bureau (1994) *China Population Statistics Yearbook 1994*, Beijing: China Statistics Press.

Rakodi, C. (1995) 'Poverty lines or household strategies? A review of conceptual issues in the study of urban poverty', *Habitat International*, 19(4): 407–26.

Rana, P.B. (1995) 'Reform strategies in transitional economies: lessons from Asia', *World Development*, 23(7): 1157–69.

Roland, G. (2000) *Transition and Economics, Politics: Market and Firms*, Cambridge, MA and London: The Massachusetts Institute of Technology Press.

Ruoppila, S. (1999) 'Residential differentiation in the transition from socialism to the market economy, the case of Tallinn, Estonia', paper presented at the AESOP Conference, 7–11 July, Bergen.

Sachs, J. and W.T. Woo (1994) 'Understanding the reform experiences of China, Eastern Europe, and Russia', in C.H. Lee and H. Reisen (eds) *From Reform to Growth: Countries in Transition in Asia and Central and Eastern Europe*, Paris: OECD.

Shanghai Municipal Statistics Bureau (2003) *Shanghai Statistical Yearbook 2003*, Beijing: China Statistics Press.

Shanghai Property and Land Resource Management Bureau (2001) Shanghai Municipal Social Housing Implementation Guidelines, Document No. 280 (unpublished government document).

Shanghai Property and Land Resource Management Bureau (2001) Shanghai Municipal Social Housing Implementation Suggestions, in Housing Reform and Real Estate Work Circular, Nos 24–26, 2001 (unpublished internal circular), Housing and Real Estate Industry Department, Ministry of Construction.

# References

Shen, J. (1995) 'Rural development and rural to urban migration in China 1978–1990', *Geoforum*, 26(4): 395–409.

Shen, J. (2002) 'A study of the temporary population in Chinese cities', *Habitat International*, 26(3): 363–77.

Shenyang Statistics Bureau (2000) *Shenyang Statistical Yearbook 1999*, Shenyang: Shenyang Statistics Bureau.

Shun, Q. (2000) 'Housing reform speeds up old and dangerous housing redevelopment, *Beijing Real Estate*, 116(June): 10–11.

Singh, I. (1991) *China and Central and Eastern Europe: Is There a Professional Schizophrenia on Socialist Reform?* Research Paper No. 17, Washington, DC: World Bank.

Solinger, D.J. (1993) *China's Transition from Socialism: Statistic Legacies and Market Reforms, 1980–1990*, Armonk, NY: M.E. Sharpe.

Solinger, D.J. (1999) *Contesting Citizenship in Urban China: Peasants Migrants, the State, and the Logic of the Market*, Berkeley, CA: University of California Press.

SPIU (Scottish Policy Information Unit) (2001) *Globalisation and Poverty*, Briefing Sheet 14, April 2001.

Spulber, N. (1997) *Redefining the State, Privatisation and Welfare Reform in Industrial and Transitional Economies*, Cambridge: Cambridge University Press.

Stark, D. (1990) 'Privatization in Hungary: from plan to market or from plan to clan?', *East European Politics and Societies* 4(3): 351–92.

Stark, D. (1992) 'Path dependence and privatization strategies in East Central Europe', *East European Politics and Societies* 6(1): 17–54.

State Council (1988) Implementation Plan for a Gradual Housing System Reform in Cities and Towns, Document No. 11, 1988.

State Council (1997) On Establishing the Urban Minimum Living Standard Protection System in the Whole Country, Document No. 29, 2 September 1997.

State Council (1998) The Notice on Further Reform of Urban Housing System and Speeding up Housing Development, Document No. 23, 3 July 1998.

State Council (1999a) Ordinance of Unemployment Insurance, Document No. 258, 22 January 1999.

State Council (1999b) Ordinance for the Provision of Minimum Living Standard for Urban Residents, Document No. 271, 28 September 1999.

State Council (2003) On Promoting Sustainable Development of Housing and Real Estate Market, Document No. 18, 12 August 2003.

State Statistics Bureau (1994) *China Statistical Yearbook 1994*, Beijing: China Statistics Press.

State Statistics Bureau (1996) *China Statistical Yearbook 1996*, Beijing: China Statistics Press.

State Statistics Bureau (1998) *China Statistical Yearbook 1998*, Beijing: China Statistics Press.

State Statistics Bureau (1998) *A Statistical Survey of China*, Beijing: China Statistics Press.

State Statistics Bureau (2000) *China Statistical Yearbook 2000*, Beijing: China Statistics Press.

State Statistics Bureau (2001a) *China Statistical Yearbook 2001*, Beijing: China Statistics Press.

State Statistics Bureau (2001b) *Report Series on the 9th FYP, Period, No 18: Urban Population's Living Standards Reached a Comfortable Level (xiao kang)*, available online at http://www.stats.gov.cn/tjfx/ztfx/jwxlfxbg/200205300091.htm.

State Statistics Bureau (2001c) *China Statistical Yearbook 2001*, Beijing: China Statistics Press.

State Statistics Bureau (2002a) Over 40 million people migrated between provinces in China, published by the State Statistics Bureau at its official website: http://www.bjstats.gov.cn/zwxx/wzxw/zzwz/200209230003.htm.

State Statistics Bureau (2002b) *A Judgement and Analysis of Urban Poverty Situation in Our Country*, available online at http://www.stats.gov.cn.

State Statistics Bureau (2003) *China Statistical Yearbook 2003*, Beijing: China Statistics Press.

State Statistics Bureau, China Statistics Information Network, (2001) *Gini Figures and the Gap between Rich and Poor*, available online at http:///www.stats.gov.cn/gqglwz/200104240017_1_0.htm.

State Statistics Bureau, Urban Economic and Social Survey Team (1995) *China City Statistical Yearbook 1993–1994*, Beijing: China Statistics Press.

State Statistics Bureau, Urban Economic and Social Survey Team (1999) *China City Statistical Yearbook 1998*, Beijing: China Statistics Press.

State Statistics Bureau, Urban Economic and Social Survey Team (2003) *China City Statistical Yearbook 2002*, Beijing: China Statistics Press.

Stiglitz, J.E. (2002) *Globalisation and Its Discontents*, London: Allen Lane/The Penguin Press.

Struyk, R.J. (1996) 'The long road to the market', in R.J. Struyk (ed.) *Economic Restructuring of the Former Soviet Bloc: The Case of Housing*, Aldershot: Avebury, published in association with the Urban Institute Press.

Sykora, L. and Simonichova, I. (1994) 'From totalitarian urban managerialism to a liberalized real estate market: Prague's transformations in the early 1990s', in M. Barlow, P. Dostal and M. Hampl (eds) *Development and Administration of Prague*, Amsterdam: Universiteit van Amsterdam, Instituut voor Sociale Geografie.

Szelenyi, I. (1983) *Urban Inequality under State Socialism*, Oxford: Oxford University Press.

Szelenyi, I. (1987) 'Housing inequalities and occupational segregation in state socialist cities: commentary on the special issue of IJURR on East European cities', *International Journal of Urban and Regional Research*, 11(1): 1–8.

Szelenyi, I. (1996) 'Cities under socialism – and after', in G. Andrusz, M. Harloe and I. Szelenyi (eds) *Cities After Socialism: Urban and Regional Change and Conflict in Post-socialist Societies*, Oxford: Blackwell.

Tang, W. and Parish, W. (2000) *Chinese Urban Life Under Reform: The Changing Social Contract*, Cambridge: Cambridge University Press.

Turner, J.C. (1968) 'Housing priorities, settlement patterns, and urban development in modernizing countries', *American Institute of Planners Journal*, November: 354–63.

UK Government (2000) *Eliminating World Poverty: Making Globalisation Work for the Poor*, White Paper on International Development (Cm 5006), London: HMSO.

Walder, A.G. (1986) *Communist Neo-traditionalism: Work and Authority in Chinese Industry*, Berkeley, CA: University of California Press.

Walder, A.G. (1992) 'Property rights and stratification in socialist redistributive economies', *American Sociological Review*, 57(4): 524–39.

Wang, F. (2003a) 'Housing improvement and distribution in urban China: initial evidence from China's 2000 census', *The China Review*, 3(2): 121–43

Wang, F.L. (1998) *Institutions and Institutional Change in China: Premodernity and Modernization*, Basingstoke: Macmillan and New York: St Martin's Press.

# References

Wang, S. (2003b) *Shenyang Issued Salary Guide for 215 Different Types of Positions*. http://www.ln.xinhuanet.com/2003–07/14/content_702745.htm.

Wang, Y.P. (1992) 'Private sector housing in urban China since 1949: the case of Xi'an, *Housing Studies*, 7(2): 119–37.

Wang, Y.P. (1995) 'Public sector housing in urban China 1949–1988: the case of Xi'an', *Housing Studies* 10(1): 57–82.

Wang, Y.P. (2000) 'Housing reform and its impacts on the urban poor in China', *Housing Studies*, 15(6): 845–64.

Wang, Y.P. (2001) 'Urban housing reform and finance in China: a case study of Beijing', *Urban Affairs Review*, 36(5): 620–45.

Wang, Y.P. (2003c) 'Urban reform and low income communities in Chinese cities', in R. Forrest and J. Lee (eds) *Housing and Social Change: East–West Perspectives*, London: Routledge.

Wang, Y.P. (2003d) 'Progress and problems of urban housing reform', in C.J. Finer (ed.) *Social Policy Reform in China: Views from Home and Abroad*, Aldershot: Ashgate.

Wang, Y.P. and Hague, C. (1992) 'The planning and development of Xi'an since 1949', *Planning Perspective*, 7(1): 1–26.

Wang, Y.P. and Murie, A. (1996) 'The process of commercialisation of urban housing in China', *Urban Studies* 33(6): 971–89.

Wang, Y.P. and Murie, A. (1999) *Housing Policy and Practice in China*, Basingstoke: Macmillan.

Wang, Y.P. and Murie, A. (2000) 'Social and spatial implications of housing reform in China', *International Journal of Urban and Regional Research*, 24(2): 397–417.

Williams, A.M. and Balaz, V. (1999) 'Privatisation in central Europe: different legacies, methods and outcomes', *Environment and Planning C*, 17(6): 731–51.

Winckler, E.A. (1999) *Transition from Communism in China: Institutional and Comparative Analysis*, Boulder, CO: Lynne Rienner.

Wong, L. and W. Huen (1998) 'Reforming the household registration system: a preliminary glimpse of the blue chip household registration system in Shanghai and Shenzhen', *International Migration Review*, 32(4): 974–94.

Woo-Cumings, M. (1999) *The Developmental State*, Cornell Studies in Political Economy, New York: Cornell University Press.

World Bank (1992) *China Implementation Options for Urban Housing Reform*, Washington, DC: World Bank.

World Bank, (1995) *Trends in Developing Economies*, Washington, DC: World Bank.

World Bank (1996) *Poverty Reduction and the World Bank: Progress and Challenges in the 1990s*, Washington, DC: World Bank.

World Bank (2001) *World Development Report 2000/2001: Attacking Poverty*, New York: Oxford University Press.

Wu, F. (1996) 'Changes in the structure of public housing provision in urban China', *Urban Studies*, 33(9): 1601–27.

Wu, F. (1997) 'Urban restructuring in China's emerging market economy: towards a framework for analysis', *International Journal of Urban and Regional Research*, 21(4): 640–63.

Wu, F. (2000) 'Global and local dimensions of place-making: remaking Shanghai as a world city', *Urban Studies*, 37(8): 1359–77.

Wu, F. (2001) 'Housing provision under globalisation: a case study of Shanghai', *Environment and Planning A*, 33(10): 1741–64.

Wu, F. (2002a) 'China's changing urban governance in the transition towards a more market-oriented economy', *Urban Studies* 39(7): 1071–93.

Wu, F. (2003a) 'Globalization, place promotion, and urban development in Shanghai', *Journal of Urban Affairs*, 25(1): 55–78.

Wu, X.G. (2002b) 'Work units and income inequality: the effect of market transition in urban China', *Social Forces*, 80(3): 1069–99.

Wu, Z.M. (2003b) *How Many Poor People in China?* Xinhua News Webpage, 16 May 2003.

Wuhan Municipal Demolition and Relocation Management Office (2001) *Good Practice in Relocation and Fund Management*, available online at http://www.cin.gov.cn/meeting/01cq/2001110213.htm.

Xiang, B. (1993) 'There is a Zhejiang village in Beijing', *Sociology and Social Investigation*, 3.

Xie, J.J. (2001) 'Seriously implement the new regulations and strength – the management of property and housing demolition and residents relocation work', unpublished report at the National Urban Property and Housing Demolition and Residents Relocation Working Conference, 16 October, Beijing.

Xie, J.J. (2003) 'Striking for new territory of housing and real estate work', unpublished report to the National Housing and Real Estate Conference, 13 January, Wuhan.

Xinhua News Agency, Shandong Branch (2003) *Exchange between 'Resource Advantage' and 'High Pressure Boiler': Concern about the problems of migrant workers*, Focal Talk Online, available online at http://news.xinhuanet.com/focus/2003–07/03/content_950816.htm.

Xu, H. (2001) 'Commuting town workers: the case of Qinshan, China', *Habitat International*, 25(1): 35–47.

Yang, D.L. (1997) *Beyond Beijing: Liberalization and the Regions in China*, London and New York: Routledge.

Yang, X. (1993) 'Household registration, economic reform and migration', *International Migration Review*, 27: 796–818.

Yang, X. (1996) 'Patterns of economic development and patterns of rural to urban migration in China', *European Journal of Population*, 12: 195–218.

Yang, X. (2000) 'Determinants of migration intentions in Hubei province, China: individual versus family migration', *Environment and Planning A*, 32(5): 769–87.

Yang, Z.H. (2003) *How to Walk Out of the Social Housing Difficulties in Beijing*, available online at http://www.realestate.cei.gov.cn//gg00/J030509A.htm.

Yao, S. (1999) 'Economic growth, income inequality and poverty in China under economic reforms', *Journal of Development Studies*, 35(6): 104–30.

Yi, S.H. (1998) *Urban Poverty in Contemporary China*, Nanchang: Jiangxi People's Publishing House.

Ying, M.Y. (2001) Experiments and Creation, Seriously Carrying out Social Housing Pilot Test Work, in Housing Reform and Real Estate Work Circular, Nos 24–26, 2001 (unpublished internal circular), Housing and Real Estate Industry Department, Ministry of Construction.

Yu, P., Pu, Q.J., Li, G.R. and Zhong, Y.Q. (2000) 'Improving social protection systems and developing social "security network"', *Chongqing Daily*, 22 November: 10.

Yu, X. and Day, L.H. (1994) 'Demographic characteristics of the migrants', in L.H. Day and M. Xia (eds) *Migration and Urbanization in China*, Armonk, NY: M.E. Sharpe.

# References

Zhang, J. (1998a) 'Informal construction in Beijing's old neighborhoods', *Cities*, 14(2): 85–94.

Zhang, J.D. (1999) *Informal Institution in the Process of Market Transformation*, Beijing, Wenwu Press.

Zhang, Z.W. (1998b) *The Minefield of Reform, Laid-off and Unemployment*, Zhuhai: Zhuhai Publishing House.

Zhong, M. and Y. Wang (1999) *The Gap between Two Poles? The Rich and the Poor in Contemporary China*, Beijing: Chinese Economic Press.

Zhou, M. and J.R. Logan (1996) 'Market transition and the commodification of housing in urban China', *International Journal of Urban and Regional Research*, 20(3): 400–421.

Zhu, G.L. (1998) *Analysis of All Social Strata in Modern China*, Tianjin: Tianjin People's Press.

Zhu, R.J. (2003) 'Government Report to the First Session of the 10th National People's Congress, 5 March 2003', *People's Daily, Overseas Edition*, 28 March: 1.

# Index

Note: Tables and Figures in the text are indicated by the use of *Table* or *Fig* after the page numbers; e.g. housing and poverty 102–6*Table 6.6, Fig. 6.4* indicates that there are both Tables and Figures relating to housing and poverty between pages 102 and 106.

Words starting with numbers are filed as though spelt out; e.g. '4050' is filed as 'forty-fifty'

# Index

# Index

# Index

change 9, 11–13; gradualism 13–16, 50, 72, 148–9; inequality and poverty 16, 19–21, 154, 159; meanings of 8–10; modes of 149*Fig. 9.1*; and political change 10–11, 23; urban 16–19, 22, 155–6

transport 118, 119*Fig. 7.3*, 161

tuition fees 61–2

Turner, J. 121

UK Government 160

Ulyanovsk 17

unemployment: benefits 128, 132*Fig. 8.1*, 136–7; insurance 124, 126–7*Table 8.1*, 130–7; in Shenyang and Chongqing 76; and state-owned-enterprise sector 3–4, 74; and urban poverty 5–6, 56–66*Tables 4.4–4.5*, 71, *see also* laid-off workers

universities, student numbers 61–2

urban change: and continuity 48–50; and economic reform 1–3; and pre-reform social structure 26–35; social and spatial change since 1978 35–48; and transition 16–19, 22, 155–6

urban minimum living standard *see* minimum living standard

urban reform: housing 88–92, 99–102, 146; literature on 6, 89

urban residents *see* residents, official

urban social class *see* class

urban villages: and poverty 69–70; and spatial re-organisation 45, 140, 146

urban–rural relationships 18, 161

villages *see* urban villages

wages: of rural migrants 64–5, 70, *see also* incomes; salaries

Walder, A.G. 32

Wang, F. 91

Wang, S. 54

Wang, Y.P. 4, 38, 89, 91; and Murie, A. 33, 48, 89

Washington Consensus 11–12

welfare provision: and employment 80; low-income support 81–2, 133–4; policies 124–8; and urban change 41–3, *see also* benefits; social support systems

Western capitalism 15

women 29, 37

Wong, L. and Huen, W. 38

Woo-Cumings, M. 154

work units (*danwei*): and employment structure 38–41; and housing provision 96, 100; integration and social structure 30–3, 49; land use and spatial patterns 35; and welfare provision 41

worker–cadre system *see* cadre–worker system; class; laid-off workers

World Bank 24, 159

WTO 157, 158

Wu, F. 32, 40, 157

Wu, Z.M. 52, 65, 133

Wuhan Municipal Demolition and Relocation Management Office 142

*xiagang* (lay off) 3–4

*xiahai* (down to sea) 128

Xi'an 35, 41, 46, 62–3, 69

Xiang, B. 37

*xiao shi ming* ('Little Citizens') 29, 30

Xie, J.J. 138, 141

Xinhua News Agency 62, 65

Xu, H. 37

Yang, Z.H. 138

Yi, S.H. 4

Ying, M.Y. 138

young people: students 61–2; unemployed 57

Yu, P. *et al.* 130

Yu, X. and Day, L.H. 109

Zhejiangcun (Beijing) 70

Zhong, M. and Wang, Y. 4

Zhu, G.L. 4, 129

Zhu, R.J. 3

zones *see* functional zones